SMILE

Particularly in Bad Weather

Dr Prudence Black is a Research Associate in the Department of Gender and Cultural Studies at the University of Sydney. Her award–winning book *The Flight Attendant's Shoe* about the design history of the Qantas flight attendant uniforms was published by NewSouth Books in 2011. As well as her academic work she undertakes consultancies relating to corporate branding heritage and is regularly asked to talk on local and national radio regarding matters to do with fashion, design, uniforms and aviation.

SMILE

Particularly in Bad Weather

The Era of the Australian Airline Hostess

Prudence Black

UWA PUBLISHING

First published in 2017 by
UWA Publishing
Crawley, Western Australia 6009
www.uwap.uwa.edu.au

UWAP is an imprint of UWA Publishing
a division of The University of Western Australia

THE UNIVERSITY OF
WESTERN AUSTRALIA

National Library of Australia Cataloguing-in-Publication entry

Creator: Black, Prudence, author.

Title: Smile, particularly in bad weather : the era of the Australian airline hostess / Prudence Black.

ISBN: 9781742589251 (paperback)

Notes: Includes bibliographical references.

Subjects: Flight attendants—Australia.
Flight attendants—History.
Airlines—Australia—Flight attendants—History.

Typeset by J&M Typesetting
Printed by Lightning Source
Cover image: Betty Baxter Anderson, 1941, Peggy Wayne, Sky Girl, New York: Cupples and Leon. Illustrator Roberta Paflin.

CONTENTS

Contents

ACKNOWLEDGMENTS

In the extremely demanding world of publishing it is an added joy to have one's book polished and shaped by a publishing house as stellar as UWA Publishing. Terri-ann White's generous enthusiasm for the book along with the team at UWA (Charlotte Guest, Kate Pickard and Katie Connolly) has made the process of turning words on a page into a fine book a truly rewarding task.

I won the lottery when I received a Discovery Early Career Research Award through the Australian Research Council: not only did the award provide funds to undertake the research for the book, it meant that for three years I was part of the wonderful world that is the Department of Gender and Cultural Studies at the University of Sydney. It is hard to imagine a better environment in which to work and think about ideas, and I extend thanks to my colleagues and the administrative staff of the School of Philosophical and Historical Inquiry.

It is fine to have an obsession with one's own material but it is another matter to ask others to share it in the same way. How lucky was I to have Jess Kean, Adam Gall and Felix Idle come on board at different stages of the project, providing insight and expertise in areas where I was lacking. It was a bonus when they too became hooked on the life of the airline hostess, and the differences between a DC-3 and a Lockheed Hudson. Thankyou to Adam Shoemaker for helpful comments about Section One and to Olivia Rosenman for her keen eye and thoughtful suggestions on the manuscript. I also want to thank my aviation buddies Jane Ferguson and Peter Hobbins for sharing their aviation expertise, and for all the delightfully focused, some may say nerdy, aviation conversations.

One can never underestimate the importance of public access to archives. Regional and international aviation museums and research libraries were fundamental to the research for the book and I extend my thanks to: David Crotty, Qantas Heritage Collection; Nigel and Paul Daw, South Australian Aviation Museum; Barbara Hanson, United Airlines Archive; Karen Johnson and Dimity Holt, Museum of Applied Arts and Sciences; John Croll, Historical Aircraft Restoration Society, Albion Park; John Hill, Dennis Sharp, Blake Summers, and Julie Takata, San Francisco Airport Museum; John Park, Aviation Heritage Museum, Perth; John Wren, TAA Museum; and Yvette Yurubi, Pan Am Archive, University of Miami.

This book could not have been written without the generosity of all those I interviewed, and people who have offered snippets of information about the profession along the way. While not everyone's story has appeared in the book, it has only been through the sharing of stories that I have been able to understand and piece together the world that is the subject of the book. I can't think of a nicer group of people. With heartfelt thanks to: Reg Adkins, Pauline and Graham Alderman, Pam Allom, Pip Asphar, Kay Barton, Jackie Benniman, Shirley Boles, Joan Bray, Juliann Breen, Pamela Brinsley, Trudy Broad, Sue Bryant, Marsh Burgess, Anne Burton, Barbara Butler, Cavell Caldwell, Graeme Cant, Owen Capp, Renate Chandler, Pat Coleman, Sammy Connellan, Lyla Cross, Pip and Nanette (Nan) Cummings, June Dally-Watkins, Janette Davie, Susan Davis, Sue de Monchaux, Flora Devery,

Loretta Dixon, Ron Entsch, Dick Evans, Betty Foster, Susan Foster, Jenny Freestone, Robin Garnett, Wendy Georgetti-Remkes, Maggie Gilet, Pat Gillespie, Mary Grant, Tricia Gubbins, Biruta Hammill, Barbara Harding Smith, Diane Harris, Dorothy Harris, Frances Herriot, Andrew Hewitt, Sir Lenox Hewitt, Michelle Higgs, Dianne Imison, Graham Jeffries, Hazel Johnson, Ron 'Sos' Johnson, Patricia Jordan, Paula Kitses, Kaye Laing, Trixie Lange, Marilyn Lawson, Mary Pat Laffey Inman, Inge Legge, Jan Lessen, Carol Locket, Sue Love-Davies, Joan McBride, Robyn McGaw, Debbie Marshall, Maureene Martin, Bev Maunsell, Darellyn Melsom, Patricia Merlehan, Patsy Millett, Kathy Minassian, Edie Morrant, Kerry-Ann Murray, Shayne Nealon, Doreen Newell, Georgia Panter Nielsen, Lorraine Nothling, Helen Nunn, Brenda Oliver Harry, Edna Payne, Anne Peterson, Anne Pfeifer, Judy Potts, Mary Powys, Betty Ralph, Michele Reid, Helen Ritchie, Elaine Rickards, Dean and Margaret Robinson, Doris Robinson, Ed Ronsisvalle, Peta Selwood, Eliza Jane Sharp, Margaret Shaw, Jean Smith, Rick Squires, Rochelle Sutherland, Pat St Leon, Teri Teramoto, Patricia Tickner, Frank Tishler, Vicki Viney, Wendy Walsh, Patricia Ward, Irma Wharton, Gillian White, Claire Williams, Faye Willis, Nan Witcomb, Pat Woodley, Connie Wright. And a thousand apologies if I have failed to include anyone on the list of thankyous. Sadly, some of the people I interviewed have died but I hope that this book is a small contribution to keep their legacy alive: Ruth Bailey, Pat Gregory-Quilter, Dorothy Lauchland, Lilian Macalpine, Lyris McIntosh, Val St Leon, Lesley Squires and Max White.

Writing this book has been a real pleasure and for once there is no need for an author to apologise to a long-suffering family. For the most part I have been well-behaved. Although, once again, Stephen Muecke had to grapple with the differences we have over punctuation and syntax as he diligently read though the manuscript. The good thing is he makes everything better. My family and friends, as always, provide the essential nourishment that supplements the other non-working side of my life.

INTRODUCTION

In 1936, the first Australian air hostesses were recruited only six years after Ellen Church became the world's first stewardess with Boeing Air Transport in the United States. *Smile, Particularly in Bad Weather* details this history of the Australian airline hostess and considers how a unique conjunction of gender, technology and labour was assembled to create a kind of profession never seen before. Airline hostesses, both individually and collectively, negotiated a new global space that was all too eagerly seen as 'glamorous', but, at its most mundane, the work itself resembled other forms of shift work, with long and erratic hours, difficult working conditions and limited career opportunities. While this contradiction can be found in many female working roles, this book describes the extreme levels of professional maturity and independence required of airline hostesses who routinely risked, and even lost, their lives in the service of an industry reluctant to acknowledge their ongoing contribution.

Air travel created a new type of modern workplace, and there was the general view that if there was a woman on board a plane, then flying must be safe. The airline hostess offered a reassuring presence not only on board, but also on the ground, articulated through forceful public promotion in airline advertising campaigns. The speed of the development of the profession meant that in the early days the airline hostesses encountered situations

Book cover, Betty Beaty, *Maiden Flight*, **1956**
From the moment the first air hostesses came on board in 1930 they were represented in films and popular fiction. Here the caring air hostess appears under the attentive gaze of the handsome pilot on the cover of the novel Maiden Flight. *Courtesy of Mills & Boon.*

that challenged the rudimentary training they had received, and had them learning on the spot. The professional maturity required of these young women meant that the 'glamour' of the job – the snappy uniform and the opportunity to travel – was continually undercut by the often extreme conditions experienced flying the world, and across Australia. At the same time the figure of the airline hostess helped create a new outward-facing image of Australian culture that reflected both national ambitions and an investment in an international world.

The airline hostess symbolised in a very particular way a new kind of modern woman. She was independent, she was trained to self-regulate as an aesthetic object, and at the same time be an expert professional. The work was thus much more than 'doing things' on an aircraft. Her feelings were a major part of the investment in the job, as she stood as a representative of a regional or national airline carrier where she was domesticated as a 'hostess' or 'eroticised' by the airline marketing campaigns.

Smile, Particularly in Bad Weather covers a fifty-year timeframe from the mid-1930s to the mid-1980s, the point when airline hostesses, along with male flight stewards, were renamed flight attendants. The new name marks the end of a struggle in which the women of the new profession had to first assert themselves, then, in a way, dissolve the importance of their own gender, by becoming flight attendants just like the men working in the same cabins. That is why the book finishes at that point; the rest of the history will be written along different lines.

This is a detailed history of the development of the profession told through the stories and the archives of the people who worked in the industry. It focuses on Australia, while referring to the profession as it evolved in other countries across the world. Indeed, the experiences of the Australian airline hostesses sat side by side with what was happening with their colleagues across the world. Training techniques, industrial awards and workplace gains matched other women working in other airlines. Yet, the Australian conditions created the need for considered responses. As a consequence of working on some of the longest and most challenging air routes in world, it was no surprise that the women would join forces to create the Airline Hostesses' Association in 1956, one of the first female professional unions in Australia. Not only did the association make an issue of the difficult physical conditions of flying, but it also responded to the threat of early forced retirement once the airline hostesses no longer conformed to the industry-promoted image of youthful beauty.

The book opens with Chapter One, 'Welcome Aboard' and introduces the domestic air hostess who first comes on board when commercial aviation in Australia was still in the pioneering stages; she emerges as an iconic modern professional, a young woman with training, prestige, glamour and mobility. The young women who flocked to the profession wanted a life beyond the routine offerings that other professions provided. Just as a generation before embraced a new workplace provided by the technology of the typewriter, this generation of women took to a new life in the skies working in planes that were, while totally 'modern', also noisy, unpressurised and, at times, unsafe.

Using material gathered through interviews with former air hostesses and flight crew, Chapter Two, 'Setting the Standard', shows how, despite the onset of World War II, Australian airlines continued to operate reduced services, and, in fact, the airline hostess profession continued to grow. An important figure was 'Matron' Hazel Holyman, who was part of the aviation industry since the early 1930s, and under her wise and professional guidance the profession took shape. As the airlines expanded and crashes occurred, so too does this chapter end by overturning many of the romantic assumptions that persist about commercial aviation.

The challenges and difficulties air hostesses faced working in the air and on some of the longest and most isolated air routes in the world is the subject of Chapter Three, 'To the Outback and Beyond'. In particular it investigates the women who flew with Western Australia's MacRobertson Miller Airlines on the routes to the Kimberley and Darwin. The vernacular conditions of working in Australian aviation, which routinely connected far-flung destinations, demanded exacting performances from aircraft and the crews who kept machines and passengers under control. Under these conditions, the figure of the airline hostess came to embody a form of soft diplomacy that promoted a modern industry while barely masking the challenges that persisted in flying across rough terrain both nationally and internationally. New airlines began operating, including Trans Australia Airlines and British Commonwealth Pacific Airlines and, despite new opportunities, the attrition rate of the airline hostesses was substantial, through air sickness, exhaustion and more significantly because they couldn't fly after they married.

Chapter Four, 'The World Comes to Australia', opens with the postwar period and the gender trouble on board the new Qantas Lockheed Constellation. Like a cat among the pigeons, the introduction of a flight hostess on board the international flights in 1948 ruffled the feathers of the flight stewards who had provided the cabin service on the Qantas planes since the late 1930s. At the same time as flight hostesses came on board the international carrier, Ansett and other regional carriers introduced air hostesses on their domestic services. Along with the everyday passengers there are accounts of the air hostesses handling wrestlers, stowaways, drunken wool brokers, Soviet spies and the intricacies of serving a 'cold collation' for Queen Elizabeth II. The implications of the new gendered nature of the airline cabin and the difficult conditions for air hostesses on board and on stopovers helped unionise the profession, with the formation of the Airline Hostesses' Association.

In the late 1950s the world of travel changed and Chapter Five, '"Slinky Sex Symbols" and the Jet Age', describes the way the Boeing 707 jet shook the industry and speed became the order of the day. Overnight the world became a smaller place with new travel destinations opening up and 'jetsetters' travelling in half the time it had taken on the older planes. The role of the airline hostess was always defined through key concepts that defined the profession from the outset, including glamour, demeanour and bodily comportment. But now, in order to cater for a new breed of traveller, the airline hostess was exoticised as a way of marketing the airlines. Her role epitomised international relations. At the same time, at a local level, Indigenous airline hostesses came on board as the everyday manifestation of Australia's national image.

The book finishes with Chapter Six, 'Goodbye Hostesses, Hello Flight Attendants'. By 1983 the outdated term 'hostess' has gone, and now all cabin crew are called flight attendants. The chapter gives the background details to the industrial relations issues associated with the 'gender trouble' of the profession in the 1970s and 1980s. Beginning with an account of the gender-based discrimination that emerged when Sir Reginald Ansett called a group of air hostesses 'a batch of old boilers', through to the introduction of male stewards on domestic airlines in the early 1980s, the conclusion to the story sheds new light on how this profession occupied an important place in changing Australia's industrial landscape, especially for women.

SECTION ONE: TAKE-OFF

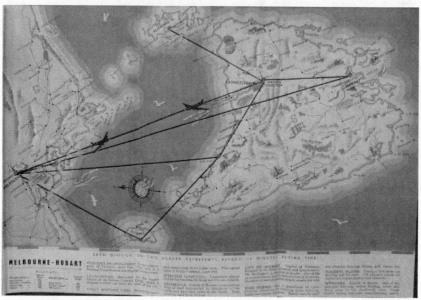

ANA Route Map of Melbourne and Tasmania, c.1946
This map was included in an Australian National Airways brochure 'Your Route Map' allowing passengers to follow the path of the plane mid-flight but also to know something about the places they were flying over. Other route maps in the brochure included Melbourne to Sydney and Sydney to Brisbane. Courtesy of South Australian Aviation Museum

Chapter One

WELCOME ABOARD

1.1. 'The Sky's the Limit': The First Air Hostesses

The newest career in the world. And, equally the strangest.

Francis Vivian Drake, 1933[1]

Do you really think you'd like flying?
There's danger, there's lots of responsibility, and there's a great
deal of work at times…You may be trapped in almost any kind
of weather – rain, snow, hail, sleet, fog. You must be calm and
resourceful and courageous. We demand a great deal of loyalty.

Ruth S. Wheeler, *Jane, Stewardess of the Air Lines*, 1934[2]

Within a year of Blanche Due and Marguerite Grueber being appointed as the first Australian air hostesses on the small regional Holyman's Airways, an article appeared in January 1937 in the Melbourne newspaper, *The Argus*.[3] Caught by the wave of interest in this new profession, the journalist Tessa Fubbs described the overwhelming number of young women rushing to apply for a job where demand far outweighed availability. She quoted one of Australia's first air hostesses negotiating her new profession:

It is interesting work and the conditions are good, but it keeps you busy all the time, and is sometimes strenuous and exacting. It is all routine. You do meet interesting people, but not as many as you would meet in a shop. It is a career that lasts only a few years, offers little or no promotion, and leads nowhere. If the object is matrimony get down to earth and stay there. Elderly, well-married businessmen are in the majority as passengers, and that young handsome passenger is probably inexperienced and will be too excited or too ill to pay any attention to you.[4]

For some, this description of the profession might take them straight down to earth but for thousands of young women in the late 1930s right through until the 1980s airline hostessing was a highly sought-after job. It was one like no other. This was the only job where young women were paid to travel, not only nationally but also across the world. It offered women a legitimate way to escape a predictable life at home with their parents, or a staid career behind the secretarial desk, or an inevitable engagement to the boy next door.

It is no coincidence that the idea of the 'hostess' took hold during this period.[5] The strong ideals of the domestic hostess were easily transferred to imagining the idea of the interior of a plane as a lounge room in the skies. For many years the popular magazine the *Australian Women's Weekly* crafted the persona of a woman's role as hostess, positively reinforcing certain skills and attributes in the everyday routines of this work in progress that was the Australian housewife. Article after article would extol the virtues of what constituted a good hostess. Indeed, just over a year after the air hostesses came on board in Australia, the *Australian Women's Weekly* made the bold claim, 'Every women enjoys acting as hostess. It is one of the gracious attributes of the feminine sex, but few have the opportunity of "hostessing" in the clouds'.[6]

The air hostess was situated in a liminal space; on the one hand she was employed to be a 'hostess' as she invited passengers into the confines of the planes, where she would serve food and drink while offering pleasant exchanges about the weather and the geography, along with gentle inquiry into the passengers' welfare. On the other hand, she was a young woman expected to manage and operate difficult technology, enforce safety procedures, and enact company policy with a degree of responsibility that might typically be expected of someone way beyond her years. The notion that the profession was a romantic one was often seen alongside the idea that the job offered an opportunity for a sense of adventure. An article from 1937, 'Exciting New Career for Girls', described air hostessing as having none 'of the humdrum of the ordinary career. It is a career of adventure, glamor [sic], travel, thrills and hazards'.[7] The association of 'thrills and hazards' with the new role of air hostess seemed an improbable fit, but this is precisely how the career played itself out in the bumpy world in the clouds.

1.2. 'An Adventurous Streak': Holyman's Airways

Smile, particularly in bad weather (1936)[8]

Early in 1936, Holyman's Airways in Tasmania had been 'flooded with applications' from 'girls' in Sydney, Melbourne and Launceston for the two positions of air hostess to fly on the new all-metal fourteen-passenger Douglas DC-2, *Bungana*. The name 'Bungana' was supposedly taken from an Aboriginal word for 'chief'. The newly appointed aviation writer in the local paper the *Launceston Examiner* wrote that many of the applicants were 'society girls', though what was required for the initial positions was a knowledge of nursing and stenography.[9] Meanwhile, the Hobart *Mercury* said that what the selectors were looking for was 'young women of some social standing, able to shoulder duties and responsibilities closely akin to those of a ship's purser and to maintain "office status"'.[10] Other requirements were physical fitness and stamina, calm temperament, a working knowledge of psychology and a pleasing personality. Blanche Due was 20 years old when she was selected for the job, which she described as appealing to her 'adventurous streak'.[11] She had completed forty hours of flying but had let her pilot's licence lapse. Her work experience included a business course, seven months of nursing at the Alfred Hospital and a first aid course at the Homecraft Hostel in Melbourne.[12] Nursing would become a qualification that was required of all Australian airline hostesses, following from the tradition set in 1930 by the first air stewardesses, as they were called in America. In preparation for the job she had collected tourist pamphlets and memorised everything possible about Tasmania and Melbourne.

Marguerite Grueber had flown as a passenger many times and completed two hours of dual-control flying.[13] Prior to joining the airline Grueber had been employed as a secretary at the Hobart radio station 7ZL.[14] It was expected that typing and shorthand skills would come in handy in the airline office on the days when she was not flying.[15] On the 11th March 1936, Grueber had received a letter from managing director, Ivan Holyman advising her that she had been selected for the coveted job. She was expected to attend the Launceston office at the end of the month to undergo a fortnight's training before commencing on the service run.[16] At that time, Holyman's Airways had flights between Hobart, Launceston, Flinders Island, King Island, Melbourne, Cootamundra, Canberra and Sydney. Late in April there was a demonstration flight on

Marguerite Grueber and Blanche Due in front of the Royal Mail DC-2 *Bungana*, Holyman's Airways, 1936
Marguerite Grueber and Blanche Due were employed as the first two air hostesses in Australia when they began working for Holyman's Airways in March 1936.
Courtesy of National Library of Australia

13

the *Bungana*. A journalist from the *Launceston Examiner* described in detail the sequence of events once the plane took off: '...a light flashed, requesting passengers to fasten their seat belts, but once off the ground the air hostess indicated the belts could be *undone*, and passengers *walked* about the roomy cabin, exchanging comments and taking photographs of the city of Melbourne...'[17] The journalist found the 'machine' exceptionally quiet in the air, and the fourteen passengers in their cushioned adjustable chairs were at times louder than the 'faint engine noise which penetrated the sound-proofed cabin'.[18] Along with morning tea and biscuits, cigarettes were offered.[19]

> *'What do you think of the uniforms?' Jane asked as they left the tailor. 'I love them. They're so trim and business like, yet feminine at the same time. What a contrast to a nurse's uniform.'*
> Ruth S. Wheeler, *Jane, Stewardess of the Air Lines*, 1934 [20]

Grueber and Due designed their own navy military-style uniform, which was made by a tailor in Collins Street, Melbourne.[21] And not only were they expected to look the part, they were required to be spokespersons for the airline. Grueber even conducted a radio broadcast with broadcaster Les Daley:[22]

> Announcer: And now Listeners, we want you to meet the hostess of the flying hotel...come and say 'How do you do', Miss Grueber!
>
> Hello everyone...this is the Hostess of the airliner speaking...I'd like to tell you all something about the plane...and the job.
>
> But first the plane. It's a marvellous 'ship' – we call her that – and travelling in the air is a lot smoother than

travelling in another sort of ship. From my seat right at the rear of the plane…just in front of the tiny buffet, I have a clear view of all the passenger accommodation… and there's a little red light over my head which shows when any one passenger happens to require my attention. Sometimes they do you know…But it doesn't take very long to get used to the motion of the airplane…and this one in particular is as steady as the rock of Gibraltar.

And now…something about passenger comfort… every seat if fitted in such a manner can be reversed, so that passengers can face one another…and each seat is ultra comfortable…being equipped with a headrest as soft as down and cushiony as the softest pillow. There is too an excellently designed arm rest and beneath that is a rack-fitting to which we attach trays when refreshments are served. Speaking of refreshments …we carry lots of things…but no alcohol…that's forbidden by regulations…but we stock everything in the soft drink line.

The interior of the *Bungana* has a definite colour scheme…soft blue leather lines the cabin…the seats are carried out in blue whip cord…and all the metal is bright. Every passenger has an individual window, also a reading light – which can be switched on or off at will – and we have air-conditioning…the very latest thing for comfort in travelling. There is also a control that allows me to alter the humidity inside the cabin at will …oh… by the way…passengers are allowed to smoke on this plane…that should tempt the menfolk ~~who usually want to go about in trains.~~[sic]

The duties of the hostess are to fix the straps around each of the passengers' legs before the plane takes off…

and remove them when it's in flight...generally we attend to the wellbeing and comfort of our passengers until they disembark. We wear a very snappy uniform and with my colleague Miss Due, share the distinction of being the first air hostesses appointed by an Australian airline. We're both fond of flying...and up to now have not been able to gratify our ambitions – but I think that hurdle no longer exists...cheerio everyone.[23]

The first scheduled flight was on Saturday 2nd May 1936 and it took two hours and fifteen minutes from Essendon, Melbourne to Mascot, Sydney with an average speed of 186 miles per hour. On board were eighteen persons including Captain Ivan Holyman and Mrs Hazel Holyman, Mr Harold Gatty of the Douglas Company, engine expert Mr W. G. Langville, two pilots, a radio operator and ten paying customers. Grueber was described as the busiest person on board, 'checking the passenger list, putting aboard the coffee and sandwiches to be served in the air, and answering questions – particularly answering questions – were her duties'.[24] Refreshments also included barley sugar, cordials and iced water. The hot drinks were served in waxed cups until it was realised the wax would melt and stick to the passengers' lips. Later they were replaced with something more suitable. The passengers chatted and smoked while they flew; they were allowed cigarettes and cigars but not pipes. While on board Captain Holyman sent telegrams outlining the delight of the passengers with 'the perfect weather and the silence of the engines'.[25]

The DC-2 had been designed and 'geared for the well to do – the mining magnates and the business tycoon'.[26] In America, on the Trans World Airlines (TWA) DC-2 service, they screened films including the newly released *Flying Hostess* (1936). The film

Collecting tickets and welcoming on board, 1936
In expectation of experiencing the elements, passengers carrying blankets and overcoats are welcomed on board the Holyman's Airways flight by Marguerite Grueber.
Courtesy of National Library of Australia.

was described as 'a romance as fast moving as the airliners around which the story is filmed'.[27] The plot was centred around 'the turbulent romance of a charming air hostess' Helen Brooks (played by Judith Barrett) and ace pilot Hal Cunningham (William Gargan) who, despite falling in love with her, had an immediate dislike for air hostesses because he felt there was no place for women in the air.[28] In a true Hollywood plot twist, Cunningham realises that an air hostess can be an asset when Brooks averts a disaster when the pilot on duty is knocked out mid-flight by a criminal. With Cunningham helping via radio, Brooks flies the plane to safety. While there is no record of it appearing on planes in Australia, *Flying Hostess* was released in 1937 and shown across the country. The film was advertised in a newspaper article, 'Would you like to be an air hostess?', that described the practical details of the working life of an air hostess as a 'modern branch of flying'.[29] The film was also advertised in the *Camperdown Chronicle* later that same year promoting what it took to be a 'flying hostess': 'Her life's record is investigated thoroughly; she must pass rigid tests for nerves and courage; and she must pass exacting medical examinations'.[30]

The introduction of the two air hostesses on the Holyman air services proved a success, so on 25th May 1936, Phyllis ('Pat') Daniels, who spoke French fluently[31] and was a trained nursing sister from Launceston, and Gladys Allan from Newport, Victoria began flying for the same airline.[32] One of the requirements for the job was nursing skills, as many of the passengers experienced airsickness, not only because of the unpressurised planes and rough crossings of the Bass Strait but also due to nervousness. The competitive nature of the position prompted the *Australian Women's Weekly* to write an article suggesting there was some bias towards selecting 'girls' from the south, 'Are southern girls more quick-witted at answering questions, or better informed than girls from NSW, Queensland, South Australia or West Australia?' they asked, 'Or are they of a lighter build and therefore less weight to carry in an aeroplane?'[33] The article acknowledged that the latest recruit, Gladys Allan, originally from Victoria, was 'a very pretty blonde, who is a very serious-minded young women with a taste for serious literature, contract bridge and amateur acting'. She was also a 'gifted pianist, and has taken her A.I.C.M. and other degrees'. Allan had flown a number of times as a passenger on a friend's plane,[34] and although she had learnt dual control she was 'never rich enough to train for a pilot's licence'.[35] This was a comment repeated by many air hostesses who would have liked to have pursued flying lessons but were without the financial means to obtain a licence.

Along with the *Bungana,* Holyman's Airways flew the de Havilland DH-86, which until the DC-2 had seemed so modern; the plane had cabin windows that were sealed, making normal conversation possible, and its four engines were equipped with an electric self-starter, so there was no longer the need to hand crank the propellers. Ivy Moore, a passenger, described her flight on the de Havilland DH-86 Express *Loila* from Sydney to Melbourne on 22nd July 1936: 'The hot tea offered by the dainty little air hostess, Gladys Allan, with her uniform cap perched jauntily on a crop of golden curls, was gratefully received. This intrepid lassie had already made twenty-eight crossings over Bass Strait, and in two months had flown more than 9,000 miles'.[36] The plane landed safely in Melbourne, and Moore thought 'a touch of glamour' was added to the bustling scene of the airport with the pilots and air hostesses in their uniforms. She described senior air hostess Marguerite Grueber taking over the next leg of the flight on the *Bungana* from Melbourne to Hobart as 'a rosy-cheeked, blue-eyed Tasmanian girl, slim and dignified' who 'marshalled us to our seats as the engines roared, and triumphantly the great Douglas was off, like an arrow from a bow, speeding towards Port Phillip'.[37] What was new, at the time, was the way such a gendered description would be immediately linked with technological enthusiasm.

Holyman's Airways Flight Schedule, Essendon Airport, 1936
Marguerite Grueber and First Officer Desmond Ditchburn set the arrival times for the Holyman's Airways planes arriving at Essendon airport from Adelaide, Sydney, King Island and Launceston. Courtesy of National Library of Australia.

> *The smoke-green serge fitted Jan snugly and the beret perched at a pert angle on her brown hair. She adjusted the seams of the new hose and slipped into dark grey pumps which were part of the uniform. With deft fingers she centred the green tie of her shirt-waist and stuck a fresh handkerchief in her pocket. Quick touches with the powder puff removed the shine from her nose and she gave her hair a final pat just as the horn on one of the field's cars blared outside.*
>
> Ruth S. Wheeler, *Jane, Stewardess of the Air Lines*, 1934[38]

The air hostess was expected to be a reassuring presence and, to help prepare them, they were issued with a volume of instructions: 'Smile, particularly during bad weather. Indeed the air hostesses' smile is her badge of service. The main idea behind the appointment of air hostesses, instead of men stewards, is that the very presence of a smiling, calm, bright young girl on an air journey is a reassurance to nervous people or those travelling for the first time'. 'She does it all year round and by choice', the passenger is supposed to reason, 'and there she is safe and sound and particularly healthy looking'.[39]

The Holyman air hostesses, when interviewed for an article in the *Australian Women's Weekly*, said that, although some of their time on board was taken up making tea and typing letters and telegrams, their work was mainly about answering questions, such as 'Where are we now?' and 'What altitude are we at?'[40] Flying over Melbourne, they would point out the university, Caulfield racecourse, the beaches of Port Phillip, and then Wilsons Promontory, and once over the ocean they would serve refreshments.[41] Pat Daniels stated that, for her, discretion was a really important aspect of the job as, 'anyone can hand out tea and barley sugar, but a good air hostess must be able to adapt herself to passengers with varying dispositions'.[42]

Before each flight the air hostesses would check the cleanliness of the plane and the supplies in the 'consumable stores'. Supplies would include towels, drinking cups, headrest covers, cigarettes and embossed stationery for writing on board. Clerical duties included checking the weight list of passengers and luggage. As well as the qualities of 'tact and diplomacy', the duties of the air hostess included making their guests at home in their 'flying drawing room' by ensuring flasks of tea were prepared and stored in a warming cupboard on board the plane. The air hostesses would welcome passengers on board in their military-style, navy blue uniforms, complete with brass buttons and glengarry cap. The tilt of the cap, cocked over the right eye, was all-important as a matter of hat etiquette. It was expected that the air hostess would attend to the passengers 'pleasantly, alertly, solicitously, and methodically'.[43] As soon as the passengers entered the plane their coats would be hung on a rack at the rear of the plane: thanks to the luxury of the heated *Bungana*, overcoats and knee rugs were no longer needed. Once seated, passengers would be strapped into their seatbelts, to prevent them 'being thrown out of their seats in the event of it being necessary to suddenly apply the brakes while the machine is taxiing'.[44] Once safely airborne the air hostess's task was to engage in conversation with passengers, explaining features of the landscape below and, if there were any signs of airsickness, a barley sugar would be offered. Airsickness was expected to be significantly reduced as the *Bungana* was designed to fly above 5,000 feet, where the air was smoother. An added feature of the *Bungana* was seats that could be turned to face each other if passengers wanted to play cards. While the DC-2s were faster, quieter and more comfortable than the de Havilland DH–86s, they were still unpressurised and, if the pilots had to fly them high to escape bad weather, it often became cold in the cabin. Grueber remembers placing sick bags over the passengers' feet to help keep them warm.[45] Other air hostesses would use newspapers.

1.3. Glamour Girls of the Air?

The 'flapper' in search of thrills is doomed to disappointment if she visualises a nice easy job, with adventure thrown in for good measure. It will be a case of sheer ability, and the Airlines of Australia and Australian National Airways, which are to run the (Brisbane to Adelaide 10 hour) service jointly, have made it plain that no 'glamour seekers' need apply.

'Air Hostesses', *The Mercury*, 19th July 1937, p. 6

While there was a general sense that air hostesses were a welcome addition to flights in the industry, as long as they were of 'attractive appearance and personality' and they had 'balance, poise, alert minds and sound commonsense', there was also the opinion that male stewards may be preferable on long flights.[46] Indeed, by July 1936, Holyman's Airways was now operating as Australian National Airways (ANA) and they were considering replacing the air hostesses with male stewards in the new year.[47] There is no record of this actually happening and it may have been in response to airlines such as Imperial Airways in the United Kingdom ignoring the hundreds of applications from 'air-minded girls' to fly with the airline, preferring instead to employ male stewards to deal with 'sick and obstreperous male passengers'.[48] The fact that males usually weigh more than women was an issue that had to be considered. Managing weight on board planes was a critical factor in preparation for any flight, and with passenger numbers on the ANA Bass Strait air services at a premium, it was becoming increasingly difficult to fly the quantity of mail needed to be delivered during peak periods.[49] As it turned out, ANA didn't introduce purser stewards until the late 1940s when they shared services with Air Ceylon and British Commonwealth Pacific Airways (BCPA). Qantas Empire Airways was the first Australian airline to introduce flight stewards when in 1938 they were recruited to fly on the flying boat services to London. Despite the relatively recent appearance of air hostesses, it was already a highly sought-after job and their presence on the planes had become so valued that the thought of removing them was increasingly remote.

Margaret Gilruth, a journalist who went on to become a famous war correspondent covering the activities of the Royal Air Force Advanced Striking Force in World War II, was intrigued by the thousands of young women applying for air hostess positions.

Many applicants didn't have the right qualifications, including a woman in her sixties who thought she might suit the job.[50] Gilruth decided to 'try' the job in the pretext of getting a good story. She was well placed to do this as she had a pilot's licence, and while working for the *London Daily Express* she became the first Australian woman to make a parachute jump.[51] She tried out for the job dressed in a borrowed uniform and a shirt her brother had lent her. She went on board with air hostess Violet 'Vi' Dethbridge, who flew as a passenger. After only one rough trip from Hobart to Launceston she decided it was 'no job for a woman', that there was no glamour in the job, and 'actually it is very hard work'. She said that she would rather take another parachute jump, a feat that involved crawling along the wing of a plane, then sitting on 'an insecure, uncomfortable perch, feet dangling into space and hands tightly clutching the struts' until given the call to fall backwards.[52] In other words, the job of the air hostess was not for the faint-hearted.

Because air hostesses had some social standing, they were the subject of news stories, representing the new culture of the airlines as it spread out through society. For many years it was typical that the appointment of a new air hostess would be reported in her 'hometown' paper, and also in a larger city paper. These were the days when a father's occupation carried some weight. For example, the Hobart *Mercury* reported, in a kind of 'coming out' language, that (the aforementioned) Dethridge, the daughter of Chief Judge Dethridge of Melbourne, who had already been working in the ANA Melbourne office, was appointed as their fifth air hostess in November 1936.[53] She would only work for two months before resigning to travel overseas with her sister by sea.[54] ANA was trying to recruit air hostesses from each state, so in January 1937 advertisements went out for air hostesses to fill the role in South Australia and Western Australia. Marjorie Anderson, a 'pretty and charming brunette' from Cottesloe, Perth, left her job as a nursing sister to become ANA's sixth air hostess.[55] She had been one of almost a thousand young women who had applied for the position and she was interviewed by Pat Daniels, who was now a senior hostess. Anderson was described in the Perth *Daily News* as having 'a capable manner, a lovely Burne Jones face, and talks well'.[56] She had spent six months working as a nanny on Murchison station, one of the oldest pastoral stations in Western Australia. The article described the highly coveted nature of the job, and presumably the comment that it was 'one of those jobs which leads to marriage' was meant to be seen as a bonus.[57] Anderson had been on many passenger flights but with her first flight on a mail run on the *Bungana* she admitted to feeling 'slightly delicate'.[58] Later that week she flew from Perth to Adelaide and then in March there was an article mentioning her on a flight on the *Bungana*, where the details of the flight were broadcast to radio listeners on the national radio station 6WF. Speaking with Anderson were Captain Baker and Lady Dorothy Haig, who was touring Australia to promote the British Empire Service League assistance for returned soldiers. Lady Haig not only expressed her delight at having an air hostess on board, she mentioned that one of her travelling companions, a white canary, enjoyed the trip so much that it sang for the first time.[59] The bird might have been happy, but Lady Haig complained that the airline refused to carry some of her luggage from Melbourne to Perth: 'It is just as well I'm used to roughing it a bit. I think that some women coming here by air from England would be very angry if they were forced, like I was, to send some goods from Melbourne to Fremantle by ship'.[60]

At least Lady Haig kept her seat. After wool sales in Hobart a passenger was preparing to fly back to Melbourne and he insisted on travelling even though he was the fifteenth passenger on the fourteen-seater DC-2. The upshot of his insistence was that the air hostess was left behind. It would seem that the concerns of the passenger would often come first. The man not only took her seat, but he also had to take over her duties.[61] Indeed, in the early days there were no hard and fast rules and sometimes they would get twenty miles out of an airport and then turn back to pick up a late passenger.[62] The matter of difficult passengers had already surfaced within three months of air hostesses coming on board. Complaints included: smoking at the wrong time, resistance to wearing a seatbelt, and sitting on the arm of the chair with limbs across the aisle. To help the air hostess if there were concerns on board, there were a number of call-buttons through the cabin that when activated would alert the first officer to come into the cabin.[63]

One of ANA's most regular passengers was Prime Minister Joseph Lyons, who would travel from his home state of Tasmania. He was a popular passenger with the air hostesses, as this comment suggests:

We all know the Prime Minister well. He is a gentle and genial passenger, usually tired and very thankful for comfort. No, he doesn't wile away the time consulting us on Constitutional matters. He goes to sleep and all you have to do is wake him at Hobart or Canberra.[64]

Lyons' wife Enid and their children were keen air travellers, but the family often travelled separately, so that in the event of a crash the children would not be 'bereft of both parents'.[65] The likelihood of a crash obviously didn't bother Sheila Lyons, the eldest daughter of the prime minister, as in April 1938 she applied for a

Prime Minister Joseph Lyons and Australian National Airways air hostesses, 15th August 1938

Prime Minister Joseph Lyons relied on the services of ANA to get him from his home in Devonport to his work in Canberra. Here he is at the opening of the new ANA building at Essendon airport with a group of ANA air hostesses.

Courtesy of Home Hill Collection, National Trust of Australia (Tasmania).

job as an air hostess with ANA. She had taken flying lessons but given them up because they were too expensive, and perhaps, like many other young women, air hostessing seemed to be the only way she could fulfil the desire to fly. The traffic manager at ANA, Mr D. Holyman, said that she had all the right qualifications, 'she has personality, appearance, and efficiency and is popular', but the one problem was she weighed 9 stone 4 lb instead of the required maximum of 8 stone 7 lb. She laughed this off by saying that, 'I will have to diet'.[66] The other issue was that, even though her father had agreed that she could apply, she was waiting on her mother for her decision. Perhaps Dame Enid said no, or losing the spare pounds proved more difficult than expected, as Sheila did not become an air hostess. Instead just over a year later, in June 1939, she was offered a position in the publicity department of ANA.[67]

There were so few air hostess positions that a new hostess could start only when someone left. Marjorie Anderson left ANA in December to marry after she had flown for almost two years, clocking up over half a million miles in 2,700 hours.[68] She was replaced by Kathleen Bonnin, a trained nurse who was described in a newspaper article as 'tall and dark with an attractive personality'.[69] Within a couple of weeks of starting with the company, Bonnin was rostered to fly on Christmas Day from Adelaide to Perth. It was a festive trip with passengers wearing paper hats and blowing whistles while being served cold turkey, chicken, ham, oysters and hot plum pudding and brandy sauce.[70] In July 1939, Bonnin was also on the historic first night flight from Perth to Melbourne on the *Bungana*.[71] It was such an exciting event that four of her air hostess colleagues made the special trip out to the Essendon airport to watch the arrival.[72]

1.4. Magic Carpet Across Australia

In December 1936, ANA had extended its services and began flying the *Bungana* on a biweekly service from Adelaide to Perth with stopovers in Ceduna, Forrest and Kalgoorlie. The first appearance of the *Bungana* in Adelaide coincided with an air pageant at Parafield airfield, and nearly 8,000 people witnessed the arrival of the 'huge, wide-winged and portholed machine. It was almost too big to fit in the hangar.'[73] Pat Daniels and Gladys Allan were in charge of victualling and passenger arrangements for the flight, and by this time the air hostesses had new summer uniforms made of beige linen. The double-breasted suit with epaulettes was worn with a navy tie, light stockings and black shoes. The navy cap had a small star-shaped ANA badge fixed on the right-hand side. In preparation for the trip across the country the air hostess had to order all the stores and provisions for the trip and arrange hotel accommodation for the passengers.

The new routes meant extended times away from the home base. On the first Perth trip Daniels and Allan felt miserable at the thought of spending Christmas away from family. Reflecting on this type of situation, Allan commented that the job of an air hostess was an excellent one for girls who have no home ties, and that 'a girl cannot have any sentimental attachments at all as an air hostess'.[74] The new run to Perth meant that some of the air hostesses would not return to their home bases for nearly a month, compared to the Sydney–Melbourne–Sydney service when they would only be away from home every second night.

Initially it was a two-day flight schedule, which would leave Perth on Tuesday after lunch, and catering was offered en route. Afternoon tea would be served after the two-hour flight to Kalgoorlie, and then there would be dinner and an overnight stay at the 'Hostel of the Desert' in Forrest, in the middle of the Nullarbor Plain. The hostel was proud of its facilities including sewered bathrooms, baths made of porcelain, and electric lights in the bedrooms. In the formal dining room, passengers and crew would sit at five small tables and were attended by maids in black uniforms with white aprons, collars and caps. Dinner would include dishes such as iced asparagus, roast duckling and apple sauce, roast mutton and red currant jelly, apple pie and cream. After dinner it was possible to play a game of tennis but only if the plane was removed from the hangar.

Forrest had been a desolate location, but in 1928 West Australian Airways (WAA), which had been formed on the 5th December 1921, had set up the hostel along the transcontinental railway to provide a stopover for the passenger and mail run to the east coast.[75] Initially WAA would fly the sixteen-seater three-engined de Havilland DH-66 Hercules on the route and the passengers would be offered a brochure 'On Airways Magic Carpet Across Australia' to read as they embarked on their journey. The brochure included useful advice such as 'good ventilation prevents airsickness which can often be cured by opening the window next to you', 'dizziness from looking downwards is unknown in an aeroplane, as there is no connection with the earth' and 'the aeroplanes used on the route are capable of continuing the journey with one engine stopped'.[76] With no air hostesses on board to assist, 'in the unlikely event of sickness, special paper bags are provided. Throw them out of the window after use'.[77] At this time it was not unusual to have animals such as cats and dogs transported across the country but more significantly there were regular shipments of gold from Kalgoorlie. The only security for the gold was that it was stowed between the pilots, and there was a mandatory pistol on board. The pistol was never loaded and the pilots were often unsure of where it was stored.[78]

> *Flying above the clouds, viewing the world through a mist, she laughed at the earthbound.*
>
> Nelly Graf, *Air Stewardess*, 1938[79]

After more than two years as an air hostess Marguerite Grueber was promoted to the new position of ground hostess for Australian National Airways (ANA). Although she was pleased with the promotion, it meant she would have to stop flying, which she regretted as she felt flying was something that 'gets into your blood'.[80] It was an occasion for reflecting on the air hostessing job she had left behind: 'Its chief charms. First the chance it gives one to observe human nature. I find an ever-fresh interest in every group of passengers. Second the travel aspect...'[81] Grueber was well aware that the air hostesses had to submit to various rules, such as not using too much lipstick, no costume jewellery and nail polish had to be of a natural or medium shade[82] and not getting too familiar with the passengers.[83] Although passengers were allowed to smoke and have a nip of whisky on board, the air hostesses were forbidden to smoke on board, or to have consumed alcohol within twelve hours of embarking on a flight.[84] Also, although frequently offered, the air hostesses could not accept tips and refusals would often lead to awkward exchanges with insistent passengers.[85] As part of the job, the air hostesses were required to have a general knowledge of the planes they were working in, including the speed, horsepower of engines, radio, airway facilities, and possess information such as why higher altitudes are smoother.

Grueber didn't comment on the irregularities of the job; for instance, most hostesses would pack an overnight bag, as it wasn't uncommon for them to be delayed for as long as three days if there was bad weather or repairs needed to the aircraft.[86] This was despite the fact that they were meant to work a thirty-hour week, with about fourteen hours spent in the air.[87] The air hostesses were allocated a ten shilling 'away from home' per diem allowance, but this didn't stretch very far, especially if staying at places like the grand Art Deco Hotel Australia in Castlereagh Street, Sydney; albeit in a small room at the top of the hotel.[88] In an earlier interview, Grueber, who had been stationed for a time in Perth, had mentioned another challenge of the job was making friends when living interstate. It was much more difficult for women in those days to make 'easy, casual friendships' in the same ways that men could.[89] It was perfectly acceptable for male crew to drink alone at the bar if they were staying in hotels. But until the 1970s, not only were women banned from bars, but the thought of them drinking alone in the 'Ladies Lounge' would have been highly unusual.

1.5. 'Don't Sleep on Duty': Airlines of Australia and Australian National Airways

The duties of an air hostess are outlined in a table of instructions occupying more than a dozen closely typed sheets of foolscap. One of the major duties is to constantly warn passengers of the risk of walking near propellers while the machine is on the ground.

'Must Retire at 35', *The Courier-Mail*, July 1937[90]

As civil aviation became more popular in Australia, new airlines were formed. Airlines of Australia (AoA), had been incorporated in 1935, and in June 1937 they advertised for young women to apply for air hostess positions for the Brisbane to Adelaide ten-hour service.[91] To be selected it was essential to be a trained nurse and the duties were outlined in a table of instructions, including 165 conditions printed on a dozen closely typed sheets of foolscap paper.[92] The young women were also expected to be proficient in shorthand and typing as the time spent on the ground would include office duties. Youth was preferred to experience so they were required to retire by the time they were 35. They were also expected to be:

...pleasant, alert, solicitous, methodical and with a clear understanding of their duties...[and] diplomats in analyzing the preferences and anticipating the wishes of each passenger. They must not chew gum or sleep on duty. Their reading during flights must be restricted to the book of regulations.[93]

A spokesperson for AoA, Mr P. Gurney, said the air hostess would be expected to regard the plane 'virtually as her home' and as such she was expected to check the cabin for cleanliness, and ensure that it and all the linen was spotlessly clean, and that all reading matter for passengers was in place. The food service on AoA was similar to ANA; morning tea was served with biscuits in individual cellophane packets and luncheon would be hot soup and crackers; cold breasts of chicken with mixed salad and mayonnaise, rolls and butter; fruit salad; tea or coffee.[94]

It was no coincidence that air hostesses were required to be nurses as there were real dangers associated with the job. One of the major duties of the air hostesses was to warn passengers of the risk of walking near propellers (and this remained a duty of air hostesses well into the 1960s). And, importantly, 'when asked to relate some of their air experiences they must refrain from mentioning any of the more thrilling or spectacular incidents'.[95] The decision to appoint air hostesses may have been a response to two fatal crashes that AoA were involved in earlier that year. On the 19th February 1937, the Stinson Model A monoplane *City of Brisbane* crashed in bad weather in the McPherson Ranges, Lamington National Park, near Lismore. The plane was not found until ten days after it vanished and, miraculously, of the seven on board there were two survivors.[96] Miss T. Casey of Brisbane, who was a regular flyer with AoA, had flown in the previous year with the copilot of the Stinson, Beverly Shepherd, and recounted the experience:

> It was a single-engine plane and the weather was frightful. Three passengers, though full of fear, were confident in the pilot, who handled the situation so well. We flew in dense fog miles out to sea, and only fifteen feet above water.[97]

She said that the recent accident in the Stinson would not alter her future bookings by air.

After another accident a month later, where the pilot and the sole passenger were killed, AoA appointed Laurie Steele as their first air hostess, possibly to shift attention away from the unfortunate spate of crashes. She was issued with the usual regulation book outlining the airline's expectations: be 'bright to all passengers without encouraging familiarity', and 'smile at all times'. Curiously, it was also specified that air hostesses were to refrain from 'making off-colour gestures towards passengers'. Steele mentioned that she didn't know what this meant and nor could she find anyone who could explain it to her.[98] Once appointed, she was issued with two winter uniforms and two summer uniforms, which she had to pay for herself, along with an insurance policy. Her uniform, like that of ANA, was a navy blue suit and it was worn with a starched white blouse and navy tie, with the wings of AoA embroidered on the left sleeve.[99]

Shortly after Steele was appointed, AoA purchased the Douglas DC-3 *Kyilla*.[100] The DC-3 would become the most successful commercial aircraft in aviation history and they would be flown in Australia until the early 1970s. The plane could seat twenty-one passengers, and had the feature of a 'robot pilot', which theoretically would allow the plane to stay on course while automatically counteracting the effects of air pockets and turbulence. It was tough, and a masterpiece of functional design. It was the only plane that could land at the same speed it could take off; perfect for landing in difficult terrain. And it transformed airline economics, almost doubling passenger numbers (in relation to the DC-2) and thereby making passenger transport profitable for the first time. Of course, this says nothing about the fact that they were noisy and unpressurised so they could only fly to 10,000 feet.[101] The airline boasted that it was steady enough to write a letter while flying, and a cup of tea could remain balanced on the floor at 9,000 feet.[102] This was a bold claim, as we shall discover in the next chapter. While it was exciting to fly on a brand new plane, the DC-3 wasn't the easiest plane to work on. The air hostesses would describe them as the plane where one walked uphill, as when they were on the ground they sat at a steep incline. Once in the air the plane would level out. After World War II, military versions of the DC-3 known as the C-47 'Dakota' were converted for use in civil aviation.[103]

In November, Steele went on a goodwill tour of Australia in the DC-3 with huge crowds greeting the plane at each city. In far north Queensland, Steele was met with an enthusiastic crowd at the aerodrome chanting, 'We want the air hostess'.[104] In Perth, an estimated crowd of 5,000 had waited for three hours for a sight of the plane and when it arrived at 5 pm they were allowed on board to inspect the 'latest phase in modern air travel'.[105] The excitement generated by the new plane extended to George A. Robinson, the director of AoA, who described a new way of commuting when he said that the new airline would make it possible for a 'man to live in Brisbane and go to his daily work in Sydney' as the service would run three return flights from Brisbane to Sydney in a day.[106] Major Victor Bertrandias, vice-president of Douglas Aircraft, who was the chief pilot on the goodwill tour, commented on the state of Australian aviation. One of the things that particularly pleased him was that in bad weather pilots were not afraid to turn back: '…[the] romantic nonsense about "the mail must go through" had been forgotten. Safety is the first and last consideration. It takes more courage to turn back and admit that weather is dangerous than to go ahead into it'.[107]

Steele shared a flat at Kirribilli with Phyllis (Phyl) Currie, who had been appointed as the second air hostess on AoA.[108] After six months Currie moved from the Sydney–Adelaide route to the Sydney–Brisbane route. She might only stay in the flat twice a week, as sometimes the trip to Brisbane would necessitate a night at a hotel in Brisbane. She described her job as 'having to do everything and be everything', and:

> People's eyes nearly pop out of their head with curiosity when they learn I am an air hostess. They seem to regard me as a being from another planet. They imagine I spend my time in daily hair-breadth escapes, enjoying a romantic life above the clouds in the manner picturised [sic] in Hollywood.[109]

It was, in fact, hard work, working on the Sydney–Brisbane route, travelling between the cities three times in one day. On alternate weekends she would work on the DC-3 *Kyilla* when it flew to Townsville. Early morning starts of 4.00 am were necessary to catch the AoA service car to the aerodrome. Along with keeping control of live freight such as crabs, canaries, rare New Guinea bugs and goldfish, she had to check for stowaways; some of the contingencies required of the air hostess that were not in the book of regulations. On one occasion she was asked to paint and manicure the nails of a Brisbane 'society woman' who had forgotten to do them before she flew. Other passengers would include businessmen and overseas travellers, but there were also lots of newlyweds, complete with bouquets and confetti. Her name, along with the captain and first officer, would be written on a notice board and placed at the door of the cockpit, and while some would call her by her name others would call her 'hostess'.

Like most airlines across the world at that time there was no cooking on board, instead tea and coffee came aboard in vacuum flasks, and sandwiches were prepared at various aero clubs.[110]

Currie stayed in Australia and eventually became chief hostess of ANA. But Steele, a year after she started flying with AoA, applied, with Robinson's recommendation, for a position to fly with the Dutch airline KLM, which she was offered.[111] Before she left Australia she wrote an account for the *Courier-Mail* of her time flying. In the article she described the many questions that passengers asked, ranging from the technical: 'How much fuel does the plane carry?', to 'Doesn't your coffee ever boil over?' And from nearly everyone came the question, 'Don't you ever get bored?' To which she answered, 'Never'.[112] She had clear opinions about the passengers, with the impression that men were the best travellers because even if they were nervous they would not admit it.

When Steele left in 1938 she became the only 'British' air hostess flying for KLM on the Amsterdam and London route. She was expected to fly six days a week, a gruelling schedule compared to Australia.[113] She mentioned that air hostesses in Europe had to keep fit, and she attended a gymnasium twice a week, went horseriding with the pilots, and played golf and tennis. One thing that impressed Steele was that ground radio and meteorological systems were in place at European airports, meaning that the pilots were constantly in touch through wireless. This meant that things ran closer to schedule and there was a greater awareness of what weather may be encountered on any route. While she was away she missed the beauty of the Australian coastline and made the observation that European women were 'generally less smart', and had none of the 'easy balance and poise of our girls'.[114] As war was approaching, the job of air hostess took on an air of intrigue, with Steele wondering what 'world-shaking secrets' were concealed in the dispatch cases of some of the notable passengers on her flights. In Australia, her passengers had predominantly been politicians, businessmen and wool brokers, but now on international flights she had refugees fleeing persecution and passengers such as Sir Harold MacMichael, High Commissioner of Palestine, who was flying to London to consult Cabinet Minister Malcolm MacDonald about the threatened war between the 'Arabs and the Jews'.[115] She described landing in airports that were full of uniformed officers, and there was uncertainty about whether they would be given permission to leave. Already on a flight from Rotterdam to Prague they had been stopped by German authorities and told they could not fly over Germany that day. In October 1939, Steele decided it was time to leave Europe after a Dutch plane was hit by bullets, killing one passenger. During the war she was chosen by the British government for the elite position of an aircraft examiner. This was a new position for women and it required a 'fine eye for detail' and exacting standards.[116]

1.6. First Air Hostess Killed

> There was the sensation of falling blindly into a great abyss and then came a jarring crash that seemed to split the cabin apart. After that there was a silence, broken only by the sobbing of the wind.
>
> Ruth S. Wheeler, *Jane, Stewardess of the Air Lines*, 1934[117]

The introduction of air hostesses in the 1930s had proved to be an unmitigated success. Alongside modelling and film-star roles, it was the glamour job of the decade, but it cost lives. Air hostesses were instructed to refrain from discussing 'air experiences of an exciting nature'.[118] This meant air crashes. Gladys Allan had experienced an 'exciting experience' in December 1936 when the de Havilland DH-86 *Loila* she was flying in − carrying five passengers − was forced to make an emergency landing in Seymour, Victoria, while waiting for a storm to pass. As the plane was landing the starboard wheel struck a fence and crumpled, the plane skidded along the ground with the starboard wing jolting and then snapping off.[119] No one was injured and one of the passengers remarked, 'I'd give the air hostess, Miss Gladys Allan, a bonus. She was wonderful, and looked after us all'.[120] Within ten minutes of the 'mishap' she had tea ready in the cabin as the passengers stayed on board seeking shelter from the torrential rain.[121]

Later in that year Allan was to experience an incident that had no happy ending. On the 25th October 1938 she had been rostered to fly on the DC-2 *Kyeema* service between Adelaide and Melbourne, but she was unwell and Elva Jones took her place. And so, tragically, it was 27-year-old Jones who became the first air hostess killed in Australia when the *Kyeema* crashed into the Dandenong Ranges killing all four crew and fourteen passengers on board. Jones had been a trained nurse from Ballarat and had joined ANA in December 1937, and until relatively recently had been flying on the *Bungana's* Adelaide–Perth run.[122] The airline described her as having a pleasant personality and being most efficient and capable. Amongst the guard of honour at her funeral was ANA's chief air hostess Miss Lorna Webb and air hostess Miss F. Stokes.[123] Allan was interviewed by the *Australian Women's Weekly* and said the death of Jones had affected her deeply but she would rather not talk about it. Adding, 'I don't believe that what happened is a warning to me' and, 'Of course, I am still going on as an air hostess!'[124]

This crash was the worst in Australian aviation history, with the loss of eighteen lives. It became particularly significant as it forced the rewriting of Australian aviation safety standards. As an air hostess, Allan would have been well aware of the difficult conditions pilots faced and she took the opportunity to comment on what she saw as a systemic failure in the system: 'If the public took a greater interest in aviation and everybody urged their members of parliament to help it forward, these accidents would not happen. They only happen because the companies are battling along without the national support they deserve'.[125] What Allan was referring to was the lack of safety aids and standards in Australia at that time. Even though navigational beacons were in place at the time of the crash of the *Kyeema*, the final adjustments to make them operational had not been completed.[126]

Allan's intervention was surprising. A mere air hostess advocating government support for the industry? Missing her appointment with the fate all her colleagues risked every working day gave her words an added poignancy. But her advocacy also presaged a later chapter in the profession's history: the pioneering role of hostesses in pushing through the industrial changes that would make their so-called glamorous jobs not only modern, but safer and fairer.

Notes

1   F. Vivian Drake, 'Air stewardess', *Atlantic*, February 1933, pp.185–93, p. 186.

2   R. S. Wheeler, *Jane, Stewardess of the Air Lines*, Goldsmith, Chicago, 1934, p. 49.

3   T. Fubbs, 'Australia's first air hostesses', Weekend Section, *Argus,* 23 January 1937, p. 30.

4   ibid.

5   See other types of hostess such as on trains in Anon. 'Transport: women on wheels', *Time*, 16 August 1937, p. 17.

6   Anon, 'Exciting new career for girls', *Australian Women's Weekly*, 29 May 1937, p. 2.

7   ibid.

8   M. Knight, 'What it means to be an air hostess: medicine and manners', *Queenslander,* 23 July 1936, p. 17; T. Fubbs, 'Australia's first air hostesses', p. 30.

9   Aviation Writer, 'Douglas plane: four strait flights daily?', *Examiner*, 6 February 1936, p. 6.

10   Anon, 'On duty with the air hostess', *Mercury*, 5 August 1936, p. 7.

11   Anon, 'New airliner's fast flight', *Argus*, 4 May 1936, p. 9.

12   Anon, 'First air hostesses', *Advocate*, 13 March 1936, (clipping); The Homecraft Hostel was established in 1929 to provide girls on leaving school with practical home training and to establish home and institutional management as a recognised profession for women. See L. Gardiner, *A Woman's Place: A History of the Homecraft Hostel*, Hyland House, Melbourne, 1993.

13   Halstead, 'Roundabout: people and events', *West Australian*, 29 July 1938, p. 9.

14   Anon, 'Australia's first. Hobart girl selected', *Advocate*, 12 March 1936, p. 7.

15   Anon, 'Tasmanian air hostess: Miss M. F. Grueber's task', *The Mercury*, 18 March 1936, p. 6.

16   Letter to Marguerite Grueber from Ivan Holman dated 11 March 1936.

17   Anon, 'A short flight: *Bungana* surprises', *Launceston Examiner*, 30 April 1936, p. 7.

18   ibid.

19   Anon, 'First air hostess', *Townsville Daily Bulletin*, 4 May 1936, p. 10.

20   Wheeler, *Jane, Stewardess of the Air Lines*, p. 54.

21   M. McRobbie, *Walking the Skies: The First Fifty Years of Air Hostessing 1936 to 1986*, Self-published, Melbourne, [1986] 1992, p. 15.

22   Anon, 'On duty with the air hostess'.

23   Marguerite Grueber, Radio Interview with Les Daley c.1936.

24   Anon, 'Douglas makes record commercial flight', *Advocate*, 4 May 1936, p. 7.

25   ibid.

26   Jean Menlove in N. Witcomb, *Up Here and Down There*, Self-published, Adelaide, 1986, p. 37.

27   Anon, 'The flying hostess', *Morning Bulletin*, Rockhampton, 22 April 1937, p. 13.

28   Anon, 'Flying Hostess at Rex Sunday', *Madera Tribune*, 24 April 1937, p. 3; Anon, 'Air Hostess', *Western Mail*, 11 March 1937, p. 32.

29   Anon, 'Would you like to be an air hostess?', *Daily News*, 17 March 1937, p. 4.

30   Anon, 'Flying hostess' advertisement, *Camperdown Chronicle*, 18 November 1937, p. 2.

31   Anon, 'On duty with the air hostess'.

32   Anon 'More air hostess: careers for girls', *Sydney Morning Herald*, 15 May 1936, p. 11. They had been placed on the reserve list (along with Evelyn Williams from South Yarra) when Due and Grueber had been appointed

in March, in Anon, 'New air hostess', *Mercury*, 4 June 1936, p. 7.

33 Anon, 'Girls from the south are in the clouds', *Australian Women's Weekly*, 30 May 1936, p. 39.

34 ibid. She had flown twenty-four hours, in Anon, 'Versatile air hostess', *Mercury*, 27 May 1936, p. 6.

35 L. Quarrell, 'Air hostesses consider work fascinating', *Advertiser*, 21 December 1936, p. 12.

36 Anon, 'Air traveller appreciates Tasmania', *Mercury*, 11 August 1936, p. 6.

37 ibid.

38 Wheeler, *Jane, Stewardess of the Air Lines*, p. 102.

39 Fubbs, 'Australia's first air hostesses'.

40 Anon, 'Girls from the south are in the clouds'.

41 Anon, 'Meet the air hostesses', *Barrier Miner*, 8 June 1936, p. 4.

42 ibid.

43 Fubbs, 'Australia's first air hostesses'.

44 Anon, 'Air hostess', *Examiner Women's Supplement*, 5 August 1936, p. 5.

45 McRobbie, *Walking the Skies: The First Fifty Years of Air Hostessing 1936 to 1986*, p. 20.

46 Anon, 'Few air hostesses: Australian lines would prefer stewards', *Courier-Mail*, 7 April 1936, p. 14.

47 Anon, 'Air hostesses to be replaced by stewards', *Mercury*, 25 December 1936, p. 9.

48 Anon, 'Hostesses banned: Imperial Airways prefer stewards', *Examiner*, 17 October 1936, p. 7.

49 Aviation Writer, 'Will additional planes be needed?,' *Examiner*, 9 August 1937, p. 6.

50 L. Quarrell, '100 S.A. girls seek air hostess career', *Advertiser*, 12 January 1937, p. 14.

51 J. Baker, ' "She turned up for work with debris in her hair": the women war reporters you've never heard of', *Guardian*, Accessed 12 March 2016 <http://www.theguardian.com/commentisfree/2015/oct/22/she-turned-up-to-work-with-bits-of-debris-still-in-her-hair-the-women-war-reporters-youve-never-heard-of>.

52 ibid.

53 Anon, 'New air hostess: Miss Dethbridge appointed', *Mercury*, 19 November 1936, p. 7.

54 Anon, 'Air hostess travels by ship to London', *Advertiser*, 15 April 1938, p. 13.

55 Anon, 'New air hostess here on Wednesday', *Advertiser*, 16 January 1937, p. 14.

56 Referencing the pre-Raphaelite artist.

57 Hepzibah, 'Pretty Perth girl gains post of air hostess', *Daily News,* 13 January 1937, p. 9.

58 Anon, 'New air hostess here on Wednesday'; Anon, 'Bungana speaking at 180 m.p.h.', *Daily News,* 15 March 1937, p. 2.

59 Anon, 'Voices from the air: Lady Haig and others', *Daily News,* 22 March 1937, p. 4.

60 Anon, 'Air services criticised: Lady Haig protests to company', *Advertiser,* 15 March 1937, p. 20.

61 Anon, 'Man makes good as deputy air hostess', *Advocate,* 30 January 1937, p. 4.

62 Anon, 'On duty with the air hostess'.

63 S. Gott, 'Flying round with the girls!', *Mirror,* September 1960, clipping.

64 Fubbs, 'Australia's first air hostesses'.

65 Anon, 'Air hostess who missed death in the Kyeema', *Australian Women's Weekly,* 5 November 1938, p. 32.

66 Anon, 'Sheila Lyons wants to be an air hostess', *Daily News,* 30 April 1938, p. 1.

67 Anon, 'Joins airways staff', *Argus,* 8 June 1939, p. 1.

68 Anon, 'Air hostess to be married', *Argus,* 19 March 1938, p. 3.

69 Anon, 'Air hostess retires', *West Australian,* 14 December 1938, p. 4.

70 Anon, 'Dinner party in the air', *Daily News,* 26 December 1938, p. 7.

71 During the war Bonnin left ANA to serve with the Australian Imperial Force as a nurse; where she excelled and acquired the rank of Captain. Anon, 'A.I.F. sister was air hostess', *Advertiser,* 10 August 1940, p. 13.

72 Anon, 'From Perth in one day', *Argus,* 4 July 1939, p. 7.

73 Anon, 'Thrills at big air pageant', *Mail,* 19 December 1936, p. 1.

74 Quarrell, 'Air hostesses consider work fascinating'.

75 Airways Museum, WA Airways Hostel – Forrest, accessed 17 March 2016 <http://www.airwaysmuseum.com/FRT%20-%20WAA%20hangar%20guest%20house%202.htm>.

76 Western Australian Airways, 'On airways magic carpet across Australia' pamphlet, c. 1930.

77 Western Australian Airways, 'On airways magic carpet across Australia'.

78 P. Yule, *The Forgotten Giant of Australia Aviation: Australian National Airways,* Hyland House, Melbourne, 2001, p. 91.

79 N. Graf, *Air Stewardess,* Gramercy, New York, 1938, book review in *Journal of Aeronautical Sciences,* vol. 6, no. 6, 1939, p. 257.

80 Halsted, 'Roundabout: people and events'.

81 Anon, 'Half a million miles flown by pioneer air hostess', *Herald,* 9 September 1938, clipping.

82 Anon, 'Air hostesses', *Mercury*, 19 July 1937, p. 6.

83 Anon, 'Would you like to be an air hostess?'.

84 Fubbs, 'Australia's first air hostesses'.

85 Anon, 'Air hostess', *Auckland Star*, 27 July 1937, p. 9.

86 Anon, 'On duty with the air hostess', *Mercury*, 5 August 1936, p. 7.

87 Anon, 'Exciting new career for girls', *Australian Women's Weekly*, 29 May 1937, p. 2.

88 Anon, 'On duty with the air hostess'.

89 Hepzibah, 'First air hostess on Perth run', *Daily News*, Perth, 5 February 1937, p. 7.

90 Anon, 'Must retire at 35: rigid code for air hostesses for Airlines of Australia', *Courier-Mail*, 9 July 1937, p. 14.

91 Airlines of Australia was registered on 4 October 1935. It had started out as New England Airways 1931–35, and in 1942 it became ANA.

92 Anon, 'Must retire at 35: rigid code for air hostesses for Airlines of Australia'.

93 ibid.

94 Anon, 'Air hostess', *Auckland Star*.

95 ibid.

96 See M. Job, *Air Crash Vol 1. 1929–1939*, Macarthur Job and Aerospace Publications, Canberra, 1991, p. 98.

97 Anon, 'Air accidents do not deter women travellers', *Australian Women's Weekly*, 27 February 1937, p. 35.

98 Anon, 'Air hostess has many duties but likes job', *Courier-Mail*, 2 August 1937, p. 17.

99 Anon, 'Australian hostess for world's airlines', *Advertiser*, 9 June 1938, p. 9.

100 ANA also purchased their first DC-3, *Kurana,* in 1937.

101 Barbara Butler, who flew with MAA in the 1960s and flew on the DC-3s, brushes this off by saying 'mountain people live that high up!'.

102 Anon, 'Goodwill flight', *Sydney Morning Herald,* 15 November 1937, p. 9.

103 The last DC-3 to fly on a commercial flight in Australia was *Tullana,* which had been purchased by ANA in 1946, taking its final flight with Airlines of New South Wales in 1970.

104 Anon, 'Will become linguist', *Courier-Mail*, 7 June 1938, p. 3; Anon, 'Goodwill air tour', *West Australian*, 16 Nov 1937, p. 20.

105 M. Hunter, 'Eve and modern sister are very much alike', *Courier-Mail*, 22 December 1937, p. 22.

106 Anon, 'Goodwill air tour'.

107 Anon, 'Aeroplane to carry 43 passengers', *Courier-Mail*, 16 November 1937, p. 12.

108 Currie became Chief Hostess of ANA c. 1945 in Yule, *The Forgotten Giant of Australian Aviation: Australian National Airways*, p. 237.

109 Anon, 'She earns her living in the air', *Sydney Morning Herald*, 12 July 1938, p. 12.

110 See an account of this regarding TWA airlines, 'Housekeeping in the clouds', *Popular Mechanics*, vol. 38, no. 5, November 1937, p. 712.

111 KLM had employed air hostesses since 1935.

112 L. Steele, 'Hostess above the clouds', *Courier-Mail*, 11 June 1938, p. 9.

113 Anon, 'Up in the air', *Evening Post*, 1 December 1938, p. 19.

114 L. Steele, 'Air hostess over Europe', *Australian Women's Weekly*, 29 October 1938, p. 12.

115 ibid.

116 M. St Claire, 'Important war post for Laurie Steele', *Australian Women's Weekly*, 10 May 1941, p. 9.

117 Wheeler, *Jane, Stewardess of the Air Lines*, p. 69.

118 Anon, 'Air hostess has many duties but likes job'.

119 Anon, 'Archbishop Wand in forced landing', *Morning Bulletin*, 4 December 1936, p. 9.

120 Anon '"Felt a slight jar": passengers not worried', *Sydney Morning Herald*, 4 December 1936, p. 11.

121 Anon, 'Archbishop wand in forced landing'.

122 Anon, 'Terrible aviation disaster', *Kalgoorlie Miner*, 26 October 1938, p. 4.

123 Anon, 'Airliner victims', *Argus*, 29 October 1938, p. 2.

124 Anon, 'Air hostess who missed death in the Kyeema'.

125 ibid.

126 Allan remained working as an air hostess for three years but in May 1939 she joined the publicity department of ANA. At the outbreak of the war, commercial aviation was severely curtailed and Allan undertook publicity work in the film industry. In October 1947 she became women's public relations officer for Trans Australia Airlines.

Chapter Two

SETTING THE STANDARD

2.1. Gimlet Eyes: Matron Holyman

The ANA air hostesses didn't even have one hair out of place,
even though they'd just come off the tarmac and propellers flying
in all directions. They still looked perfect.

Patricia (Martin) Tickner, ANA air hostess, 1956 to 1965

In February 1940, the starboard engine of the ANA DC-2 *Bungana*
burst into flames as it was flying over Dimboola. Air hostess Mavis
Matters had reported the strong smell of petrol to the captain and
copilot before the engine fell out of the nacelle and dropped to the
ground.[1] The plane lost altitude fast, with the eleven passengers
holding hands, but it was reported that Matters, who had been
with the airline for eight months, was 'superb' as 'she moved
calmly to each passenger fastening safety belts'. And while she
appeared calm, apparently there were beads of perspiration on
her forehead.[2] It was thought that a bird had struck the engine.[3]
Matters' experience saw her as part of an editorial feature in the
Australian Women's Weekly about brave Australian women, appearing in the article alongside a woman who rode for four days by
horseback from a small mining town to Cloncurry to save the life
of her six-year-old son, and a woman from Yass who gave birth to
a baby while bushfires raged around her outback hut.[4] The heroic

air hostess would appear again in the *Australian Women's Weekly* with the tale of an American air stewardess who swallowed the key to the aeroplane's safe in order to prevent an onboard robbery. As the article said, 'this spirit of duty knows no frontiers!'[5] Wartime had changed circumstances for many professions and, despite previously strict rulings that an air hostess could not be married, Matters became the first, acting as a senior hostess while her husband Geoffrey Sheppard served in the RAAF.[6]

Dramas in the air were not restricted to real life; they also made for good viewing for film audiences. *Flight Angels* (1940) starred Virginia Bruce as the 'White Angel of the Airways' and Jane Wyman as the 'Blonde Dynamite Looking for a Place to Explode'. They appeared as air hostesses in a story about a pilot who, due to failing eyesight, takes a job as an instructor at an airline hostess school. Originally the film had the working title of *Tough Angels*, as it was to be about the rigours of training at the Chicago air hostess school. The emergence of this Hollywood genre was a sign the profession in America was gaining momentum. More airlines were employing stewardesses, with Delta Air Lines employing their first in 1940, ten years after Ellen Church had been recruited as the world's very first stewardess for Boeing Air Transport (later United Airlines).

In 1940 there were only eighteen air hostesses working at ANA, and they were under the charge of Hostess Superintendent 'Matron' Hazel Holyman. She was not a real matron, but thought she had been given that name to differentiate her from all the other Holymans associated with Holyman's Airways.[7] Matron would seem an appropriately formidable handle to borrow for the air hostessing profession, as the nursing matron could be characterised as someone who was responsible for organising work, training, and providing discipline in work and the private life of her charges.[8] The matron would also look for and develop the qualities of a 'good woman' that included 'quietness, patience, endurance, obedience, unselfishness and devotion'.[9] Many of the air hostesses would attest to feeling Matron's eyes on them; to not wanting to disappoint her even if they didn't always agree with what was asked of them.

Matron had been married to Victor Holyman, the founder of Holyman's Airways, who disappeared tragically with ten others on the 19th October 1934 when the de Havilland DH-86 *Miss Hobart* he was flying went missing over Bass Strait. Not only did the airline lose its founder and one of its most experienced pilots but the crash had a damaging impact on the finances of the airline with few passengers flying for the next year.[10] The perception that air hostesses promoted feelings of security may have encouraged Holyman's to bring air hostesses on board to boost passenger numbers. Since the incorporation of Holyman's Airways in 1932 'Matron' had played a central role, driving the passengers in her own car from Launceston to Western Junction airfield, which at that stage was more of a paddock than an actual landing strip. She would provide passengers with a thermos of tea and she would pack a tin full of biscuits for them to share on the often very bumpy flight to Flinders Island. Years later she recalled having to 'practically push the passengers into the plane'.[11] After Victor's death she travelled to Europe, and in 1939, while in London, she received a request from Ivan Holyman to come back and help train flight hostesses for ANA.[12] Before returning to Australia, she prepared by visiting air hostess training schools in England, Holland and America.[13] She reported from her study tour, which included visiting United Airlines in Chicago, that three American airlines each had 150, 125 and 100 air hostesses and that they had training schools, something she aspired to have in Australia.[14] When she took up her new duties in November 1939 ANA training would be conducted in her office.

Matron Holyman was assisted by Mavis Gardiner, who had started flying a couple of years earlier, and Phyllis Currie who had transferred from AoA.[15] Matron described her new role as 'Housekeeping in the Air' for, as well as directing the activities of the air hostesses, she planned all meals served on the planes and those served at the Essendon passenger hostel. As part of her superintendent role Holyman would fly interstate to what were then considered far-flung places such as Townsville, Mackay and Cairns to interview would-be air hostesses. Matron stated that there was a great deal more to the air hostessing profession than the appearance of 'a shining perm beneath the forage cap', even though everyone who applied for a position had to supply a photograph. But Matron was adamant:

> Contrary to most opinions, this is not a job for glamor girls. The kind of pleasing appearance that is acceptable to all types of travellers is more satisfactory. The girl we choose must be efficient, intelligent, cool and level-headed, and she must also be charming. She must speak nicely, and must show signs of being able to adapt her conversation to suit her passengers.[16]

At this time the formal requirements to be an ANA air hostess included nursing qualifications, aged between 22 and 35 years of age, no taller than 5 foot 4 inches (162 cm) and not more than 8 stone 7 pounds (54kg).[17] Training was over three weeks and included learning about the engines and flying, handling passenger reservations, serving hot and cold meals, controlling the ventilation on the planes, geographical and historical points of interest and the best possible connections with trains, boats and other planes. Initially, the ANA air hostesses were expected to pay for their own uniforms, the winter uniform costing £7.7.0 and the summer dress (from Myer) £4.4.0 but later on Matron implemented a policy where they would be issued with uniforms free of charge.[18] An average day included six hours in the air, and it was expected that the air hostesses would fly about thirty hours a week. On the longer east–west run the air hostesses could clock up nine hours of flying time. Adverse weather conditions often meant that it was necessary to land the plane and wait until the weather cleared. This could include an overnight stop, and it was expected that the air hostess would have to assist passengers during these stopovers.[19]

When plane arrives at aerodrome, the hostess is expected to check everything and see that passengers do not walk off with rugs, spoons etc.

ANA air hostess pre-training course notes,
September to December 1948

The air hostess had many responsibilities, including accounting for 'every salt and pepper shaker, every knife, fork, and spoon', which if lost she had to pay for out of her own pocket. Keeping charge of the cutlery and crockery helped create the general impression that the air hostesses fulfilled the roles of a domestic hostess in the sky. An article in *The Argus* in March 1940 compared her role to that of a domestic hostess preparing for a dinner party. The only difference was that meals were served 10,000 feet above the air and on metal trays:

...the thought of serving twenty-one meals, and two more for the pilots, from a space about three feet by two and a small bar doesn't appal her. She may, sometimes, remark, 'Oh, dear, I'm quite exhausted, I've been on my feet all day', just like any housewife. One is apt to forget that, on a long run, such as the Perth–Adelaide section, she has also travelled 1,410 miles, effortlessly.[20]

Cynthia Loxton had decided to join ANA in 1939, even though it was her friend Elva Jones who had been the air hostess killed in the DC-2 *Kyeema* crash the year before. When she joined there were no meals provided for air hostesses: she claimed the hostesses would sometimes ask the pilots to fly through cloud to make it rough and thereby discourage at least one passenger from their meal. Once again, it was Matron who came to the aid of the air hostesses by insisting that they be allocated an in-flight meal.

2.2. War Interrupts

Within a year of Matron starting with ANA she had to travel to Brisbane to recruit new air hostesses to replace a number who had left to get married. During wartime a fair proportion of the air hostesses would be lost to marriages and engagements.[21] By 1942 most civil air services in Australia were suspended and civilians were only able to travel by air if there was an emergency. For those who were considering travelling there were posters asking everyone to consider, 'Is Your Journey Really Necessary?' With air services reduced to a minimum, air hostesses were required for different roles. ANA air hostesses were required to help with the evacuation of civilians from Port Moresby. They would fly from Cairns to Port Moresby, stay the night and then travel on to Rabaul where they would land on the golf course, and the passengers who had been brought in from outlying plantations by smaller planes would be ushered on board. For the air hostesses left at home, with their flying hours reduced, some tried to find other things to do. Jean Menlove and a couple of her colleagues hoped that the spare hours waiting for a flight could be filled with voluntary work at the Adelaide Children's Hospital. What seemed a good idea to start with ended badly. A write-up in a local paper about their voluntary work led to the air hostesses being ordered to return to nursing until the end of the war.[22] In 1943, because so many nurses were required for the war effort, the rules were changed and air hostesses no longer had to have nursing training. This was also the case in the United States. At De Paul University, Chicago a psychology course was developed in conjunction with Trans World Airlines (TWA) with the aim of recruiting students; this meant the prerequisite of a nursing qualification could be substituted with a year of college education.[23]

Matron continued to recruit and train air hostesses on an individual basis throughout the war, but since this was labour intensive she put in place her earlier plan to train air hostesses in groups. This was something she had wanted to do since visiting the stewardess training school in America. With the shift away from using trained nurses, there was also the view that a specially designed training course could instil a sense of discipline, which was proving a more important aspect of the job than nursing skills. Group training would mean a six-week intensive course, with lectures prepared by Matron, the chief engineer, a flight super-intendent, the operation superintendent and the public relations officer. Despite the war, ANA and AoA (who had some shared services) were making other changes, and they employed Kathleen Wise as the first female publicity officer. The plan to create a training school would require some expense and it was not as if the airlines were flush with money at this time; ANA had to farm its own land near the Archerfield airfield in Brisbane, growing potatoes and carrots to supply food for their flight services.[24]

Matron Hazel Holyman and some of 'her girls', Adelaide, 1945
Matron Holyman, Air Hostess Superintendent of ANA, photographed with some of the new recruits in Adelaide, 1945. Anne (Oxenham) Burton is seated at the front on the left-hand side. Courtesy of Anne Burton.

Anne (Oxenham) Burton was 22-years-old when she was interviewed by Matron Holyman in 1944, and she described her as 'very beautifully dressed and very correct, and pretty tough'.[25] For her interview, Burton 'got dressed up in my best bib and tucker', and over seventy years later she could clearly remember what she wore:

> Well in those days we used to dress-make...I made myself a soft green woollen suit, buttoned down the front...you made the button holes very carefully, high

neck. It was a pale green, and I had a hat made, covered in the same material. On it I wore a little lily-of-the-valley brooch, I suppose it was made of glass, but it was white and green and it was the most delicate thing, and I've still got it, some of the bits have fallen off, but it was the prettiest thing. I had some shoes, Parker shoes; they were very in…at that time, which I had bought the year before for 4 guineas (£4.4), which was a lot of money.[26]

It *was* a lot of money. When Burton started the average wage for a young woman such as herself was about £4 a week, and she bought the shoes on layby, paying them off over six months. Parker shoes were sold at David Jones and the exclusive high-end department store Georges of Collins Street, and in 1944 they could be purchased with the use of eight coupons. Despite the expense, the brown suede shoes were a good investment and stayed in her wardrobe for many years.[27] Burton remembers Matron interviewing her:

…she wanted to know where I went to school or what my education was, and a few other things like that, and first aid. She'd talk to me, the idea was I had to be a lady, I had to be worthy of being an air hostess, flying in their planes, welcoming their passengers, but also have a bit of common sense.[28]

She was selected in an intake of five and she said that 'Gert' (the girls' name for Matron) wasn't selecting on the basis of looks, describing her intake as all 'looking alright, but we weren't models'. Some of the senior air hostesses, such as Bernadette 'Barney' Lalor had been nurses and Burton thought they were pretty tough, as they were used to ordering people about in their previous jobs. For the first few days the new recruits all stayed at the YWCA.

There wasn't much training, just a few lectures and the trainees had a day acting as ground staff, standing at the foot of the plane and smiling and waving when the plane took off. Burton's first flight was to Hobart on the 30 June 1944. She was meant to have a senior hostess on board the first time she flew but this didn't happen, nor was her pale grey uniform ready in time. She was told to wear her 'civvies' and as it was wartime there was a lack of seamed stockings, so on occasion she used tanning lotion over her bare legs and drew a line down the back of her leg to simulate a seam. When her uniform finally arrived she wore it with carefully sourced nylon stockings. With rationing in place, she would send her stockings to a small shop where they would be mended for a penny an inch. Rather than wear a corset ('they were for the rich and fat, or else terribly smart women'), Burton wore step-ins, a light elastic garment.

After graduating, Burton and one of the other new recruits found a bedsitting room in Albert Park, Melbourne. It was a large room and they shared a double bed, and down the hall was a bath-room which they shared with about half a dozen other boarders. She was there for about three months and then she was transferred to Adelaide, where she lived on her own. The other air hostesses were living elsewhere in a five-bedroom house, but it was full. While in Adelaide, she would fly on the Douglas DC-3 long-haul flight to Perth. In Perth they would stay at The Esplanade Hotel in Fremantle, and Danny, the night porter, would wake Burton at 4am with a cup of tea so she could get ready for the bus that would take her, plus the rest of the crew and any passengers, to Guildford airport.

Because it was wartime the flights might only have five or six passengers on board, often military personnel, and most of the plane was taken up with mail freight. The flight to Perth would often be a bit rough, as they would have to fly at about 4,000 feet to avoid the headwinds. Working in turbulence would test your physical strength:

> Well you'll always hang on, because just in case, you might get a sudden drop. I was often on that route in summer, it would be very rough, and you'd need to hang on. I can remember doing some flights in the DC-2s where there were only fourteen passengers, and I would always hang on with my right hand. I remember getting quite a sore shoulder after some trips, because the centrifugal force would be very hard when you're standing and fighting against it. It would be very diffi-cult to stay upright, and be walking, perhaps answering a bell or carrying a tray.[29]

As it was 1944, the food wasn't anything 'too fancy': 'an orange drink, a roll, and a little cap of butter, a chicken leg, and some tomato and lettuce, perhaps a bit of beetroot, and maybe cucumber. Then some sort of a sweet'.[30]

On the 25th August 1945, Burton remembers opening the door of the plane, after landing in Adelaide to a lovely sunny day, and hearing someone announce, 'the war's over'. She left ANA shortly afterwards. She had been flying for fifteen months and had asked for leave to spend time with her sister who was having another baby and was living in Kalgoorlie, but Matron refused, saying too many of the air hostesses were wanting leave: 'So I resigned, and I was quite happy to go. It was hard work, it wasn't a great deal of fun getting up early in the morning…intellectually it wasn't very stimulating'. Later Burton applied for the first Qantas flight hostess intake in 1947, and was in the final cut but missed out even though she had provided a letter from Prime Minister Robert Menzies saying that he remembered her from a flight he had been on.

2.3. The Gulf Run and the Territory

Throughout the 1940s and 1950s ANA flew on the weekly 'Gulf Run' to far north Queensland. The route took in a big loop starting from Cairns then on to Normanton via Abingdon Downs Station, Van Rook Station, Dunbar Station, Rutland Plains Station, Mitchell River Mission, Galbraith Station, Delta Downs Station and back to Normanton. In Cairns the air hostesses stayed at the Strand Hotel, a grand two-storey affair built in 1915 on the Esplanade along the Pacific Ocean shore. They would occupy rooms on the ground level, and when the tide went out it would be a bit smelly. While the air hostesses would have their own room with handbasin and cupboard space, the toilet and showers were upstairs and along the wide verandah.[31] It wasn't until the late 1950s that ANA provided a flat for the air hostesses, as by then they were permanently based in Cairns for up to four-month periods. At Normanton they would stay at the old wooden National Hotel, sharing the accommodation with shearers and roustabouts. The entrance to the hotel was through the front bar or the billiard room and to go to the toilet and shower out the back, it was necessary to dodge the odd duck or chicken on the way there.[32] The shower was under a high water tower pumped full of bore water; and the water stored in galvanized tanks was usually too hot to stand under, so instead it was a matter of soaping oneself and splashing water over the body.[33] While the accommodation was often a bit rough and ready, the hotel would try to keep standards up with white tablecloths on the dining tables, to keep the commercial travellers happy.[34]

Dulcie North was stationed in Cairns in 1950 and remembers that most of the passengers on the Normanton run were Indigenous, using the service to move from one station to another. On landing in Normanton the passengers would be collected by a ute and any white passengers would get a place in the cabin, while any of the Indigenous passengers, crew, cargo and the air hostess would go in the back.[35] Indigenous staff were used at the station and they would sometimes cook local delicacies, such as duck baked in the ground, as a lunchtime meal for the crew and passengers. When Betty Ralph, another ANA air hostess, was stationed in Cairns she remembers Wednesday as the day they would fly into Mitchell River Station and that would be the day the women would put lipstick on. There was a kind of ritual for arriving at the station. The crew would fill two brown paper sick bags with lollies, and:

> We'd stand on the back of the truck throwing lollies out
> for all the Aboriginal kids on the way. I can remember
> saying to the skipper, 'this is disgusting, fancy throwing
> lollies to them. Go and offer them, offer them the bag',
> he said, 'Righto, go on, off you go, offer them the bag'.
> They all just looked at me and walked away. He said you
> just wanted to spoil all their fun, didn't you?[36]

Ralph remembers the lunch as a 'beautiful hot roast beef lunch in an iron shed but it was stinking hot, absolutely stinking hot'.[37]

The cyclonic conditions of the tropical north made for challenging flying, it was not unusual for the passengers to use blankets to protect themselves from the leaks in the planes. When it was too wet to land, the mail and freight would be thrown off the plane. It was a fairly risky procedure. The pilot would slow the plane down by dropping the wheels, then the first officer would tie a leather belt around his waist, attach it to the luggage rack and, on hearing the Hostess Call Button ring, the first officer would open the door of the DC-3, and the air hostess who was hanging over the two rear seats would push everything out as fast as she could.[38]

You know you're young. As they say twenty feet tall and bullet-proof at that age.

Trixie (Henderson) Lange, ANA air hostess, 1954 to 1957

Trixie (Henderson) Lange, who began flying with ANA in 1954, remembers being stationed in Cairns and doing the Gulf runs.[39] There were very few air hostesses who didn't love the station runs, as they were a unique opportunity to see remote country. At Abingdon Downs, halfway between Cairns and Normanton, 'They'd have to send somebody out on a horse to clear the strip of horses and kangaroos and see if there was any termite mounds being built up over the period…because it was only a weekly flight'.[40] For people living on the stations, bad weather could keep them isolated for weeks and these flights kept up their mail and supplies; 'If there was going to be a birthday party the week before, they'd tell me what they'd like. It would be candles or icing sugar or something that they might have run out of. Tomatoes were always very sought after'.[41]

Before Lange began flying she was 24 years old, living at home and working as a dressmaker on the family's strawberry farm in Wellington Point, Queensland.[42] Her dream, if she didn't marry by the time she was 30, was to buy a sheep farm with her father. She had applied to TAA about twelve months before, and it was after a fight with her boyfriend coincided with her mother seeing an ANA recruiting advertisement in the *Courier-Mail* that she rang the airline. She was offered an interview, and ten days later was at the Essendon flying school wearing a new black cardigan protecting her against the Melbourne cold. She stayed at a 'hostel' in an old terminal at Essendon airport with two other Queenslanders, Beth Sneyd and Rae Pritchard, and June Sawtell from South Australia. The accommodation was pretty rudimentary, a single bed and small cupboard on a brown lino floor. From next door, all through the night, came the clanging of the overnight maintenance on the planes. Perhaps the only advantage of staying in the hangar was being able to go from their rooms to the second floor and watch everything happening on the airfield, which they considered a rare treat. Lange remembers being trained for about three weeks, and learning comportment skills, like how to balance on a balancing board (a circular board on a roller). Matron asked the girls to wear bloomers, as the thought of falling and exposing their 'scanties' was not acceptable. Lace-up shoes were also preferred for safety reasons and because they were seen to have a sense of 'decorum'.

It would not be until Matron retired in 1955, and Nell Meyrick took her place, that the ANA air hostesses could stop wearing the old 'matron-like' lace-up shoes. Meyrick also let the trainees spend a day at the Elly Lukas School of Elegance in Collins Street, learning how to do their nails and hair and how to wear the uniform. The uniforms were made by a tailor and a dressmaker,

Australian National Airways, Graduation Day, August 1956
Every Graduation Day was cause for great celebration and here sixteen new ANA air hostesses pose in front of the ANA DC-4 Loongana. Robin Garnett (third from the left) started with ANA as a 23-year-old, then went on to work as a secretary for Ansett for 36 years. Courtesy of Robin Garnett.

upstairs in the old terminal building. The winter uniform was a grey woollen suit with no lapel on the jacket. Instead, it buttoned to the neck and the white collar of the shirt folded over the neckline. The summer uniform was a grey dress with a navy blue jacket. They were issued with one pair of stockings a month, possibly a fifteen denier, not too sheer but not coarse either. And on the first Monday of the month, Janet Haley, the senior regional hostess, had them all on the scales. Lange remembers clearly the physical requirements for the job:

We had to be between 5 foot 3 and 5 foot 7 and the maximum weight was 9 stone, so I was minimum height, maximum weight. I think it was because on the DC-3s you couldn't be too tall but you couldn't be too short that you couldn't reach into the luggage racks.[43]

She graduated on 1st March 1954 with seventeen others, and her first flight was to Swan Hill to collect an unaccompanied minor. She remembers families crying at both ends of the flight, the child being transported as a result of a broken marriage. 'Everybody' wanted to be an air hostess in those days and Lange said it was a great feeling, 'You'd go into Myer in Melbourne and they'd just about bow down to you'.[44] She was based back in Brisbane and she shared a flat with three other ANA air hostesses at Oxlade Drive, along the river at New Farm. If 'the girls' were overnighting from Melbourne and she knew them, then rather than stay in a hostel they would come and stay at the flat. It wasn't unusual to have a party. To get to the airport she might catch the passenger bus from the city, or Joan Ruby had a car and she would drive her. Failing that; there was a pilot who lived opposite and sometimes they would go with him. Returning late at night was sometimes more difficult, but Lange didn't mind the walk back from the bus station. Eventually her father bought her an Austin A30, not only so she could drive to the airport but also so she could drive up and visit the family when she had leave. It was a busy weekly schedule:

Monday Cooktown return, Tuesday Cooktown to Thursday Island return, Wednesday the station run to Normanton where they would overnight, and back to Cairns on the Thursday, Friday a repeat trip to Thursday Island. Saturday a flight to Brisbane with a return flight to Cairns on the Sunday.[45]

Her routine when she arrived at work was to check the food and the passenger list. Cutlery was kept in a tin and brought on board along with blankets and other supplies. The Cairns run on the Thursday was known as the 'Milk Run'. They would leave at 6am on a DC-3, with stops at Rockhampton, Mackay, Bowen, Home Hill-Ayr, Townsville, Ingham and Cairns.[46] It was tiring because of all the stops. The other run was to Thursday Island, flying from Cairns to Cooktown, Coen, and Iron Range (near Lockhart). Sometimes it would be a direct flight back from Thursday Island if there weren't any passengers. There were no ticketing offices at the stations on the outback posts so the air hostess would write out a ticket for each leg of the journey. Passengers would remember and appreciate the air hostesses on these trips. Lange remembers she had one admirer:

On a Thursday Island flight I brought a stockman to Cairns for his leave. I took him back to Coen, then a month later, and on a following flight he had left me some Cooktown orchids. They looked like a bundle of sticks to me. The pilot said he had ridden 50 miles to give me those, so then I appreciated them a bit more. I brought them home to mum who put them in a tree and they flourished. Wherever I have been I have taken some with me. Now sixty years later I still have them flowering.[47]

On the Monday mornings there would be a flight from Cairns to Cooktown taking on businessmen, lawyers, doctors, dentists, the Karitane nurse for the day, then returning late that afternoon. During the day the crew would sometimes go fishing on the wharf, or the stationmaster, Bill Gladwell, would take them up the railway line on a fettler's trolley to the Endeavour River to fish. Lange would also crew on the DC-4 with forty-eight passengers and two hostesses but her fondest memories are flying on the DC-3s, recalling they were a bit rough; if they didn't get up to a certain height, they tended to sway a bit:

> Once I can remember serving breakfast on a DC-3 and coming into land and I thought, 'What happened?' Well, one engine had cut out, we had turned around and come back and straight into Cairns and I hadn't even noticed.[48]

There was always a supply of blankets on board, as the heaters were a bit tricky to get working, although a good kick would often make them work better.[49]

> *Pilots, by the way, are the answer to every novel reader's prayer. Men's men, every one of them, and by the same token women's men, too. Masculine in the true sense of the word; terribly responsible, dependable-looking people. The kind who cause women to swoon appealingly in times of stress, murmuring, 'my hero!' Who wouldn't be an airline hostess, or failing that, air-minded?*
>
> 'Taking the Air', *Australian Woman's Mirror*, 15 June 1937

Despite the difficult conditions, the air hostesses had utmost faith in the pilots. They were older ex–World War II pilots and Lange repeated what other air hostesses would say about them: 'they treated you as their kid sister…they looked after you'.[50] Marsh Burgess had been a pilot during the war and joined ANA for a short time, before leaving to have a long career with Qantas.

He remembers flying on the DC-4s and the lack of oxygen as the planes reached around the 10,000, and sometimes 12,000 feet mark, as they climbed to avoid bad weather. The fatigue would set in but, as he said, 'Well, if your life's on the end of it and the lives of all people on board you make yourself stay awake'.[51]

Lange thought there was an independence to the job, which came from living away from home and sharing experience with other young women who:

...were all young and enjoyed the life. It was very free. I mean it wasn't as restricted as nursing. There wasn't really that much you could do [professionally at that time], you were a school teacher, a nurse, a telephonist or a stenographer, that's about the only positions... and then most of them you had to leave when you got married anyway.[52]

The independence the young women had was not without incident. The general impression that after hours the air hostesses were all at home painting their nails and setting their hair ready for the next flight was challenged when one of the air hostesses ended up in court. Miss Brigid Crotty, a joint-owner of a block of flats in Leichhardt, appeared in the local Magistrates' Court complaining about male visitors drinking and having 'night parties' with the three air hostesses who were living in one of the flats. One of the air hostesses, Mary Stanley, denied that her visitors were anything but gentlemen, one of whom was in fact the secretary to General Thomas Blamey. Crotty was having none of this and said 'these flats are run on my standard of moral and not yours or the other inmates'. Later Stanley in a forthright manner was said to reply, 'I will have whom I like, when I like and as long as I like'.[53] General

Thomas Blamey was known to the air hostesses. On his way to attend a War Advisory Council he tried to defend his aide, who was attempting to take a window seat from a fellow passenger. The air hostess intervened and warned Blamey that while he may command an army, she commanded the passengers' seats on that plane.[54]

2.4. Daly Waters and Guinea Airways

There were other airlines travelling north, including Guinea Airways. The airline had been started in the 1920s with the purpose of flying from Adelaide to the goldmines in New Guinea.[55] It was only in 1939 that they employed a ground hostess, as they would have up to twelve passengers on the new Lockheed Model 14 Super Electra. The ground hostess was Nell Meyrick (later, air hostess superintendent of ANA), who before joining the airline, had run a dance school in Port Pirie, South Australia.[56] There was no room for an air hostess on board the Electra, so she would supply the passengers a bread roll, a boiled egg and a piece of fruit, which they would have at the first stop, Mt Eba, near Woomera. The service to Darwin ran three days a week and it meant that she had to get to the city by 5am if she were to get the car to Parafield airfield, north of Adelaide. Meyrick commented on the number of women and children travelling and mentioned that she did not 'remember any full-blooded Aborigines travelling from the north, but half-castes are sometimes passengers'.[57] Freight on the service would include mail but also 'luxuries' such as shellfish, lettuces, celery, eggs, cakes and fruit, which were delivered en route to Alice Springs, Tennant Creek, Daly Waters and Darwin.

While air freight was crucial to outback Australia, not everything could be shipped by air. Henrietta Pearce, who with her husband Bill 'Boss' had set up the hostel and shop at Daly Waters in 1932, would have to order in bulk. For example, she would order two tons of flour to be delivered by road freight. This would be enough to last six months in case the roads or the landing strip became impassable during the wet.[58] Daly Waters was an inland stop for domestic flights, for Qantas Empire Airways flights and Royal Netherlands Indies Airways (KNILM later KLM) flights heading to and from the Dutch East Indies. The KNILM Lockheed Electras were quite luxurious, and the stewards in their white serving coats would come to the hostel with fluted silver thermoses each engraved with coffee, tea, milk, iced water, soup and lemonade. Pearce would refill the thermoses as best she could, often using goat's milk. It was not unusual to have three planes landing at once at Daly Waters, and young indigenous boys 'Jerry, Lennie, Stumpy and Micky' would help with refuelling and the mail.[59] For many years it was common practice to use Indigenous labour on the airstrips of the outback stations and towns. The aerodrome was a mile from the house but Pearce would be there to greet the passengers, and invite them in for a breakfast of boiled eggs, homemade bread, hot scones, various kinds of cakes, honey-in-the-comb, marmalade and tea and coffee. Lunch would be sausage rolls or pasties, cold ham and beef, cakes, homemade biscuits, cheese and dry biscuits and fruit if they could get it.[60] If flights were delayed, the eighteen beds in the hostel were made up for the unexpected guests. The beds were made up as needed as the departure of any plane in the dry inland conditions would create a huge dust storm even though the runway was so far away. Given the calibre of the international guests – Lady Edwina Mountbatten was one of the first passengers to fly into Daly Waters – the specially fly-proofed dining room with a concrete floor must have seemed primitive.

2.5. The War Ends

By the end of the war, there were eighty air hostesses working for ANA, and a further eight undergoing training and attending lectures by Matron Holyman, Chief Hostess Phyllis Currie and Senior Hostess Mavis Gardiner.[61] The airline was still receiving hundreds of applications; ANA spokesperson Mr J. N. Walsh thought there had been an increased air-mindedness of young women as a result of the war. The main reason that an applicant wasn't successful would be because they had poor poise, lazy diction or careless speech – sure indicators of selection by class.[62] Preference would be given to ex-servicewomen provided they had the minimum requirements for eligibility. For example, 24-year-old Winifred Brown had been a radar operator for three years before she became an ANA air hostess in February 1946.[63] Not only would ex-servicewomen be given preferential treatment, but widows of servicemen or air hostesses who were married to men serving overseas could be employed. An ANA air hostess at this time would be paid £4/10s a week as they attended the six-week training course, of which three of the weeks involved in-flight training with a 'flight-training girl', and then after this they would be paid £5 a week. After a probation period of about thirteen weeks the air hostess would receive £5/10 a week, with insurance, superannuation and one winter and two summer uniforms provided. They would become permanent if, after a maximum of five supervised flights, they proved themselves suitable for the job.[64] As soon as they graduated they would be the only air hostess on board, unless a trainee was flying with a more experienced hostess.

Having survived the gruelling war years, Matron Holyman thought that ANA had done well, believing that ANA had more air hostesses than any other airline in the world. And her advice for every hostess who left the training school was, 'No matter what happens, girl, always face the passengers calmly and smile'.[65]

2.6. When Things Crash and Burn

The huge silver bird winged on through the night, on its errand of mercy. At times, the sleet rattled against the windows of the cabin like thousands of small shots. It was the roughest flight Peggy had taken. Most of the time, the grave-faced passengers were content to sit quietly, with seat belts fastened, conserving their energies for whatever lay ahead.

Betty Baxter Anderson, *Peggy Wayne, Sky Girl*, 1941[66]

By the end of the 1940s, ANA had significant plans for expansion. The airline had bought land in Brisbane, Sydney and Melbourne with the view to providing accommodation for their passengers. Even more ambitious were the plans to build model towns with homes, shops, medical facilities and child welfare centres on land purchased by the airfields at Guildford, Perth, and at Parafield, Adelaide. The plans were never realised. Instead, the postwar period proved a challenging time for ANA with six major air crashes between March 1946 and June 1950, and in three of them all on board were killed.[67] There were a number of different reasons for the crashes, including faulty instruments and bad weather. An analysis of the accidents that occurred in 1948 also found that there was a lack of flying skills and discipline among the pilots.[68]

The first major accident happened on the 10th March 1946 when the ANA DC-3, crashed into the sea at Seven Mile Beach soon after takeoff from Cambridge Airport, Hobart, on a return trip to Melbourne. The flight had been delayed earlier that day as the scheduled plane, another DC–3 had mechanical problems and had to be replaced. The plane took off at 8.50pm on a runway lit with a flare path of kerosene lights.[69] It reached a height of about 400 feet, and then turned slightly and, as one witness Elsie May Bender described it, 'became a mass of orange light' before it crashed into the sea.[70] All twenty-five people onboard were killed, the twenty-one passengers, and the four crew, including air hostess Pauline Trimmer.[71]

Killed on first duty of flight, 1946
The glamorous portrayal of the air hostess betrayed the dangers of working in the air. Air hostess Pauline Trimmer was killed along with twenty-four others when the DC-3 she was flying in crashed soon after take-off from Hobart, 10th March 1946. Courtesy Betty Ralph.

For the 20-year-old Pauline Trimmer on board the fatal DC–3 it had been a bad trip from the start. Eric Hyland, a porter for ANA in Hobart, reported that 'Miss Trimmer, the air hostess, told him she had had a "rotten trip" on the way down from Melbourne because the heaters were not working'.[72] And this can be confirmed as one of the passengers on the flight said Captain Spence 'walked into the passenger cabin, and remarked to witnesses that it was very cold, and he intended to bring the plane down to 4,000 feet or 5,000 feet.'[73] There was also a report of a flash of lightning, which the captain described as a 'hell of a crack'.[74]

After news of the crash a ground mechanic with ANA, in a brave and touching gesture, had gone to the crash site thinking that Trimmer might be trapped in the tail piece. He swam out through the rough surf, clambered on board and tied a rope to the protruding wheel so that the tail could be dragged on to the beach.[75] Later, her body was found when it was washed ashore along with the rest of the passengers and crew. The cause of the accident was never confirmed. There was an 'open finding' made in July 1946 – speculation included an insulin-dependent pilot, a lightning strike to the nose of the plane on the earlier flight out of Essendon Airport 'only strong enough to knock a packet of cigarettes off the ledge of the windscreen in the pilots cabin', and suspicions that a massive gannet (a bird around 3 feet long with a wing span of about 6 feet) had flown into the plane.[76]

Pauline Trimmer had graduated from ANA, along with seventeen others, on the 4th February 1946.[77] This was the largest intake that ANA had trained and 21-year-old Betty Ralph graduated from the same course. Ralph and Trimmer shared a flat at St Kilda, so it was no surprise that Ralph still had an old newspaper clipping about the accident. It has a photograph of Pauline Trimmer with the headline, 'Killed on First Duty of

Flight'. Straight after the accident, Matron had called Ralph in to the office to counsel her in regard to Trimmer's death, but Ralph said, 'I didn't need it. I felt I was quite safe'. Despite the tragedy, Ralph described the DC-3 as a 'very friendly little aircraft and you knew the passengers. We were always encouraged to remember their names'.[78]

Urgent telegram for Miss Betty Ralph, 1945
One can only imagine the excitement of receiving a telegram requesting attendance at an interview for the position of air hostess with Matron Holyman of ANA. Courtesy of Betty Ralph.

So it was Betty Ralph from Jamestown, a small country town in South Australia, about 50 kilometres east of Crystal Brook where Trimmer had lived, who was able to tell the story of her flying career. As a 10- or 11-year-old, Ralph had seen a plane land in a nearby paddock and had walked there with her younger sister. Someone offered to shout them a joy flight, which they accepted, her parents having no knowledge of where the two girls were. Her next flight was on a family holiday with Guinea Airways to Port Lincoln and Mildura. Seeing the air hostess on board cemented her future career in her mind. In December 1945, she was interviewed by Matron at the Oriental Hotel in Rundle Street,

Adelaide. It was a boiling hot day with a dust storm blowing:

> I thought this is crazy, getting dressed up in all of this. I
> remember that quite well. So I had quite a pretty blue-
> and-white linen dress. I decided that a better idea would
> be no hat, no gloves. I was dressed for the day [laughs]
> but there was a very glamorous girl who arrived in this
> gorgeous pink dress. She had a black hat and gloves, the
> lot. I felt like little orphan Annie in my little linen dress
> and flat-heeled shoes.[79]

Ralph's concerns were unfounded and she was accepted into
the training course, and then flew for three months in her civvies
as her uniform wasn't ready. This was often the case with uniforms, and there was talk that it was to give the new recruits a trial
run to see if they 'lasted the distance' before outlaying the expense
of a uniform. The grey linen dress was made by Ida Fountain, a
dressmaker who lived in Essendon. According to Ralph, it was 'a
bugger to iron'. Each air hostess would have to provide their own
stockings, and a two-way stretch girdle, because their 'bottoms
were eye-level height for the passengers'. It was recommended that
they wear fingernail polish because that would allow any grease
to come off easily. Despite the silver service in the cabin, with
china cups and saucers and silver pots for tea and coffee, the planes
would leak oil and were pretty dirty to work in. Ralph went on
to fly for twelve years, and during this time she was promoted
to senior hostess in Melbourne but declined the position of chief
hostess as she 'was happy in what she was doing'. For her, every
flight was a 'great thrill'.

On the 4th September 1948, a party at the famous Sydney
nightclub Romano's went ahead without the planned special guest

Brenda 'Peggy' Wise. Entrepreneur Harry Miller had organised the party as a way of thanking 'Miss Peggy' for the special attention she gave the wrestlers from his Rushcutters Bay stadium on their regular flights between Sydney and Brisbane.[80] But two days before the party the 23-year-old ANA air hostess, who had been with the airline since January, was killed when the ANA DC-3 *Lutana* crashed into Square Top Peak, Nundle, New South Wales. The area had experienced extremely cold conditions, including snowfalls, and the pilot had reported difficulty in maintaining height because of severe icing. The plane was way off course when it crashed, killing all thirteen persons on board. Anne Chandler had been rostered for ground duty at Brisbane's Archerfield airport on the day of the *Lutana* flight:

> The day had been uneventful and I was packing up to go home when the captain of the 5pm Flight 331 *Lutana*, a DC-3 bound for Sydney, told me the scheduled hostess had not turned up for the flight. 'Anne, it looks as though you will have to come with us', he said, 'Could you put the passengers on board please?' It was apparent by now the hostess was not going to show, so I was designated to hostess the flight. Captain John Drummond and copilot John Atkinson carried out the pre-flight checks, and we were now ready for take-off. As the aircraft started to roll into the wind, the throttle was closed just before lift-off. The captain had sighted the scheduled hostess running her hardest towards the aircraft. The tail of the DC-3 was not far off the ground, so the exchange was fairly easy. Within minutes, *Lutana* VH-ANK was airborne, flying into the north-east wind

heading for Sydney, and so I went home. But the aircraft did not reach its destination.[81]

These kinds of stories, about the arbitrary hand of fate, are among those told by many of the air hostesses from this period.

Just over a month later, ANA suffered its third accident in a period of ten weeks when the DC-3 *Kurana* crashed near Mt Macedon, Victoria, on the 8th November 1948.[82] The pilot and copilot were killed, but miraculously the nineteen passengers and Elizabeth Fry, the air hostess, survived. Fry had been flying for nine months when she experienced the 'unfortunate mishap'. She described the event:

After the seatbelt sign was turned off, I went to the cockpit to see when the captain and copilot wanted breakfast. By the time I got back to the galley – less than a minute – I was flat on my back with thermos bottles, luggage, etc, hurtling everywhere. My first reaction from the rotating floor was that we had hit a ghastly electrical storm, but by the time I had staggered to my feet I realised we had crashed. The tail was off the plane and the door was gone. The plane was on fire up front, so my main concern was to get the passengers off safely before the whole aircraft blew up.[83]

On impact, Fry had asked the passengers to remain in their seats while she opened the rear door, and then quickly evacuated everyone before the plane caught fire. She attributed the high standard of training and the standards set by Matron as the reason she could, in 'that split second decision', get the passengers out of the smashed and burning aircraft.[84] After the crash she counted all the passengers and proceeded to administer first aid, including putting a splint on a broken leg. In May 1949, ANA managing director Ivan Holyman presented Fry with a silver salver from the insurance company Lloyds of London. Fry was modest when she accepted her award saying, 'I did no more than any other airline hostess would have done. I just happened to be the hostess on the day'.[85] Lloyds were no doubt relieved that they didn't have to pay out for the lives of nineteen passengers who had been endangered in the crash. By June, Fry had married and left the airline.

It was not only accidents that created deaths on board; sometimes passengers would die mid-flight. Mostly these occurrences would be kept quiet, but a 59-year-old passenger from Sydney made the papers when she died en route. The air hostess had noticed her pallor, and enquired after her health, but was assured that she was well before she fell asleep; never to waken.[86] In preparation for these instances training would include instructions on how to pull the eyelids down and to place a blanket over the passenger so they would look as if they were asleep.[87]

2.7. ANA Goes International

There is no doubt the series of fatal air crashes damaged ANA's reputation, but it didn't stop Ivan Holyman trying to expand ANA's services and fly internationally. The Australian government, protecting Qantas and their capacity as Australia's international airline, had refused ANA permission to fly international services in its own right, but in June 1948 ANA signed an agreement with Cathay Pacific that included a 35 per cent share in the company. This was a financial arrangement and did not include any flying services, although ANA staff were seconded to Cathay Pacific for training purposes. Also that year ANA acquired a 49 per cent interest in Air Ceylon, and by January 1950 a regular service between Sydney and London had begun via Ceylon using ANA's DC-4s and their crew. Betty Ralph was one of the first ANA air hostesses to go on the Air Ceylon trip. They would fly from Australia to the capital Colombo and stay at the Mount Lavinia Hotel, which was an old colonial hotel on the coast. ANA also set up a base in Cairo as the long flight would mean the pilots' 'flying hours would be up' and they would break up the shifts by having one crew fly from Colombo to Cairo, while another would fly the Cairo to London leg. In Cairo they would stay at the Heliopolis Palace Hotel, 'it was a quarter of a mile long', said Ralph who was stationed there for three 'wonderful' months. Her independence was slightly curtailed as it was not considered safe to go out on her own, and she would also have to ask the captain for her overseas allowance money before she ventured out. Margaret (Brown) Shaw had been with ANA for a year when she was selected to fly on the Air Ceylon route. She had to have three weeks' special training before she started and she was stationed in Colombo for three and half months, staying there until the service finished around the time of the Coronation in June 1953.

While Shaw was flying there were four air crew and two air hostesses, and initially they would fly to Cairo but that became dangerous with the 'Black Saturday' riots in January 1952. Patricia Deverall who would later fly with Butler Air Transport and Trans Australia Airlines (TAA) was the air hostess on a BOAC flight from London to Sydney when the crew were ordered off the plane by armed police at Cairo airport during the unrest. On board were nine children and a 3-month-old baby with its mother and, while the crew were taken off the plane, initially the passengers remained on board, with Deverall sending instructions about where to find food and water on the plane.[88] With the risks of flying into Cairo seeming too great, the ANA Air Ceylon flights began flying to Cyprus, which proved even more dangerous. Finally they moved to Tel Aviv (where they would often be escorted by a fighter plane until they got out of the territory over Jordan); they would then fly on to Colombo.[89] Shaw realised the posting was a unique opportunity, travelling into countries on the edge of war, having experiences that were far removed from those of her colleagues back home. In addition to the adventures on board, friends and family would ask her to bring back things, but they were not always as exotic as one might imagine: 'I had a long list of things I was to bring back from London, which was a blooming nuisance because we only had thirty-six hours there. But you know, three people wanted umbrellas'.[90]

She remembers returning from her time overseas and reporting to Matron, who inspected her with her 'gimlet grey eyes', '"Miss Brown, how did you get on, on your flight?" I said, "It was lovely". "We didn't send you overseas to have a lovely time" was her answer, but that's Matron [laughs]'. Shaw was sympathetic to Matron and her role as superintendent, as under her wing she had so many girls who had left home for the first time, and she felt responsible and protective of all of them. But she also 'insisted that they did the right thing'. Before her overseas posting, Shaw had been stationed in Brisbane, where it was fun living with three other air hostesses, 'we would all have stories to tell because you didn't see that much of each other'. While in Brisbane she felt:

...we relaxed the rules slightly up there. You were sup-posed to wear lace-up shoes...[but] everybody wore court shoes and...you didn't wear nail polish, your hair had to be above your collar...word would come through that Matron was flying north – suddenly all the court shoes went, the nail polish would go off and everything would be spic and span.[91]

Shaw thought the conditions for air hostesses were not optimal. After there had been a couple of murders in Brisbane, a few of the air hostesses were feeling unsafe, and some of them called a meeting:

We asked if we could have taxi cabs for the early morning air hostesses because it was lonely walking up to catch a tram or a train or a bus because very few people had cars, and it wasn't allowed. That's not a called-for expense. Our salaries, I mean, we had to provide our own shoes and stockings, handbags, overcoats. You just got the uniform.[92]

Other issues included having to share rooms on overnight stops, or staying in a hangar at Mascot. She thought that most of the air hostesses liked the odd hours because they had time off, and there were advantages travelling between cities: '...you wouldn't wash your hair in Brisbane because the water was too hard. So you washed your hair in Melbourne where the water was soft. I mean, that sounded terribly glamorous. We bought our shoes in Melbourne'.[93]

When Shaw returned from Colombo she became a trainer, before she left in 1953 to marry a passenger she had met on a flight. Reflecting on her time flying she clearly felt it to be character building:

...it took you away from home – it taught you to be independent, I think and perhaps think for yourself and know that you're more capable than you thought you were of handling different situations...there's a feeling of comradeship, a bit like the army or anything like that I think. You share. It's a shared experience'.[94]

By 1949, ANA employed 170 air hostesses, and it was still a highly competitive job. The training school had changed with the introduction of Stephen Kentley. He had been manager of the Hotel Australia in Melbourne, and had been so disappointed with the service he had received on an ANA flight that he had written Ivan Holyman a four-page letter criticising the service.[95] The upshot was he was appointed catering manager, later renamed passenger services manager. Working alongside Matron and her assistant Elma Adams he lectured the air hostess recruits about cabin service during the six-week training course at the Essendon training school.[96] Anne (Sloman) Peterson began with ANA in 1949 and remembers that it was a 'rather hectic training program'.[97] She was only 19 when she joined, even though 21 was meant to be the starting age. She had borrowed her sister's birth certificate and joined under her name, which proved a bit tricky at times, forgetting her name was 'Judeth', not 'Anne'. Her sister had also applied, but was not accepted as she was only 4 foot 10 inches.

Peterson remembers being the first air hostess allowed to wear 'court shoes'. She had a very high instep and, after she received doctor's advice, she was allowed to stop wearing the 'ungainly ugly lace-up shoes' which Matron favoured and 'all the hostesses detested (including the pilots)'. Her doctor recommended a court shoe would be preferable. Peterson purchased a rather glamorous pair of navy court shoes, with a stacked leather heel, but was informed by Matron that such a heel was not permitted; all heels had to be plain.

As a junior air hostess, Peterson was earning approximately £9 per week plus overnight allowances, and she found she had to have other means of support. So she continued, on her days off, to work for the legal firm she was with before joining the airline. After about eighteen months with ANA, Peterson was grounded for six months due to a reoccurring dislocated shoulder caused in part by a misplaced hot water urn. In those days laid off air hostesses did not receive workers' compensation. On hearing this, Peterson's irate father decided to take the company on and demanded that some compensation be paid. After a lengthy battle, ANA agreed, so Peterson, in another first, received workplace compensation. The amount was three-quarters of a weekly pay, which at that time was £11 a week (as she was now a senior hostess). After surgery on her shoulder, Peterson was allowed to do reception work at Essendon Airport until judged fit to fly again. A refresher course was required prior to her resuming flight duties.

2.8. A New Decade: A New Disaster

With things returning to normal after wartime, and the hope that the crashes of the 1940s were behind them, ANA started the new decade anticipating more growth This was not to be, as on the 26th June 1950 they had their fourth fatal crash in five years. Edgar Forwood, the managing director of Forwood Down foundry in Adelaide, was the sole survivor after the ANA DC-4 Skymaster *Amana* crashed near York, Western Australia.[98] He was a regular traveller and coincidentally a firm favourite with many of the ANA air hostesses. When the plane crashed he was sitting in his favourite seat, number twenty-nine on the port side, directly in line with the wing. He described the crash: 'I felt the plane suddenly going down. Then there were screams from the passengers. They were terrifying. We hit and I fell out. Then I found that I was on fire. I put out the flames by hand'.[99] Sadly, Forwood died a few days later from his injuries. There were two air hostesses among the crew of five: Jane Winsome Graham from Port Pirie, who had started in April 1948 and Margaret 'Alison' Britton, who had joined the airline four months earlier. The twenty-three passengers who were killed received an insurance payout of £2,000, the captain £3,000, while the air hostesses' lives were valued at £1,000.[100] Anne Burton remembered Forwood as an elderly man who would take the air hostesses on outings:

Edgar Forwood and ANA air hostesses, Adelaide Hills, c. 1949
Edgar Forwood, who was killed in an ANA plane crash in 1950, had been a regular passenger on ANA flights. He would often take air hostesses on outings in his Cadillac, and here he is in the Adelaide Hills with a group of them including Betty Ralph (second from the left). Courtesy of Betty Ralph.

He had a big Cadillac or something like that. He more or less adopted the hostesses, and I only had a drive a few times with him, as they would be jealous about his trips (not wanting a newcomer to share). He would take them out and he would give them a day out, quite often. There was nothing sexual about it, he was a very nice man, and they were all very fond of him, and he was on that flight. But that was after I left.[101]

Betty Ralph was also friendly with Forwood and she has a photograph of him with her and four other ANA air hostesses, taken on an outing to the Adelaide Hills. It was not unusual for a passenger to be attentive to the air hostesses as many of the passengers were regular fliers and would build relationships with the crews, particularly as it might be the same few air hostesses flying specific routes. Ralph remembers up in far north Queensland travelling on the DC-3s on the Normanton cattle station run, they would regularly be given four parcels of beef; two for the pilots and two for the air hostess. Inside the parcel would be a 'beautiful' piece of steak, which she would share with the three other air hostesses who were based in Cairns.[102]

Ralph loved the Queensland routes. On the Townsville route they would take off very early out of Brisbane on a DC-4, serve breakfast at Rockhampton, then fly on to Mackay and Townsville, landing at about 11 o'clock in the morning. The crew would go to the hotel, and Ralph would iron her uniform and get everything ready for the next day and then the crew would all go up to the Townsville swimming pool before lunch and swim with the Olympic swimmers, who were practising for the 1956 Melbourne Olympics.[103] Ralph was stationed in Cairns for six months, which was longer than usual, but she had heard there were 'rumblings' going on down south and thought she wanted to stay clear of what was happening. The 'rumblings' would eventuate with ANA merging with Ansett to form Ansett-ANA in 1957.

Eventually Ralph had to leave Cairns and she cried all the way home; she was to miss the independence of being up north. She returned to Melbourne with a good tan and was immediately told to replace her uniform, which was looking the worse for wear. The grey fabric had faded from frequent washing and drying in the hot Queensland sun. Her hat and gloves were in good condition as she had barely worn them up north, keeping them in her handbag just in case a check hostess came on board. With ANA now merged with Ansett, Ralph sensed that the Ansett air hostesses wanted to 'rule the roost', even if the ANA air hostesses outnumbered them by far.[104] Ralph resigned in 1958, as Ansett did start getting rid of ANA staff, and she thought that she may be next. She left to work at Myer as the personnel manager for the shoe section, where her training and experience were no doubt highly valued.

One cannot underestimate the importance of old 'gimlet eyes', Matron Holyman, in the forging of the very character of the air hostess as the quintessentially modern professional woman. Never before had women been able to bring the charm of the domestic hostess, shackle it to the ultra-modern technology that made mass air transport possible, and present themselves as the very image of their nation in a cosmopolitan global world. Matron Holyman set the standards that others built on for this creation of this new kind of person.

But at the same time there was a baptism of fire through which the airlines, as well as their crews, had to battle – World War II itself. The resources and demands of the war upgraded the aircraft and associated technologies dramatically. 'Airmindedness' was on the rise and, as postwar reconstruction began to kick in, the airlines began to play a much larger communication and transport role. And in a sense they were still learning, because the frequency of accidents was higher in these infant years of commercial air travel. In future years, because of these crashes, air safety standards would improve, and regulation and control provide a tighter safety net to support the growing industry.

Notes

1   The nacelle is the casing that holds the engine.

2   Anon, 'New air hostess', *Argus*, 9 June 1939, p. 8; Anon, 'Fire on Bungana at 6,000ft', *Daily News* (Perth), 8 February 1940, p. 1.

3   Anon, 'Amazing plane landing', *Argus*, 9 February 1940, p. 1.

4   Anon, 'Three Brave Women', *Australian Women's Weekly*, 2 March 1940, p. 20.

5   Anon, 'Failed in their duty', *Australian Women's Weekly*, 24 August 1940, p. 14; Anon, 'Foiled bandits', *Sunday Times* (Perth), 8 December 1940, p. 5.

6   Anon, 'Growing importance of women's jobs in the air', *Advertiser*, 11 March 1941, p. 6.

7   Interview with Hazel Holyman, in M. McRobbie, *Walking the Skies: The First Fifty Years of Air Hostessing in Australia 1936 to 1986*, Self-published, Melbourne, [1986], 1992, p. 27.

8   A. Game & R. Pringle, *Gender at Work*, Allen and Unwin, Sydney, 1983, pp. 99–100.

9   ibid.

10 P. Yule, *The Forgotten Giant of Australia Aviation: Australian National Airways*, Hyland House, Melbourne, 2001, p. 32.

11 Anon, 'Matron Holyman retires: she set a world standard', *Air Travel Magazine*, November 1955, p. 14.

12 Charles Kingsford Smith and Charles Ulm formed Australian National Airways in 1928, and in 1931 the company closed because of financial difficulties, partially attributed to the collapse in the economy but also a loss of customer faith after the loss of the *Southern Cloud* in inclement weather over the Snowy Mountains on 21 March 1931. In August 1957, ANA merged with Ansett to become Ansett-ANA, and then in 1968 it became Ansett Airlines of Australia.

13 Anon, 'Let's talk of interesting people', *Australian Women's Weekly*, 27 July 1940, p. 2.

14 Anon, 'Air hostesses: They fly for their living', *Australian Women's Weekly*, 18 May 1940, p. 2.

15 N. Witcomb, *Up Here and Down There*, Self-published, Adelaide, 1986, p. 15.

16 Anon, 'Air hostesses: they fly for their living'.

17 ibid; Anon, 'Two S.A girls are air hostesses' *Mail* (Adelaide), 19 August 1939, p. 2. By 1954 it had changed to 21 to 26, between 5 foot 3 and 5 foot 6

and maximum weight of 9 stone, in Anon, 'Charm of air hostess, *Barrier Miner*, 23 January 1954, p. 1.

18   Witcomb, *Up Here and Down There*, p. 33.

19   Anon, 'Sick woman's flight', *Argus*, 7 August 1939, p. 4.

20   Anon, 'Tea at 10,000ft is "Grand Fun"', *Argus*, 9 March 1940, p. 13.

21   Advertisements to recruit air hostesses had been placed in newspapers and further information was supplied at ANA offices. In William Street, Perth information could be found at the office of the Orient Line shipping agents who also acted as agents for Australian National Airways. In M. Ferber, 'Picking petals off a daisy', *Daily News*, 4 March 1940, p. 9.

22   Witcomb, *Up Here and Down There*, p. 37.

23   Anon, 'Train air hostesses: they need to be among other things, psychologists', *Daily Journal-World*, 19 March 1942, p. 12.

24   S. Catling, 'This flying business is not all flying', *Courier-Mail*, 13 August 1949, p. 2.

25   A. Burton, interview with the author and Jessica Kean, 8 April 2015.

26   ibid.

27   Anon, 'Parker Shoe advertisement, Georges of Collins Street', *Argus*, 19 August 1944, p. 11.

28   A. Burton, interview with the author and Jessica Kean, 8 April 2015.

29   ibid.

30   ibid.

31   Witcomb, *Up Here and Down There*, p. 50.

32   ibid., p. 59.

33   T. Lange, interview with the author, 28 July 2015.

34   P. Merlehan, interview with the author, 27 July 2015. Air hostess with TAA from 1957 to 1965.

35   Witcomb, *Up Here and Down There*, p. 56.

36   B. Ralph, interview with the author, 6 August 2013.

37   ibid.

38   T. Lange, interview with the author, 28 July 2015.

39   ibid.

40   ibid.

41   ibid.

42   ibid.

43   ibid.

44   ibid.

45   ibid.

46   There was also a mail run to Townsville that would be full of *Courier-Mail* newspapers on the way up, so the air hostess could sleep on the back seat or chat to the crew, but on the flight back the plane would be full of

passengers. The crew would stay at the Queens Hotel and during the day they would go to Magnetic Island to swim and laze on the beach.

47 T. Lange, interview with the author, 28 July 2015.

48 ibid.

49 P. Alderman, interview with the author, 20 February 2014, ANA air hostess 1951 to 1955.

50 T. Lange, interview with the author, 28 July 2015.

51 M. Burgess, interview with the author, 18 April 2014. ANA Pilot 1948 and Qantas 1949 to 1979.

52 T. Lange, interview with the author, 28 July 2015.

53 Anon, 'Objected to noise at flats', *Courier-Mail*, 17 May 1944, p. 5.

54 Anon, 'Air hostess told General Blamey', *Sunday Times* (Perth), 16 August 1942, p. 3.

55 Later, Airlines of South Australia, 1959.

56 McRobbie, *Walking the Skies: The First Fifty years of Air Hostessing in Australia 1936 – 1986*, p. 27. In November 1955 Meyrick replaced Matron as Hostess Superintendent of ANA.

57 Anon, 'Ground hostesses at Parafield', *Mail* (Adelaide), 26 July 1941, p. 9.

58 Anon, 'Pioneering at Daly Waters', *Mail*, 18 September 1943, p. 13.

59 E. George, *Two at Daly Waters*, Georgian House, Melbourne, 1945, p. 71.

60 ibid., p. 73.

61 Anon, '10th year of air hostess service', *Mercury*, 10 October 1945, p. 8.

62 Anon, 'Aspiring hostesses: lack poise and diction', undated newspaper clipping c. 1945.

63 Anon, 'To be an air hostess', *Daily News* (Perth), 25 February 1946, p. 5.

64 Yule, *The Forgotten Giant of Australia Aviation: Australian National Airways*, p. 237.

65 ibid., p. 238.

66 B. Baxter Anderson, *Peggy Wayne, Sky Girl*, Cupples & Leon, New York, 1941, p. 149.

67 Catling, 'This flying business is not all flying', p. 2.

68 P. Yule, *The Forgotten Giant of Australian Aviation*, p. 175.

69 ibid., p. 167.

70 Anon, 'Heard "Terrific Bang"', *Mercury*, 1 May 1946, p. 10.

71 Between March 1946 and June 1950 ANA aircraft were involved in six major incidents, with four leading to loss of life, including three in which all on board were killed. In Yule, *The Forgotten Giant of Aviation*, p. 146.

72 Anon, 'Bird possible cause of air crash' *Mercury*, 1 May 1946, p. 1.

73 Anon, 'Bird might have collided with cockpit of Plane', *Mercury*, 2 May 1946, p. 10.

74   ibid.
75   Anon, 'All aboard airline believed killed in sea night crash', *Central Queensland Herald*, 14 March 1946, p. 12.
76   Anon, 'Bird might have collided', p. 10.
77   B. Ralph, interview with the author, 6 August 2013. Ralph joined ANA in December 1945.
78   ibid.
79   ibid.
80   Anon, 'Party held without air hostess', *Daily News*, 4 September 1948, p. 1.
81   Anon, Nundle Community Newsletter, 26 March 2012, Accessed 12 June 2015 <http://www.tamworth.nsw.gov.au/ArticleDocuments/1277/Nundle_Community_Newsletter_March%20_2012.pdf.aspx>.
82   Anon, 'Airliner crashes on Mt Macedon', *Examiner*, 9 November 1948, p. 1.
83   Witcomb, *Up Here and Down There*, p. 123.
84   ibid., p. 124.
85   Anon, 'Air heroine to be rewarded', *Advertiser*, 21 April 1949, p. 3.
86   Anon, 'Woman's death on ANA plane', *Sydney Morning Herald*, 11 March 1946, p. 4.
87   W. Georgetti-Remkes, interview with the author, 5 September 2015. Air hostess from 1964 to 2015.
88   N. Adam, 'Australian air hostess guarded children', *Advertiser*, 29 January 1952, p. 1.
89   M. Shaw, interview with the author, 4 March 2015. This was the build up to the Greek-Cypriot attempts to remove the British from Cyprus.
90   ibid.
91   ibid.
92   ibid.
93   ibid.
94   ibid.
95   M. Gibson, 'A tribute to Stephen Kentley', clipping.
96   Anon, 'Positions as air hostesses in keen demand', *Cairns Post*, 9 September 1949, p. 1.
97   A. Peterson, telephone interview with the author, 5 May 2015.
98   Anon, '28 deaths in Skymaster crash', *Mercury*, 28 June 1950, p. 1.
99   Anon, 'Air crash near York', *Geraldton Guardian*, 27 June 1950, p. 3.
100 Anon, '28 deaths in Skymaster crash', p. 1.
101 A. Burton interview with the author, 8 April 2015.
102 B. Ralph, interview with the author, 6 August 2013.
103 In preparation for the 1956 Melbourne Olympics the swim team trained in Townsville, as they had done for the Helsinki games in 1952.
104 For example, in the early 1950s Ansett only had eighteen air hostesses compared with ANA, which had two hundred.

SECTION TWO: MID-FLIGHT

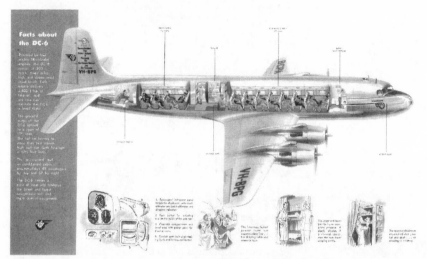

BCPA Brochure showing the interior of the Douglas DC-6, c. 1948

British Commonwealth Pacific Airlines (BCPA) flew the 'Southern Cross' Route across the Pacific from Sydney via Auckland, Nadi, Canton Island, Honolulu, San Francisco to Vancouver. The planes offered the luxury of the seats converting to berths for the overnight flights. Courtesy of Queensland Air Museum

Chapter Three

TO THE OUTBACK AND BEYOND

3.1. Keeping the West Connected: MacRobertson Miller Airlines

> *It was good to be home, to be back with old friends and with the*
> *prospect of doing again the work she had loved. Now she could*
> *forget the years of endless plane loads of sick and wounded men,*
> *of misery and suffering…Her gratitude was that peace was real*
> *and that she could resume her part in the most thrilling of all*
> *professions – civilian flying.*
>
> Alice Rogers Hager, *Janice Airline Hostess*, [1948] 1949[1]

The war over, it was not until 1946 that the national regulations prioritising which passengers could fly were removed and full passenger services resumed. Almost immediately, the Australian airline industry opened up; Trans Australia Airlines (TAA) began services on the 9th September 1946, British Commonwealth Pacific Airlines (BCPA), operating through ANA, began services on the 15th September 1946, and Ansett Airlines, which had stopped regular services during the war, returned to commercial aviation, employing their first air hostesses in May 1946.

If there was any reluctance to travel by air before, the extensive use of aircraft during the war had increased people's sense of 'airmindedness'. An agent for ANA recalled that in 1937 the twice-weekly passenger service on the DC-2 between Perth via Kalgoorlie and Adelaide was often empty, but by 1946 there was a total of 469 seats available each week for air travellers flying from Perth to the eastern States, and there was good demand for them.[2] He described the flight he had taken between Perth and Kalgoorlie and marvelled at the speed of the flight as it passed an east-bound train below; 'like a greyhound racing a poodle'. Joan Hudson, a senior hostess with ANA, was on board serving coffee, sandwiches and fruit, and the agent again marvelled at the size of the serve after wartime rations. With the increased passengers, even babies were being catered for with ANA providing a souvenir flight logbook. The hostess would fill out the baby blue or baby pink book stating the route taken, and the book would then be signed by the crew.[3]

Australian air hostesses continued to face working on some of the longest and most isolated air routes in the world, and this included the Western Australian routes from Perth to the Kimberley and on to Darwin. The vernacular conditions of working in Australian aviation, which routinely connected far-flung destinations, demanded exacting performances from aircraft and the crews who kept the machines and the passengers under control. Writer Ernestine Hill had experienced the isolated conditions and the importance of pilots when she travelled to the Kimberley in 1937. She described this in detail in the *Great Australian Loneliness*:

By carrying crayfish and prize Pomeranian dogs to the Never-Never, bringing down the dying and sometimes the dead, and scattering a small snow-storm of weekly letters over a country that was once out of the world for five months at a time, they have brought the Great Australian Loneliness well on to the map.[4]

Hill was probably flying on an Airlines (WA) flight. The airline had been formed in 1935 by Charles Snook to provide a service between Perth and the goldmining towns of Wiluna and Kalgoorlie. Over ten years later, in March 1946, the airline appointed Nelle Borbridge as a ground hostess. She had worked for the Women's Australian Auxiliary Air Force (WAAAF) as a wireless operator, and then served with the Royal Australian Air Force (RAAF) in Melbourne, and at air force bases in Bullsbrook and Cunderin, Western Australia. As a ground hostess she helped passengers on departure, and on occasion she was required to help out in emergencies such as bringing a passenger on a stretcher from Sandstone in the mid-west to Perth.[5] Marjorie 'Marge' Ellershaw, who had been in the Women's Royal Australian Naval Service (WRANS) during the war, had also joined the airline shortly after the war to work as a clerk, but became a ground hostess with the introduction of the four-seater Dragonfly DH-90. Ellershaw recounts how hard the work was:

> We would leave home at 3.30am, call at the GPO and pick up the mail. Then we would weigh it, and the passengers, and drive them all out to the airport. At the airport canteen we would make lunches. Then we had to be in the aircraft to welcome the passengers, give them barley sugar, and fasten their seatbelts.[6]

Ellershaw changed her role as a ground hostess to air hostess when Airlines (WA) purchased a de Havilland Dove DH-104 in 1947.[7] The Dove could seat eight, and the Department of Civil Aviation had ruled that a crew of two would be required to operate the plane, so it was decided that air hostesses would be employed and they would also double as radio operators. To work on the Doves, the hostesses had to have a knowledge of morse code, with a competency of sixteen words per minute. Training included passing the post office exam as well as climbing to the

Darellyn (Goss) Melsom, radio operator and air hostess, on board the Airlines (WA) de Havilland Dove, 1955
The de Havilland Dove was a one-pilot plane and air hostesses were employed to double as radio operators, a first for women in the world of aviation. Courtesy of Darellyn Melsom.

top of the very high radio tower at the airport. The multi-tasking Dove hostesses thus became the first women in the world to combine the roles of radio operator and air hostess.[8]

The reason women were selected for the dual roles was because, as women, the airline could pay them less. Weight was also an issue; the lighter the crew, the more freight could be carried. The 'Dove Girls' also had to be shorter than other air hostesses, preferably under 5 foot 3 to manage the height of the cabin. As radio navigators, they would keep a logbook, don earphones and occupy the right-hand seat for take-off and landing and then, depending on the next position report, they'd go into the cabin to offer tea and coffee to the passengers. They would fly from Albany in the south to Wallal Downs station, between Port Hedland and Broome in the north, and inland stops at Kalgoorlie, Leonora, Marble Bar, Geraldton, Meekatharra and a number of sheep stations in between.[9]

In those days it was difficult to get home telephone lines connected, but the 'Dove Girls' would have priority in case flight times changed and they needed to be contacted. Every six months they would have a medical, including important hearing checks because of the morse code. One of the perks of the job was three days off after the exhausting station runs. They could stay at a cottage on Rottnest Island, as the airline flew there. Working two roles sometimes made the job challenging. If the weather was bad they would have to stay in the cockpit with the pilot furiously 'trimming' to keep the plane level, while casting glances back at the passengers holding their sick bags, who would be wondering why they weren't getting any assistance. While there were scones and other treats to look forward to at the outback stations, it was difficult terrain, and on occasion it would be necessary for the crew, the passengers and the locals to help dig a bogged plane out of the mud. The Dove had its idiosyncrasies. Sometimes the undercarriage came down but the cockpit indicator didn't work, so the pilot didn't know if the wheels were down but not locked, or if they hadn't come down at all. Darellyn (Goss) Melsom, one of the 'Dove Girls', encountered this on a flight she was on: 'So we had to fly over the tower and they put up a searchlight to see if the wheels were down. We had to fly around, and I'm doing the radio at that stage, the passengers were all strapped in, to get rid of the last of the fuel. We said, "righto, we're coming in now, we're coming in". At the airport someone asked, "Just a minute, how many souls on board?"'[10] In the meantime, a radio station had reported that there was a plane flying around and it was in trouble, so Melsom's family got in their car and went out to the airport to watch, and hoping no doubt that 'the souls' on board would land safely.

If you weren't sick you were an air hostess.

Edna (Higgs) Payne, MMA air hostess, 1951 to 1953

The other major passenger airliner operating in Western Australia was MacRobertson Miller Aviation (MMA).[11] The airline had been set up in Adelaide in 1927 with Horrie Miller as pilot and with the financial backing of Sir Macpherson Robertson of confectionary fame. Robertson had a long history with aviation. He had sponsored the MacRobertson Centenary Air Race from Mildenhall (near London) to Melbourne in 1934. It was an important event as it opened up air travel as a viable means of international travel. In the same year MMA transferred their main operations to Perth, taking over the route flown by the mail service provider, West Australian Airways.[12] As well as flying in Western Australia, MMA provided a mail service from Perth to Daly Waters in the Northern Territory, arriving in time to connect with the Qantas Empire Airways flights, which would be taking mail through to the UK.[13]

Ann Shooter was appointed as the first air hostess for MMA in November 1945. The airline was hoping that the addition of an air hostess would improve passenger comfort on the new Douglas DC-3 passenger service from Perth to Darwin. Although MMA had been flying the route for some time, their planes were mostly carrying freight, but now the charter of the converted Douglas DC-3 from the Commonwealth meant that it was possible to cater to passengers, especially women travelling with children, to the far north.[14] It was expected that the older children would be travelling unaccompanied to schools in Perth and an air hostess would be required to help, as well as provide a food service.[15] Shooter's name had been on a waiting list for ANA for some time and they had given her some training when they recommended her to MMA. Along with the training, she was qualified in first aid, had bush nursing skills, and she had worked at a hostel in Perth. Shooter lasted only a few weeks in the job as she suffered from chronic airsickness, and was replaced by Kitty O'Neil, who was working at MMA as a clerk. She had been recruited by Horrie Miller, who got to know her after seeing her each day as he passed by her counter at Foy & Gibson department store.[16] MMA didn't have a training program although O'Neil had passed a first-aid and home-nursing course with the St John Ambulance Association. By September 1946 she was already a senior air hostess with MMA, with responsibilities for training. This may have suited her, because at just under 5 feet and weighing 6 stone she may have struggled to reach the hat racks on the DC-3.[17]

In March 1946, an MMA air hostess with the nom de plume Blue Bird of Happiness wrote an article for the *Western Mail*. She was in Broome with time on her hands as she was on an enforced layover; the Douglas DC-3 she was rostered on had experienced engine trouble on the Perth to Darwin run. She had been in Broome for four days (probably staying at the Governor Broome Hotel), but expressed confidence in the 'ten tons of shining silver' battling through whatever it might encounter.[18] She recounted an 'amusing incident' that happened the week before. On approaching Darwin, they had run into a cyclone. The weather was so severe it was impossible to see the wing tips of the plane. There were seven other aircraft in the air at the same time, waiting to land. The plane circled for one-and-a-half hours, constantly being tossed about. Fortunately, there were no passengers in the plane but oranges were rolling everywhere, spilt from a broken case. Instead of remaining strapped in, she tried to retrieve them, hitting her face on the floor with the turbulence. It is not known if she flew long after that, as she revealed that she had just become engaged to a man from Bluff Point, Geraldton.

Travelling through the north-west of Western Australia was particularly challenging in unpressurised planes because they had to fly below 10,000 feet to maintain adequate oxygen levels. With no radars, the planes would often encounter unexpected turbulence, in particular clear air turbulence (rapid movement of air with no visual cues such as clouds). MMA hostess Elizabeth (Bartlett) Foster recalls the difficulties of flying on the DC-3s with no weather radars:

> We were always late…But some of the experiences were terrifying. We never really knew about cyclones until we blundered into them. There were so few ships to radio us of their approach, but the Aboriginals knew.[19]

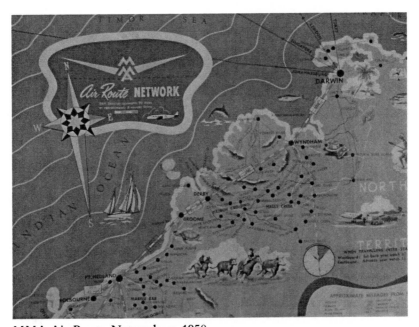

MMA Air Route Network, c. 1950

Passengers on board the MacRobertson Miller Airlines were handed out this brochure on the Douglas DC-3 and the de Havilland Doves. This detail from the brochure shows the main routes and the different stations the airlines would service in far North Western Australia. Courtesy of Eliza Jane Sharp

During the 1950s, there were meteorologists based in Port Hedland, and the pilots relied on shipping reports to warn them of any imminent weather issues. It wasn't until 1957, when MMA starting flying the Fokker 'Friendship' F-27, that the planes were fitted with weather radars. It wasn't just the weather that might be a bit rough. Stanley Brogden, a well-known aviation writer, travelled on a DC-3 flight between Darwin and Perth and described the catering. While a cup of tea was served at most ports:

> Passengers who must get up at 4.30am to 5am at Broome or Derby get a piece of heated-up fried fish (fried the previous night at Broome) and according to

my experience get nothing at Derby. For the passenger who gets aboard at breakfast the sight of a cup of tea is exhilarating at 9am, but the fruit cake with it is less exciting as a breakfast.[20]

The DC-3s were wonderful in that you were at a height that you could observe the topography of a place whereas now you just get above everything don't you. You don't see anything.

Patricia Jordan, MMA air hostess, 1948 to 1951

Patricia (Fidler) Jordan was 20-years-old and had just started working with MMA when she won the 'Miss Kimberley' competition. The following year, in January 1949, she was announced 'Miss Western Australia', with Olympic runner Shirley Strickland coming fourth.[21] She went on to be placed third in the 'Miss Australia' contest, with TAA air hostess Joan Easey 'Miss Victoria' coming second. As part of the Miss Australia competition they had to write 'a ten to fifteen minute essay about Australia, its resources and the opportunity it offers migrants'. Along with the swimsuit parade there was also a 'rigorous' physical culture examination, where 'the girls had to pick up pencils off the floor with one hand, and then both hands, while keeping their knees stiff and straight together'.[22] One can only wonder if skills of manoeuvring her way down the narrow aisles of the MMA planes may have helped Jordan with this particular trick. As a result of the beauty competition, Jordan was offered both a job as model and a position with British Commonwealth Pacific Airlines (BCPA) flying on the Sydney–Vancouver route.[23] But she wanted to consult with her mother before making a decision, and there was also a 'romantic attraction' in Perth weighing heavily in her decision making.[24] In the end she chose to stay with MMA.

Jordan's career with MMA had begun when she had been travelling from her home in Broome to Perth along with Cyril Kleinig, who was assistant manager, later general manager, of MMA. He dropped the suggestion that she try out for an air hostess job with the airline. She agreed, somewhat reluctantly, and on her first training flight she felt very airsick but was grateful that a passenger from Wyndham, who had been an ANA air hostess, offered her a few suggestions about managing the flight. This trip was almost the extent of her training but she did learn other tips from the five air hostesses in the company, and she made sure that she carried a St John First Aid book on all her flights. As she lived in Broome she was rostered on the Broome–Darwin run, and she suggested this was the airline's way of saving on accommodation costs. A tailor in Northbridge, Perth, made the white gabardine uniforms for the air hostesses and the uniform for the pilots. The dress was worn with a half-wing badge, which was so sharp that when bending over it would invariably pierce through the uniform. Flying on the DC-3s, there was no power in the galley, so two huge urns would have to be filled with boiling water and carried on board to make tea. At one point, Kleinig decided that, instead of the usual cold meat and salad, a hot meal would be served between Derby and Wyndham. Jordan had to work out how to manage 'these enormous urns of stew or whatever it was, braise in one and mashed potato in the other'. By the time she got to the bottom of the urn, as she put it, 'you had gravy under your armpit'. The service didn't last long because they struggled with it over the ranges, one of the most turbulent parts of the journey.[25]

By the time Jordan was 23 she was chief hostess and felt right at home on the Western Australian routes:

You got to know a lot of the regular passengers, like commercial travellers and people from up north who came down. We had all the boarding school kids that used to come up regularly. It was rather funny because a lot of the Kimberley people had known me since I was a kid.[26]

But drunk passengers were an issue.[27] Jordan again:

We had to more or less frisk them for liquor when they got on, you know, no hipflasks or anything [laughs] because you didn't have onboard drinks. You'd shoo the flies away too as they got in. Wax matches were collected also. When I was helping them do up their seatbelts...they're a bit plastered...one fellow who sort of knew me, he said, 'Quit your tickling, Pat'.[28]

On the flights from Darwin, MMA would sometimes pick up migrants who had flown in on the Qantas Empire Airways flights. The crew and the passengers would stay at the Berrimah Hostel, eight miles out of Darwin. The hostel had been set up during the war as a hospital to treat Australian soldiers and Japanese prisoners of war, and after the war it was used by Qantas and other airlines to accommodate crew and transit passengers. As an entry point to Australia one can only imagine what the international passengers thought of the place, as Jordan remembers staying there and being eaten alive by mosquitoes and sandflies. The tropical heat would get to the migrants and she remembers Greek women wearing black stockings just above their knees, and once on board they would lift up their skirts to keep cool, and looking down the aisle of the aircraft all one could see would be rows of pale thighs.

*She must watch her conversation at all times outside the
Company as regards delayed aircraft, service difficulties, engine
trouble or any other matter that might cause public concern in
regard to using air transport.*

MMA *Air Hostess Manual,* 1965

Jordan was on holidays when MMA was involved in Western
Australia's worst civilian aviation accident. On the 2nd July 1949,
eighteen people were killed when the DC-3 *Fitzroy* crashed in
driving rain shortly after take-off from Guildford, Perth. She
recalled the events leading up to the disaster:

I had gone on a holiday from Darwin. I went down
to Alice by bus and by the old *Ghan* to Adelaide, and
stayed with friends in Lenswood and then came on the
old *Stratheden* across to Fremantle. But I sent a telegram
in those days requesting an extra three days, I think it
was, because it fitted in with the ship. Had I been back I
possibly would have been on that aircraft because that's
the way it happened.[29]

The plane had taken off at 2 am, en route to Darwin, where
it was expected to arrive in time to connect with the Sydney
to London Qantas Empire Airways flight. George Forbes, an
occupant of a flat in the former army camp of South Guildford,
said he watched the plane crash a short distance from where he
lived. He heard a roar and a screaming sound before the crash.
At first he saw nobody and went and called the police, but when
he returned to the plane he saw 'some onlookers attempting to
recover a body from the cockpit with a long pole'. He went to
the site and discovered two figures in the cockpit in uniform, one

103

of which appeared to be a woman, presumably the air hostess.[30] She was Sylvia Seymour, who had worked with MMA for only nine months. The impact of a crash such as this on a small airline affects everyone but, despite the distressing nature of that accident, Jordan says that she never worried about crashing. There was even an expression – if there was an unusual bunch of passengers on board – they would be described as 'a crummy lot to die with'. Jordan left the airline in July 1951 to marry Sturdee Jordan, an MMA pilot with whom she had shared many flights, finding him 'caring and courteous and good to fly with'.[31]

Edna (Higgs) Payne and Trudy (Edwards) Broad joined MMA the year Jordan left, and by then there were only six air hostesses working for the airline; as Broad says, 'they were desperate'.[32]

Service with a smile on board the DC-3, c. 1951
Edna Payne on board the 'workhorse of the sky', the DC-3, serving a simple meal of salad and fruit to the MacRobertson Miller Aviation passengers. Courtesy of Edna (Higgs) Payne.

Broad was sorry when Jordan left as she thought that she was a very good chief hostess and 'she represented the company with style and aplomb and had always looked so neat and tidy'.[33] Broad had been working at the State Government Insurance Office as a shorthand typist, and was feeling a 'bit trapped' in a relationship with a local boy, when she met a friend who was an air hostess with MMA who encouraged her to apply. She went to the MMA office in Yorkshire House, St Georges Terrace, and the upshot was she was told to go to the airport that Friday night and fly on the Derby run. The plane would return the next day, leaving at 5.45am. She couldn't believe her luck, to go to Derby overnight! Soon after that flight she started work, without the usual first-aid certificate. Payne did the first-aid course on her first day with the airline.

Like other keen young women wanting to be air hostesses, Payne told a 'white lie' and put her age up from 20 to 21 so she could join. The airline turned a blind eye to this, even when, on a flight back from Carnarvon, she found time to sew the buttons on the dress for her 21st birthday party that was happening that night. Payne was trained by Broad, even though she had only been flying for six weeks. Broad made no claims about her expertise: 'we were so short of hostesses, then Payne came and she did the flight – I trained her – and I didn't really know what I was doing'.[34] Procedures were much more relaxed in those days, especially on a relatively small airline. When Payne was on one of her training flights she was allowed to sit in the captain's seat while he was having a rest at the back of the plane. Meanwhile, Broad, who was training her, was having a look out of the window at Darwin passing under the wing. They had overshot the landing. She grabbed the 'skipper' and he raced back to the cockpit, hauled Payne out of the seat and 'had a word' to the copilot, who had been so busy chatting to Payne that he had failed to notice Darwin below. With the captain back in the cockpit the plane was landed with none of the passengers aware of the slight detour!

While Broad and Payne were still flying together, they were issued with new summer uniforms, made by a dressmaker who lived near the airport. They were of linen, and not very good quality according to Broad, who said they would crush. Plus, the dressmaker had a habit of fitting them a bit too tightly, no doubt unaware there was a tendency for bodies to swell at altitude. Stockings were another issue; travelling in the high humidity of the tropical north, it could take almost twenty minutes to get one's stockings on. The pilots were fortunate enough to be allowed to wear shorts.

Any change in personal weight of 3lbs, must be notified to the Booking Supervisor. It is the Hostess' duty to keep her weight below the maximum permissible.

MMA Air Hostess Manual, July 1963

Working on the DC-3 required a certain amount of physical strength as it was a tail wheel plane, as opposed to the later nose wheel planes. This meant it sat low at the rear when on the ground. The door to the cabin was at the back of the plane, and because of the steep incline the air hostesses would have to hold on to the seats to pull themselves forward to get to the front. It was difficult for the air hostess while the plane was taxiing, but once it had reached a certain height it would naturally level out. The other plane that created difficulties for the air hostesses was the Lockheed Hudson, a converted bomber. East-West Airlines, a regional airline flying out of Tamworth, New South Wales, introduced them into their fleet in 1949. The first air hostess for

East-West was Carmel Paul, who, unfortunately, was continually airsick and left after a relatively short time. Joni Upjohn started with the airline after Paul left and commented that the air hostesses didn't have to worry about gaining weight on the Hudson as it would rattle and shake from take-off to landing. The other peculiarity of the plane was that the air hostesses would have to navigate the rear-wing spar, also known as the 'axle', traversing the cabin. Upjohn again:

> It was 2 feet high, and to reach the cockpit or the first four passengers, the hostess was forced to step over it. With a tight skirt it was difficult to negotiate without showing a considerable amount of leg. The local wags who travelled frequently knew all about the spar and they were all bottom pinchers.[35]

The Lockheed Hudson carried sixteen passengers. To distribute the weight, the air hostess would position the heaviest passengers in the centre of the cabin.[36] The issue of weight was a constant for all airline companies. Before an MMA flight everyone (the passengers, pilots and air hostesses) would hop on big old commercial scales at Guildford, so they could estimate the amount of petrol for the trip. Even the actual weight of the plane was considered. The DC-3s were all bare-skinned metal and Kleinig, who was now MMA's general manager, thought the cleaner they were the less friction, so about every six weeks the whole plane would be polished with wadding, cloth soaked with the Duraglit product. One of the reasons they stayed bare-metal was that a coat of paint would have added 80 pounds to the weight of the aircraft.[37]

Of course, the girls are just the marriageable age, attractive, and have opportunities to meet the most eligible men. Perhaps it's just as well the company like youth. And the older girls get, the more liable to fat. Some pilots suggest we cut down on the weight regulation of 120 pounds. You see, the heavier a girl is, the more disturbance she causes when walking about the ship (plane).

Nelly Graf, *Air Stewardess*, 1938 [38]

While it may seem extreme that the weight had to be so finely calibrated, Payne remembers there was one air hostess who had put on a lot of weight. As a consequence, the pilot had to trim the plane according to where she was in the cabin. One can wonder if this is an apocryphal story, but on another occasion one of the booked passengers was a no show, so more fuel was added to the plane. When he turned up at the last minute the petrol tanker had to come back to remove the fuel.

The job demanded specific qualities, as Broad said: 'You had to like people, to be friendly to people. You had to work like a dog. You had to be mighty quick'. She recalls that 'you rarely had a woman passenger unless she was the matron going to Halls Creek, or one of the wives of the station people flying to Perth. Many of the passengers were travelling salesmen and government employees, and the occasional shearer. Most of them were polite and if you offered them a cup of tea, 'You'd think you'd given them the world'. Being able to cook a boiled egg seemed to be an important requisite of the job, as it was a staple food for many years on the MMA planes. The eggs, two for the men and one for the women, would be placed in calico bags and then cooked in urns filled with boiling water that had been collected at the stopovers. The rest of the food was pretty basic. The trays were prepared on board, a serviette was put on the tray, and then ham and salad were placed on a plate, and, as there was no plastic wrap in those days, an upturned bread-and-butter plate was placed on top to keep things fresh. If the food stayed fresh between Perth and Carnarvon it was seen as a minor miracle. These conditions need to be seen in the context of the times, and it has to be remembered, as Payne recalled that for her generation, which had just been through the horrors of war and endured years of rationing, 'anything' seemed so much better than that.

MMA ran charter flights to transport personnel to mining camps; shearing teams on their rounds between stations; and even Norwegian men, who would arrive in the country and have to get to the whaling stations. Depending on what the charter was for, they would offer a greater selection of foods and drinks, including savouries and cheese, beer, whisky, gin, rum and brandy. MMA also ran special flights for a number of months to transport Royal Navy personnel who were stationed in Onslow in preparation for the nuclear testing at the Montebello Islands in the early 1950s.[39] All air traffic was stopped on the day of the testing as they weren't exactly sure what would happen with the atomic cloud. Robert Drewe wrote about this in *Montebello: A Memoir*, where his mother had her own concerns:

> 'Listen to me,' she says. Her voice becomes firm and serious. 'They've let off an atom bomb today. Right here in W.A.' I can visualise her anxiously blowing cigarette smoke out the side of her mouth so it doesn't pollute the telephone mouthpiece. 'Atom bombs worry the blazes out of me, and I want you at home'.[40]

Patsy (Miller) Millett, who was Horrie Miller's daughter and later became an MMA air hostess, remembers the secrecy surrounding the testing. When she was a child flying down on the DC-3 from Broome the first officer collected everybody's box brownie cameras, 'in case they got a misty picture' of the islands.[41]

The station and mission runs were a favourite with many of the MMA air hostesses. They would be based in Derby for a month, flying out of there with their fingers crossed, as these runs would often involve rough flying where one would be 'bucketed around in the sky' for hours on end. They would land on graded airstrips, and pull up alongside bower sheds made of a mesh of fronds or twigs. There was always a warm welcome on landing as you would offload 'a bag of mail, a workman or two, or some big box of something they were waiting for, parts or something'.[42] Tableland Station was often mentioned by the air hostesses. If all had gone to schedule the plane would usually land at the station at about 1.15pm, catching the heat of the day when temperatures could be over 100 degrees Fahrenheit (37.6°C).[43] Despite the searing heat, the station owner's wife would set up afternoon tea for the crew and passengers, serving hot scones, butter and jam on a tablecloth and with tea in china cups.[44] The station runs weren't economical, even though MMA was subsidised to do the mail run. Elizabeth Foster explains at one point: 'The bigwigs in Perth [flight operations] tried to stop the practice because it was messing up the schedule. But these station women were tough biddies, [they had to be] to live up there. They weren't going to take any notice of people in Perth'.[45] And the service continued.

The experience of flying on the station runs meant that many of the air hostesses met Indigenous people for the first time. Indigenous people living in towns and in traditional communities would rely on air services when seeking medical help,

Bower shed, Tableland Station c. 1961
Passengers on the MMA station runs didn't expect anything too fancy although they could be assured of a hot cup of tea and other refreshments under the shade of a bower shed at Tableland Station, Western Australia. Courtesy of Elizabeth Foster.

or as workers flying between stations. Wendy (Moir) Georgetti-Remkes was from England and was on one of her first flights as an MMA air hostess when a young Indigenous woman and her baby came on board. They had been in Derby hospital and were returning home:

> She had a tiny baby on the hip. We stopped at one of the stations and she disembarked as all passengers did, just to stretch her legs. She wouldn't reboard! She was one stop short of her destination. I went straight up to the pilot and said, 'She won't reboard'. She said she's had enough. He said, 'Leave her, she'll turn up at her destination'. I watched this native. Only a young woman. Bare feet, baby on hip and she disappeared into the scrub. The heat was shimmering. It was surreal. I thought, she's going to perish.[46]

She turned up a couple of days later. The pilot passed on the information to Georgetti-Remkes, just to put her mind at rest, saying, 'She did turn up, they always do'.[47]

Many natives, especially half-cast, are of course conversant with civilised habits and all the Hostess needs to remember is to seat them at the front of the passengers.

MMA *Air Hostess Manual*, September 1964

In their training manual for air hostesses, MMA made it quite clear that, 'It is essential, except in the case of sickness, that the hostess gives equal attention to all passengers'.[48] This was articulated in relation to the Indigenous passengers who would fly with the airline. Despite this call for equality, there were discriminatory practices such as using 'China Cote' plastic cups for the Indigenous travellers rather than the china cups used for the other passengers.[49] The manual also suggested that the Indigenous passengers should have sandwiches rather than a meal, 'as they would only be confused by the cutlery and crockery'.[50] The air hostesses had to recognise the different behaviours and also understand that many of the Indigenous passengers were quite fearful when travelling in a plane. Even though there were adjustments to be made in relation to caring for them, the air hostesses would describe the experience of travelling to the missions and the stations as one of the benefits of flying in outback Western Australia.

Be a good listener, ask leading questions and show a genuine interest in the conversation. However, avoid conveying to the passenger, any inquisitiveness of your part. Do not talk about yourself. Rather, encourage passengers to talk of themselves.

MacRobertson Miller Airlines Air Hostess Manual, 1962

Anyone who flew with MMA remembers Port Hedland. In the early days the landing strip would be lit by a single row of kerosene lamps. MMA pilots thought their job could have been much easier if there had been two rows of flares, so the plane could land between them.[51] It was a tough town, and the crew would stay at the Esplanade Hotel, which offered 'A Cool Drink and a Warm Welcome', and promised to 'especially cater for plane passengers'.[52] While Broad and Payne were flying there was a water shortage, so water was sent up by train from Marble Bar and, on arriving at the Esplanade Hotel, they would pick up an ewer and take it upstairs to wash themselves. The hotel seemed to serve a steady diet of cabbage and mashed or baked potatoes, as they were the only fresh produce to be had in town. There weren't always enough rooms available, so it became a first-in-first-served basis with the rest of the crew sleeping on the balcony. The beds were lined up side by side, and Doreen (Gardiner) Newell, who started flying with MMA in 1955, remembers being forewarned not to take see-through pyjamas.[53] Fortunately, there were no lights on the balcony so if the 'girls' had to get out of bed they would wrap a sheet around themselves, leaving only a little gap for the nose, to prevent sandfly bites. Most of the flight crew were older than the air hostesses, and they were generally protective, especially as the towns they were flying into had 'men everywhere'. This may have been the reason the local policeman would come out to the airport to collect the air hostesses and take them into town, rather than have them travel on the old bus. Newell remembers the policeman being a 'very nice young man', even going out to catch a huge mango crab for her when she told him how much she loved them. While the local policeman might have been benign in his behaviour, not all of the crew were perfect gentlemen. They might try something such as suggesting a walk along the jetty to 'get a bit of ozone'. Aside from walks on the jetty, and swimming, there were the 'Deck Chair' theatre nights and a real bonus was the Port Hedland Cup race day if one was lucky enough to be in town, and all the pastoralists would come from far and wide.

> *You never knew what was going to happen so that in a sense made it more exciting.*
> Doreen (Gardiner) Newell, MMA air hostess, 1953 to 1955

Newell was on her first flight when she recognised the copilot was from Brunswick, her hometown near Bunbury. Seeing him on board comforted her, which was just as well as they lost an engine on a flight from Port Hedland to Wyndham, and by the time the plane landed in Halls Creek she was 'an awful shade of green'. It was the 'friendliness of the crew' that Newell remembers, and with only about twelve air hostesses it felt like 'one big family'. She would have stayed longer with the airline but she met her future husband and being away for up to ten days on the Perth/Darwin run meant it was 'a long time to wait and see my sweetheart'.

> *Avoid any type of unladylike conversation.*
> *MMA Air Hostess Manual*, June 1962

The Kimberley port town of Derby was pretty basic as well. Initially the crew stayed at the corrugated-iron Port Hotel but then accommodation was arranged at Patterson Hostel, a rambling old house surrounded by trees and, like at the Esplanade Hotel, the crew would escape the heat and sleep on the verandah. There wasn't much to do in Derby, but the crews would play tennis at the local courts. Later the airline helped build a new hostel, with separate wings for the women and men, and there was a recreation area where the crew played table tennis. It still wasn't ideal as Patsy (Miller) Millett describes; it was 'overstuffed…you could hardly get a room in there. That was a great difficulty for the hostesses. Having to wait for a room after a long flight. Having to get the key from the kitchen, rooms not open. It was the last thing you wanted'.[54] Accommodation in Darwin was much better, and the crew would stay at the 'Raffles of Darwin' the Hotel Darwin. It seemed a luxury having rooms with ensuites, even though the hotel was still peppered with bullet marks from the Japanese invasion during the war.[55] The crew would dress for dinner, unlike in Derby or Port Hedland, and instead of 'a stew or whatever was going' here they would eat fresh barramundi served with a 'pink sauce'.

There wasn't great value in being thrown around the sky every day. But the value was in the people that were there and what you could do for them. You were, very often, their lifeline.

Pat Ward, MMA air hostess, 1962 to 1967, 1968 to 1982

Barbara Butler started with MMA in 1961 and flew for four-and-a-half years.[56] On the north–south trips, Butler remembers staying at Shepheard's Hotel in Geraldton. The hotel was run by Mr and Mrs Shepheard, and Mrs Shepheard reminded Butler of Sybil from *Fawlty Towers*. It was a 'posh hotel' having 'hot and cold water in all rooms', and there was a lounge and cocktail bar as well as a beer garden.[57] The dining room had white linen, polished silver, polished glasses, and flowers on every table. Compared to Shepheard's Hotel, staying at Meekatharra was 'a bit grim'. It was an old hotel, with criss-cross metal springs on the iron-frame beds, with uncomfortable mattresses. It was mostly men who stayed there and therefore Butler had to share the family bathroom: 'It was unbelievable, with all the rubber duckies in the bath and the squeezed out flannels and all the baby clothes and the whole bit'.[58] Flying to the outback towns meant that air hostesses' sense of duty went beyond the rostered hours. One of Butler's passengers was a woman from Kununurra with tuberculosis who was travelling to the Sir Charles Gairdner Hospital in Perth. Over the coming months, after returning from trips up north, Butler would visit the hospital bringing her 'cards and things her children had made' and passing on details of how the family was coping.

> *I remember going to a dance at the Continental Hotel in Broome,*
> *there were sixty men and five women!*
> Elizabeth Foster, MMA air hostess, 1960 to 1963[59]

Elizabeth (Bartlett) Foster just made the minimum height requirement of 5 feet, and she was aware that, as well as being single, 'a neat, well-groomed appearance was more important than beauty and glamour'.[60] She had been a dental nurse and travelled overseas by herself for two years before joining the airline. Her sister Mary had also been an MMA air hostess but left after ten months as there had been too many engine burnouts and near misses. Mary (Bartlett) Grant was 22 when she started with MMA, having left a nursing job at Mount Magnet because of a bad staph infection. She barely had any training: 'I was shown the plane and where the hammock was and how to do it up. I flew with another girl for a week and I was on the roster'.[61] It is doubtful that this was a great comfort, but she remembered there was a first aid kit containing morphine in case of a crash landing in the desert.

When Foster joined in 1960, the ground training was a six-day course, and then there were three weeks of flight training with a training hostess.[62] Not long after graduating, she and her training hostess were marooned at Wittenoom Gorge as the gravel landing strip couldn't handle the huge flows of water created by a cyclone they encountered en route. They had to wait for a whole week, staying with 'thirty fellas' at the old two-storey Fortesque Hotel. There were no cyclone warning systems at the time, and she was marooned again on her next trip there. When the weather cleared, they would play a round of golf at the Wittenoom golf course, on the 'blue asbestos' greens made from the filings from the mines. The first year that Foster flew she spent Christmas Day in Darwin and was touched to receive a big box of chocolates from 'MacRobertson' (Sir Macpherson Robertson) with a personally autographed card. To fill in the time while staying at the Hotel Darwin she sent a letter to her family in Perth describing her life as an air hostess in the far north-west:

> The stations in the Kimberleys are going through a drought, there was not a blade of grass anywhere but it should break, even this week, as we received the first monsoonal weather in the mission run to Arnhem Land. So probably next week, half the stations will be out. Less work for me; because you can't land.[63]

Flying on the DC-3s was always a challenge. Not only were the aisles so narrow that one would have to develop a 'side bottom waddle', to get the meal service done between ports; one had to be quick. For catering, everything was taken out of the drawers one by one, and if the weather was bad there was not enough time to get the meal service done. MMA decided they would employ someone, for a $10,000 fee, to find out how they could improve the 'time and motion' of meal service in the DC-3. The upshot was they couldn't, saying that it was impossible, given the hours, 'to serve twenty-eight people with sixty movements in every tray'.

Foster's response was that she thought she could do a better job. Marge Ellershaw allowed her to take up the challenge, and Foster found the solution:

> So what I did is I separated the drawer into different sections, and put everything in it. So you took the whole drawer out and put it on top. If it got rough, all you had to do was put the drawer back and the couple of things that were on the right-hand side. I never got any money for it, though I got a letter from the company to say, 'well done'.[64]

By the end of the 1950s, MMA had introduced the thirty-six seater Fokker 'Friendships' F-27.[65] They could travel almost twice the speed of the DC-3s, and they were pressurised and fitted with weather radar.[66] There were now two air hostesses on board and they had the luxury of using a built-in oven and being able to press a tap, rather than lug the heavy and cumbersome urns around. Contrary to what one might imagine, the new planes created a nostalgia for the experience of flying on the DC-3. Foster describes this feeling:

> The DC-3s move with the wind, they don't shudder. It's a whole sort of feeling you're one with nature in a DC-3. But when you get in these modern aircraft where they shudder and shake, I wasn't as happy. In the Fokker you didn't have time for passengers. On the DC-3 you did have. So I met a lot of people on the DC-3. I could sit down beside them and talk to them. You had time and you learned their stories.[67]

Foster also preferred the DC-3 because, as a keen photogra-
pher, she would take photos with her East German Werra camera
from the back window of the DC-3. Even though there was good
vision from the 'Fokker', as it had high wings, it flew so much
higher that it was impossible to get any clear detail for photographs. In 1963, one of her photos taken from the DC-3 was used
in the September issue of *National Geographic* magazine. She was
paid £101 for the image, which at the time was a small fortune,
especially as by then she was living in London and earning only
£4 a week.

*Passengers may be introduced to each other when, in the opinion
of the Hostess, it is desirable.*

MAA Air Hostess Manual, June 1962

*They worked their butts off; they really did. They were always
pleasant. Some of them were characters. But they were always
very loyal to the company.*[68]

Ron 'Sos' Johnson, MMA employee 1971 to the collapse
of Ansett 2001

*The work of air hostess with MacRobertson Miller Airlines
Limited is a most interesting career. Girls are chosen for their
smart and trim appearance, pleasant personality, tactfulness and
general adaptability.*

MMA Air Hostess Manual, 1965

Good kid but her teeth were lousy. I told her to get 'em capped.

Robert Sterling, *Stewardess*, [1982] 1983[69]

While many of the MMA air hostesses possessed a natural beauty, such as Pat Campbell, who was selected as Miss Air Hostess 1962, and Francene Maras, who won the Miss Australia quest in 1977, there were others who had to work to meet the standards. One young woman who applied and met all the other criteria was asked to have orthodontic treatment, which she did, before she was formally accepted into the airline. The application form for the airline in the 1960s included a two-page form asking for personal details such as: religion, flying experience, training in deportment or speech production, sporting activities, club activities, hobbies, foreign languages, living with parents, father's occupation, away from home for any long periods, experience in the preparation and serving of meals, your place in the family, family ties or obligations, medical knowledge (details of nursing experience), possession of a current St John first aid certificate, health, including seasickness or fatigue as a result of early rising, experience handling children and/or infants and a guarantee as to the length of service.[70] At the end of the form was a scant four lines for the interviewer's report, indicating that the consideration about who was suitable may have been 'short and swift'.

Pat Ward, a senior air hostess for MMA, reflected upon the type of air hostess they wanted for the airline in the 1960s:

Well, we certainly weren't looking for any glamour, which I think, perhaps, the other airlines were. We were looking much more for an individual, someone who has got some character and personality, who seemed dedicated to what they really wanted to do. Perhaps they'd previously done nursing or, they'd already worked in some other field. Yes, I think, really, just their character, their personality.[71]

Being an air hostess requires tact, good humour, infinite patience and a genuine liking for humanity. It's like being a nurse — you must have a sense of vocation or you'll never have another happy moment.

Evadne Price, *Air Hostess in Love*, 1962[72]

Pip Asphar, who was head of recruitment with MMA in the 1960s, remembers conducting interviews with Pat Ward and Avril Shilkin, who was third in charge. After the interviews a group of three or four prospective air hostesses would go on a familiarisation flight to somewhere like Geraldton or Kalgoorlie and back. They would see how they would relate to each other, and how they would relate to the passengers in the aircraft, as 'what they would show us in an office situation would be totally different to what they would show us in an actual situation. This was excellent because it used to set some apart from the others'.[73] Asphar agreed that ex-nurses:

> ...or girls from the country that had come up and finished their schooling in private schools in Perth would often make the best hostesses. These young women were a little bit above the others in terms of their manners, their decorum and presentation and secondly, they had that terrific country ethic and natural ability about them.[74]

An independent personality helped, as it was difficult to have a social life with long and fragmented hours of duty. The familiar relationships of family and friends were sidelined, and a strangely fleeting social life was patched together from moments sitting on the edge of an armrest talking to passengers, meeting the roustabouts and cockies at the stations, and taking tea with the families at the Christian missions. Sacrifices were made, yet the novel and unique conditions generated new professional values for these western pioneers of the air. As Patsy Millett said:

> What we did was vital to what had been an extraordinarily isolated community in the north for many decades. It was very important that they had that airline coming through, particularly to the stations. Of course, we did have an idea that this mining boom was terribly important too. That this was the future of the State and all that sort of thing. Since then, over the years, I've become terribly involved in the environmental movement and I do not quite see it that way. I went into places that were pristine and gorgeous and now they are just great pits in the ground.[75]

The mining boom in Western Australia in the 1960s caught MMA a bit on the 'back foot', as they didn't have enough planes, or the ones they were flying were antiquated. Nor did they have enough pilots or air hostesses for the increased services. The airline needed to inject more funds into the company to purchase new aircraft, and the result was that in 1963 they became a division of Ansett Transport Industries. MMA continued to operate under their own banner until 1969 when Ansett took them over completely, renaming the airline MacRobertson Miller Airline Services.[76] Patsy Millett started flying during the boom years, thinking she would help out for the year and then go back to university. She had been encouraged by her sister Julie, who was an air hostess with the airline. Millett chose to fly on the old DC–4s as she wanted the Broome run, and that was the plane that was used on that route. She was critical of the condition of the old planes. They would leak oil, so the uniforms were always dirty, but more serious was her lack of confidence in the machine: 'every time I closed the door on that DC-4 I started to get the idea that I was closing the lid on my coffin, I really did. I thought this is going to crash, nothing surer'.[77]

It wouldn't be the DC-4 that crashed, but another MMA plane did. On New Year's Eve, 1968, Australia experienced its third-worst civil aviation accident when a MMA Vickers Viscount, flying from Perth, spiralled out of control and crash-landed at Indee Station near Port Hedland. All twenty-one passengers and five crew were killed. The air hostesses on board were Georgette Bradshaw, Gail Sweetman and Kay Aubrey. They were all in their early twenties, with Aubrey travelling as a passenger for the purpose of familiarisation training. Millett had left the airline just before the accident, but she knew the plane and, as the accident investigation report confirmed, the crash occurred because the plane 'was bloody worn out. It was in fact — it was structural failure that took it out — metal fatigue'.[78] Pat Ward had come back to work for MacRobertson Miller Airline Services as Hostess Superintendent after having a year off to go to university and she had to go with Julie Miller to inform the families about the deaths of their daughters: 'I had been concerned, strangely, when I accepted the job of Hostess Superintendent. It was something that concerned me — I knew if anything happened — I would have a big responsibility to the team. So I had considered it when I took the job'.[79]

3.2. TAA 'The Friendly Way'

'What I would like to find,' says Miss Wilson, 'Is a few girls of the shy, retiring types with no glamour or dress sense and less

than average intelligence. Then I could relax. There used to be a lot around and I can't believe they've all disappeared'.[80]

Nan Wilson, Air Hostess Superintendent TAA, 1949

Can you do it? Of course you can. Hostess, go aboard. Wear the TAA smile of friendly service all the time. Good luck to you, and happy landings.

TAA promotional training film, Fortune Productions, c. 1948

It was Trans Australia Airlines (TAA) that proved to be the main competitor to regional operators in the Australian domestic airline industry. There had been a referendum in August 1944 in an attempt to nationalise the Australian airline operators, but this was defeated and ultimately the bid was ruled unconstitutional by the High Court. In reaction to this decision, the Labour government set up the Australian National Airlines Commission, which in turn set up TAA as a government-owned airline responsible for handling the domestic network. The first service on the 9th September 1946 was a publicity flight from the Laverton RAAF base in Victoria to Sydney, in the DC-3 *Joseph Hawdon*, complete with bullet holes in the fuselage. Like other DC-3s, it had been converted to a civilian plane after World War II, then leased to ANA by the Commonwealth Government. It was reclaimed by the Australian National Airlines Commission for TAA.

One of the first slogans TAA had produced for the first services in October 1946 was 'One Fare for All – The Lowest'. This slogan, and low-cost airfares, drew a fast and furious response from ANA. By May 1947 they were forced to drop their fares to match TAA's.[81] It would be TAA's next slogan that would become the most well-known: 'Fly TAA – The Friendly Way'.[82] It was suggested that the slogan had come about as a response to

Doug Laurie, TAA's traffic superintendent, saying that their main competitor ANA, with their monopoly on the east coast, had a 'lousy reputation for service'.[83] But Ian Sabey, who was TAA's publicity manager, said the phrase was a bid to capture some of the success of the phrase, 'friendly service' which Melbourne's Myer department store had been using since before the war.

There was nothing friendly about the pressure TAA put on ANA and the other interstate airlines, which were significantly disadvantaged by the new competition. TAA took over the delivery of much of the airmail, which had provided a steady subsidised income for the other airlines, and the airline also secured the steady passenger clientele of senior government employees.

Helen Sommerville was 29 years old when she was appointed Air Hostess Superintendent for TAA in July 1946.[84] She had plenty of experience as she been an air hostess with ANA since 1940. After her appointment, the next step was to place advertisements in newspapers across the country welcoming young women to apply for air hostessing positions. By late August over 800 women had applied for the fifty positions.[85] Applications had been received from Hungarian, Norwegian, Scottish, Dutch and French women, but the most applications by far came from Western Australia.[86] The advertisement for the position outlined the requirements:

- Qualifications – personality, intelligence and good appearance
- Age – should be between 22 and 28 years
- Height – 5 foot 2 inches to 5 foot 6 inches
- Weight – not exceeding 120 pounds
- Knowledge of nursing or first aid essential
- Ex-service personnel who fill the above description

will receive preference

- Selected personnel will be required to carry out training in Victoria
- Remuneration – trainees £4.10 shillings per week
- First three months £5 per week
- Thereafter £5.10 per week until the completion of eighteen-months' training, when £6 per week will be paid
- Photographs should be supplied wherever possible[87]

The first three successful applicants were Veni Vernon and Sheila Briscombe, who had flown with ANA, and Patricia Deverall, who had flown with Butler Air Transport. They commenced flying on the 26th August 1946, wearing uniforms and were photographed all which were a few sizes too big and held together by pegs.[88] A second course commenced in September, and by the end of the year there had been six courses in total. The inclusion of ex-service personnel was stretched to include Gwladys Fogden from Wales, whose Australian husband had been killed in active service five weeks after they had married.[89] She generated a good deal of publicity for TAA as the 'airman's widow'.[90] She was also selected to undertake promotional activities for the airline, such as addressing the Overseas Wives Club about air travel and how it affects mothers and children.[91]

To promote the airline and its services TAA had also recruited one of the original ANA air hostesses, Gladys Allan, now Mrs Gellie, as their Women's Public Relations Officer. She gave talks to women in Sydney and Melbourne about air travel and flew to Cairns in order to advise prospective passengers on the types of clothing to pack for flights to the tropical north, and also to see what was available in the local shops.[92] She became the youngest

Welcome aboard TAA

Many of the air hostesses kept scrapbooks and this clipping is from a scrapbook that TAA air hostess Rochelle (Miles) Sutherland made during her time flying from 1960 to 1963. Courtesy of Rochelle Sutherland.

member of the Business and Professional Women's Club, Sydney, before she left the airline in 1948 to accompany her academic husband on an exchange to England.[93] Another TAA air hostess, Miss T. Rogers–Uff, was also given promotional duties and her talk was at the Brisbane branch of the Business and Professional Women's Club, held at the Lyceum Club. In her talk she wanted to dispel a few of the myths about air hostesses. As she told her audience:

> An air hostess' life is definitely not a glamorous one. It is
> plain hard work. Young girls who are full of enthusiasm
> at the beginning of their first trip, are tired out and free
> of any ideas about glamour when they land.[94]

The first TAA air hostesses attended a three-week training school, but by September it was a six-week course and on graduating they were paid a starting salary of £4.10 a week, rising in increments, where after eighteen months of service they could receive £6 a week.[95] Audrey (Kitching) Bussell was in the second intake of TAA air hostesses, and she thought the salary was good at the time, even though she would have to catch trains for any holidays as she couldn't afford to fly by air.[96] Also, there were no allowances then for food, laundry or stockings. The air hostesses would go to the Commonwealth Government Clothing Factory in South Melbourne to be fitted for their uniform. The uniform was similar to ANA's with a summer uniform of a belted white dress with brass buttons and an embroidered half-wing badge above the breast pocket on the left-hand side. The winter uniform was a navy, military-style suit with epaulets, worn with a white shirt. Bussell flew on the inaugural flight to Adelaide, and her overriding impression was of the smell of Dettol and fishing false teeth out of airsickness bags. The food was a barley sugar on take-off and then a salad tossed with ham and a few canned peaches served with custard.[97] It was only later when TAA flew the Douglas DC-4 on the eight-to-ten hour Perth route that a hot roast dinner was offered to the forty-eight passengers on board. Like the experience of most air hostesses, it wasn't all plain flying.

On occasion the cabin door would blow open on take-off and she would have to hold on to the first officer's jacket while he leaned out to close it.

By July 1947, TAA was still receiving between eighty and 100 applications a week. To help with the training TAA made a film that described the type of 'girl' they were trying to shape to suit the corporate culture. The hostess-to-be was described as:

> ...an ambassador with the public reputation of the air-line largely in her hands. Her success will come from a special TAA personality – a mixture of human qualities, which do not come only from the study of our rules and routines. Those qualities can be developed deliberately by an intelligent girl, they are exhibited in her deport-ment and in an easy cordiality which, while pleasantly friendly, allows the hostess to retain an agreeable dignity at all times.[98]

The voice over mentioned that 'some qualities are physical'. For instance, her overall appearance of 'fastidiousness comes first from a clean, well-dressed uniform', and the air hostess would use her 'smile as an asset'. Also:

> The human qualities come into use from the moment of embarkation, when the smile of welcome at the doorway sets the tone for the whole journey...Passengers must be made to feel welcome and important. That is the first and most important duty of The Hostess, who can turn a disgruntled passenger into a happy one by her manner. Where possible, use the passenger's name in a word of welcome, the name on the ticket will help you, and you

should come down the aisle to meet the person on the forward seat.[99]

Within a year of the TAA air hostesses first coming on board, twelve of them received a refresher course with Air Hostesses Supervisor Mrs A. Macandie and publicity director Ian Sabey.[100] They were asked if they could suggest 'workable improvements to the service'. Some of the improvements suggested were that a bottle of eau de cologne be included in the equipment of each plane for spraying after airsickness; that plane seats be allocated when tickets were bought to save the trouble of 'trying to please' passengers who insisted on window, back or front seats. As an aside, the air hostesses mentioned that they were disappointed that overseas passengers often 'treated them as waitresses' and were 'disinclined to recognise their status'. Another idea was marking a person as a 'FF' for their first flight, as that would help identify them especially if it was necessary to call on the captain 'to give reassurance'.

Ian Sabey, along with introducing 'The Friendly Way' slogan, was responsible for one of Australia's most iconic advertisement campaigns. In April 1948, Sabey noticed Nola Rose while he was sunbathing at Bondi Beach. Rose was 19 years old and she had just won the title of 'Miss Pacific' in the Australian Surf Girl contest. She was a photographic model and mannequin for David Jones, Sydney, and Sabey enlisted the Noel Paton advertising agency to create a poster, thinking that it was important to include images of pilots and hostesses in their advertising campaigns. Ralph Warner created a painting of Rose wearing the white summer uniform, and the image was used on a simple layout designed by Jim Haughton-Jones.[101] Arthur Cole, the chair of the Australian Airlines Commission, thought the image of Rose was 'too sexy' and the poster wasn't released until he retired in April 1950.[102]

Despite Cole's reservations, the striking advertisement went on to win an international poster award. The image of Rose was to influence the TAA air hostess graduation photos: the air hostesses would be posed with their faces beckoning out of the frame, shoulders receding and their arms out of view. There were various versions of the poster, usually modified to include the introduction of a new plane to the TAA fleet, such as the Vickers Viscount 700 in 1954. The image of Nola Rose was used in TAA advertisements until the 1960s.

Air hostessing was something new and when something new happens everybody wants to be in it.

Dorothy Lauchland, TAA air hostess, 1952 to 1954

After the war, Dorothy 'Dot' Lauchland went to work with TAA in their finance department in Brisbane, and the air hostesses would come to her office and collect their pay. It got her thinking, as she was keen on getting some free travel, she decided to move to Sydney and it was from there that she applied to be an air hostess. After a successful interview with Mrs Margaret Hughes, she moved to Melbourne and started flying with TAA as a 27-year-old in 1952. The training was organised into three parts: inflight services, emergency procedures and first aid. The air hostesses had to know quite a bit of history because the aircraft in those days were named after Australian explorers, and people would look out the window and they'd want to know where they were, and they also expected to be told something of the history of the country.[103]

Lauchland lived in an old Edwardian-style boarding house at 295 Dandenong Road, Windsor, with eight other TAA air hostesses and remembers it would be freezing in winter, as she stood on Dandenong Road early in the morning waiting to catch the first tram – with only the regulation TAA uniform on – to take her to the city. Once in the city, the TAA bus would pick her and any passengers up and take them to the airport. Finding accommodation was always an issue for the air hostesses. When Kay Barton started her training with TAA in the late 1950s she shared the same boarding house with thirteen other air hostesses. She stayed there after her training finished and then she moved to a big two-storey house in Lumeah Road, Caulfield. Air hostesses would find their own accommodation by placing advertisements in local papers, 'Two Air hostesses urgently require self-contained Flat. Ring FU9430'.[104] Or, 'Air Hostess from Perth, like full board, private family, near city'.[105] The policy for many of the airlines would be to station the air hostesses away from their hometowns, as in those days many of the air hostesses would have lived at home, and the airlines didn't want families ringing up asking why their daughters were five minutes late home, when in fact they may be a few *days* late getting home.[106]

Lauchland would sometimes fly the Darwin route and stay in the Hotel Darwin. If the open-air picture show was screening, she might go by herself or with one of the TAA air hostesses who had flown up from Adelaide. There would also be overnights at the Imperial Hotel at Longreach, and the town could be packed if it was show week and Lauchland would have 'country boys' sleeping on the balcony outside her room. She would be told, 'if those bloody jokers are making too much noise and waking you up, you call out and we'll shut them up'. TAA would fly through Queensland up to Papua New Guinea, via Townsville. Initially nobody wanted to be based in Townsville, so TAA would send air hostesses there for six-week blocks staying in a flat behind the Seaview Hotel. Lauchland remembers the parties in the flat and the air hostesses became 'palsy-walsy' with some of the boys who worked at the Seaview who would visit after work with leftover chicken and other food from the hotel. Eventually there were four air hostesses permanently based in Townsville.

Sometimes there was trouble on board. Wool buyers and tax agents were part of the steady trade of airline passengers but it was the wool buyers who were the worst drinkers:

> They'd be late on the aircraft, they'd be in the bar and
> of course they made a lot of money in those days. You'd
> be taking them things and you'd hardly have any time
> to serve the food.[107]

One day Lauchland had had enough of running backwards and forwards to the wooden box that kept the little bottles of spirits and beer: 'I was sick of this, so this time I got the box and I put it up in the middle of the aisle and I came and said to two or three at a time, 'You can drink as much as you like or you can finish it off but I want that money, I haven't got time to do that myself'.[108] Lauchland was not alone in her thoughts about the wool buyers. Pamela (Farrell) Brinsley, who flew with TAA from 1949 to 1950, described the wool buyers as 'by far the most obnoxious' of all passengers. She thinks they were 'emboldened by their numbers' as: 'They flew en masse from town to town wherever the wool auctions were held. The liquor flowed and they became more and more noisy, and they were known for patting and pinching one's bottom when we bent forward to pass food or drink!'[109] With the difficult passengers Lauchland would refer to her training for clues about how to handle them remembering it didn't matter what they did, 'be nice and be sweet, don't worry about it'. And 'if you're nice enough and they keep complaining, they will be the ones who will apologise; and it's a fact, they did'. After two-and-a-half years flying, Lauchland left to marry a pilot.

As well as flying to Papua New Guinea, TAA air hostesses got the opportunity to fly overseas when the airline began charter flights to New Zealand on the Skymaster DC-4s in 1947. They took over the service from Tasman Empire Airways Limited (TEAL) while they were having their flying boats modified.[110] For TAA air hostesses Peg McGill and Elizabeth Cox the possibility of flying overseas was anticipated with great excitement. They flew up from Melbourne to Sydney for the onward journey and all went well, but the return flight, which commenced after only a two-hour break in Auckland, was horrendous. The unpressurised plane was buffeted around the skies for hours, items fell from the hat racks, the passengers were ill, and an engine failed halfway across the Tasman, with the second 'on the blink'. By the time McGill got back to Melbourne, returning to her home on the all-night tram at 4am, she had been forty-five hours without sleep. Cox resigned from TAA shortly afterwards.[111]

The next international link happened the following September when TAA introduced the first of its new Convair planes, which had been purchased in order to transport migrants from the United Kingdom. The plane could seat forty, and it had radiation wall heating, sound-proofing, large square windows and a built-in stairway in the tail. The plane was faster than the DC-3s and the DC-4s Skymasters. Inside the main cabin was a smaller cabin area where one air hostess would prepare the food while the other would do the running back and forth to the passengers. Ansett also flew later versions of the Convair and the twin-engined plane featured in the opening chapter of pulp fiction novel *Flight Hostess Rogers*:

The Convair Airliner, flight fourteen out of Chicago, settled down on Runway Four of La Guardia Airport like a graceful homing pigeon returned with a message. Hostess Ceil Rogers hardly felt the soft whomp-whomp of the landing gear as it slued up the smooth landing strip...The twin engines belched and went silent, a dying wheeze as the gasoline supply giving them life was cut off. Ceil saw the huge props cease churning the evening New York air.[112]

The migrant passengers who flew on the TAA Convairs paid £260 and they were subsidised by the British government (£75) and the Commonwealth government (£32.10). While relatively expensive it was far cheaper than flying with any other commercial airlines but by June the following year the scheme was deemed a failure because of a lack of passenger numbers.[113]

While there were individual differences between the airlines, the basic training for air hostesses was almost the same the world over. The key differences would be specific training to work on particular aircraft. The demand for air hostessing did not abate, and in January 1948 the Australian Air League announced they were going to launch an advanced training program for women who wanted to be air hostesses. There were conditions about who could apply regarding age, weight and height similar to that of the airlines but other than that if they were 'self-possessed and have some understanding of human nature' they could apply to attend the six-month course, which would have lectures two or three times a week. A representative of the league was going to attend an air hostess training course, but already they knew that the course would offer map reading, knowledge of planes and a voice production course, as a pleasant speaking voice was considered essential.[114] Helen Sommerville, TAA air hostess superintendent, endorsed the course by recommending that women wishing to become air hostesses join the school at 54a Pitt Street, Sydney.[115]

3.3. Navigating the Pacific Islands: British Commonwealth Pacific Airlines

You are a highly trained member of an International Airline, and as such, you will be continually in the public eye. Dwell on this aspect, and realise just what it means. Your Country and your Company will be judged by you, who are in closest contact with the Passenger. Your conduct, both on duty and off, whether in uniform or not, will be subject to the most stringent criticism, and any indiscretions on your part will reflect upon your Company and Country.

BCPA Hostess General Rules, December 1950

In 1948, British Commonwealth Pacific Airlines (BCPA), which had been flying to North America since 1946 using ANA services, began flying in its own right.[116] It started a 'Southern Cross' service flying to Vancouver via Fiji, Auckland, Canton Island Atoll, Honolulu and San Francisco. It employed Bernadette 'Barney' Lalor, who had been an air hostess with ANA since 1941, to become hostess superintendent.[117] BCPA was a small airline with a fleet of four DC-6s and there was a purser on board as well as two air hostesses.

Pat (Chrystal) Gillespie had worked at TAA for two-and-a-half years when she received a telegram asking if she would like to apply for BCPA. She moved to Sydney to undergo special training, as the DC-4s and the DC-6s flew over water.[118] The DC-6s could

Ditching Procedure brochure, BCPA c. 1954
The serious issue of an aircraft going down is lightened by this illustrated brochure which was handed out to passengers on the BCPA DC-6 flights across the Pacific Ocean. Courtesy of Patricia Coleman.

seat forty-four passengers during the day, but at night, between Fiji and Honolulu, the seats were converted into single and double bed berths. Four bottom seats could convert into a double bunk and above that was a single bunk, which could be accessed by a ladder. If the two people sharing a bed weren't a couple they would put a 'bundling board' between them, and a curtain would be drawn across the bunks for privacy, as in a Pullman railway sleeper. It would be intriguing to see what people chose to wear to bed, the BCPA information booklet suggested one could change into full night attire, 'although most experienced travellers prefer to remove or loosen outer clothing only'.[119] One of the air hostesses on board the DC-6 had to be a nurse and Anne (Lynn) Pfeifer, who had been a trained nurse, started flying with BCPA in 1953. She remembers the 'blue babies', with congenital heart defects, they had to carry for surgery in the United States.[120] While the air hostesses would take care of the passengers the purser would take care of the paperwork and the practique (the documentation required to allow passengers to disembark in another country). Gillespie recalls that sometimes the purser would also 'look after' the air hostesses, bringing them a cup of tea while they had their break.[121] Gillespie would leave for work in a uniform described by aviation writer Stanley Brogden as 'out of this world' and 'surely the smartest and most chic in the world'.[122] Actually, the uniform was not so different from any other air hostess uniform, as it was a double-breasted suit worn with a distinctive beret. The fact that it was taupe coloured may have made a difference.

The 'Southern Cross' trip to Canada was a long flight, which, in total, took forty-nine hours, and the crew was away for three weeks at a time. The best thing about the trip was the compulsory rest period in Hawaii. This break was enforced by the Department of Civil Aviation to avoid fatigue, with air hostesses restricted to twenty-five flying hours a week, or 100 hours a month.[123] The break could be up to five days, so the time was spent shopping and lying on the beach, while staying at the Moana Hotel (later the Royal Hawaiian Hotel).[124] Gillespie recalls on one trip a very difficult headwind encountered while flying into Fiji. She was flying with an air hostess who had recently secretly married, and it may have been her mind was elsewhere:

There was no visibility. So we were going around and around and around. I was going around checking people and they were saying we seem to have been close to that hill before. I said, 'Oh yes, we always do this when we come to Fiji'. Then the air hostess who was with me; she'd just got married. She's sitting in the seat with the *Herald,* and she said, 'I haven't even had a honeymoon'. She's looking at the Situations Vacant. She wasn't much help to me, I can tell you.[125]

By the time the plane landed the crew were shaking so much they couldn't sign the papers but the air hostesses were asked to count the cutlery, something that was always checked on arrival at each destination. Given what they had just been through Gillespie thought this seemed like the 'final insult'.

…most hostesses marry within the first year or two, and there is one girl's explanation for that: 'their boyfriends, back home, get tired of being "grass widows", and pop up with a proposal they might otherwise have held back'.

Anon, 'It is the Glamour Job Every Girl Envies',
Sunday Mail, 5 April 1953, p. 11

Never show favouritism with your passengers, five minutes conversation with all passengers is better than half an hour's talk with one.[126]

BCPA Hostess General Rules, December 1950

Patricia (Stokes) Coleman became an air hostess with BCPA in 1954, just before it was absorbed by Qantas. She had trained at Miss Hale's Business College in Sydney and, after working at a number of secretarial jobs, the 20-year-old went to work at BCPA as the secretary for the chief engineer, John Mills, in a hangar at Mascot. They used to conduct test flights, and, when she could, she would hop on board. Her dream was to become a pilot but it was too expensive so, at the suggestion of flight engineer William 'Billy' McMahon, she applied to be an air hostess. They thought that she was too young and so she had to wait until she turned 23, which was the requirement of BCPA at that time. While waiting at BCPA, she applied for Qantas and was interviewed by senior hostess Marjorie 'Marj' de Tracy, but wasn't accepted. She never wavered from her desire to be an air hostesses, even after seeing the impact on her colleagues at BCPA when the DC-6 *Resolution* crashed in heavy fog near San Francisco airport on the 29th October 1953. All nineteen on board were killed in the crash, including the purser Walter 'Wally' Knight and the two air hostesses Amy 'Kay' Lewis and June Elder.[127] Finally, early in 1954, Coleman became a BCPA air hostess, and remembers the airline commonly being referred to as 'Barlow's Circus of Performing Animals'. As they were taking off from Sydney they used to sing a song:

> Bye-bye Sydney
> Stick your bridge and stick your quay
> San Francisco is the place for me

On the 1st April 1954, BCPA amalgamated with Qantas. When Coleman moved across to Qantas with the rest of the BCPA crew, Marj de Tracy said that she remembered her, right down to the cream felt hat she had worn at the interview.[128] The BCPA air hostesses proved popular with the Qantas stewards as they had been used to handling and preparing the food, and would often pitch in and help out with what was then the stewards' main responsibility. And while Coleman hadn't lost any of her desire to be 'up the front' of the plane, she accepted that being an air hostess was the next best thing. Her father thought that she had given up a good job to be a 'flying waitress'.[129] Despite this attitude 'nine times out of ten' he would come out to the airport to see her when she returned from an overseas flight. BCPA had been aware of families farewelling and greeting the air hostesses, and in one memo warned, 'When hostesses are departing from Sydney, on duty, all farewells must be said in private. Hostesses must not be waving to friends and relatives, once they have emplaned'.[130] The families of the air hostesses often took a keen interest in their comings and goings. Margaret (Brown) Shaw's father was thrilled when she joined ANA in 1952 and, while he didn't come to the airport, he would keep charts of where she had flown, how many miles and what her weekly rosters entailed.[131]

Coleman thought that being an air hostess on an international airline required special qualities:

> You had to be a bit intelligent, you had to know what was going on in the world because you had to speak to people. People asked you different things about your own country as well as the countries you were going to. [And]…there's some little thing inside the girls that flew that set them apart…I can't quite hit it on the head, I'm not quite sure what it is but maybe they were a bit gregarious. Being able to slot in and being able to adapt to different circumstances, different people.[132]

When Coleman joined Qantas she met Barry Coleman, who was a Qantas flight steward, and they flew together for fourteen months before they married in secret in 1957. She continued flying until she was six-months pregnant.[133] Fellow crew members commented that she was 'getting thick around the waist', and even when she said that she was pregnant they didn't believe her.[134] Eventually the telltale signs were too obvious and she had to leave, but was only given two weeks' severance pay as she had not given Qantas a month's notice, and it was with regret that she had to return her uniform.[135]

3.4. Natural Attrition

Even though I do have to fly with Adam Murray, that man made such a fool of me, setting up a blind date with me and letting me talk all about my job without ever telling me he was an airline pilot. And there was I telling him how it felt to fly, oh! I could cheerfully strangle him…even though he is young and good looking.

Peter Yeldham, 'Air Hostess' radio play, Episode One, 1954[136]

Throughout the 1940s and 1950s, there continued to be a steady flow of air hostesses who left to marry. There was a well-held notion that air hostesses left flying to get married to passengers or pilots, and they sometimes did. But Mrs Margaret Hughes, who was TAA air hostess superintendent in 1952, said that the air hostess barely had time to get to know passengers and there were not many single pilots left, as most of them were a bit older and already married.[137] Pamela Brinsley came from England and joined TAA in 1949, thinking an air hostess job would be a good way for her to see Australia. While she noticed a bit of flirting amongst the crew, she said the job 'didn't lend itself to serious relationships because [the] two parties were on the move all the time, usually in different directions!'[138]

Air hostesses resigning to get married and contributing to the postwar baby boom was not just a problem for Australian airlines. In 1949, BOAC considered not employing any more air hostesses, saying that the £250 spent training them was proving to be a false economy. This didn't happen and in April 1950, *The Londoner* reported, 'A convent charm school where thirty-six girls learn tact and deportment, how to serve food without spills when travelling at speed, how to deal with wild animals and survive in jungles, is run by B.O.A.C. at Heston, Middlesex'.[139]

Air hostesses also left their jobs to travel the world, or work for international airlines. Others left as they were able to use skills they had gained in new professions. Davida Nowland left TAA to undertake 'pioneering, strenuous and dangerous' work as a first-aid worker for the Red Cross assisting the resettlement of Chinese in Malaya.[140] And during the Korean War, Lorraine Jarrett who had flown with ANA, left to return to her nursing duties when she became an air evacuation sister on the Korea–Japan–Australia run.[141] There was always a small number who found the job too demanding, or the conditions too difficult and left to undertake other work. Air hostesses were still flying on unpressurised planes, and the lack of oxygen at altitude made the work exhausting, as they were on their feet for most of the flights. It was less of a strain for pilots, who were seated, and passengers, who could snooze. By the 1960s, as part of the training for MacRobertson Miller Airlines, air hostesses would be taken to the RAAF Base Pearce just north of Perth to endure a decompression chamber to check how they managed with a lack of oxygen. The effects of lack of oxygen are described perfectly in Pamela Hawken's novel *Air Hostess Ann:*

The pressure in this chamber is the same you would get in a non-pressurised plane flying at 10,000 feet. At that altitude the air is very thin and there is less oxygen...after a minute she was talking disjointedly and the watching girls were surprised to hear broken sentences...They noticed that Pat's pencil was wavering uncontrollably all over the page.[142]

There were other health issues. Nanette Cummings, who started work with TAA in 1948, flew for only a year as she became ill. She thinks she may have been 'burning the candle at both ends' with the demands of the job. On one occasion she flew the ten-hour flight from Melbourne to Perth only to find that the arrival air hostess was unwell and she had to get back on board and make the return journey.[143] Most of the airlines had their own doctor not only to assess the new recruits but to manage ongoing medical issues. Like Dr E. Anderson with ANA. He would give the air hostesses a six-monthly health check that would include an x-ray,[144] vaccinations for overseas flights, and he administered airsickness tablets.[145] Irma (Wharton) McLaren, who flew for ANA and then Qantas, remembers being told by the doctor that the abnormality of spending a long time in the air could stop menstruation. The issue of menstrual cycles would be a challenge for many of the air hostesses, and in later years many would go on the pill to regulate their cycles.

It is well known that Australian aviation developed in part to conquer the challenges of the wide open spaces of the outback, with its interminable rough roads. After World War II, Australia was still heavily invested in its rural industries, and these supplied income and products for the burgeoning cities in the south-eastern fringe of the continent. It was no different in the west, but with

Perth as an isolated city, the nation's largest state had just as much need to move people and goods quickly if it was to move with the twentieth century. Domestic airlines such as MMA provided the crucial links in the west that connected all the points of the national compass, and also on to Singapore and Europe. The memories of the pioneering air hostesses call for a rethinking of the myth of the world's most glamorous profession as it encountered another myth, that of the great Australian outback. They were constantly at the interface of the demands of the machine, their routine, and the expectations of their passengers. They saw things as they were, and met the challenges, as always, with a smile.

Notes

1 A. Rogers Hager, *Janice Airline Hostess*, Julian Messner, New York, [1948] 1949, p. 18.

2 Anon, 'Two hours travel by air to Kalgoorlie', *West Australian*, 2 August 1946, p. 9.

3 Anon, 'Log book for flying babies', *Sunday Times*, 8 September 1946, p. 6.

4 E. Hill, *The Great Australian Loneliness*, Robertson and Mullens Ltd, Melbourne, [1937] 1945, pp. 17–18.

5 Anon, 'Horses to planes', *West Australian*, 15 March 1946, p. 9.

6 Anon, 'Dragon in the tree-tops', *Australian Women's Weekly*, 3 February 1960, p. 3.

7 Marge Ellershaw would later become chief hostess of ANA.

8 The first two air hostesses employed were Connie Brooks and J. Sutton, as they had both been radio operators during the war.

9 D. (Goss) Melsom, written correspondence with the author, December 2015.

10 D. (Goss) Melsom, interview with the author, 15 April 2013. Melsom joined Airlines (WA) in 1953.

11 Airlines (WA) merged with MacRobertson Miller Aviation on 1 October 1955.

12 Western Australian Airways had been set up in 1921 and was based out of Geraldton.

13 Queensland and Northern Territory Aerial Services (Qantas) was registered in Brisbane on the 16th November 1920; in 1934 it became

Qantas Empire Airways with Imperial Airways (later BOAC) owning 50 per cent; in 1947 the Australian government purchased all the shares. Qantas was privatised in 1995.

14 The DC-47 Dakotas were military planes converted for civilian use after the war.

15 Anon, 'North-West air service', *West Australian*, 28 November 1945, p. 4.

16 F. Dunn, *Speck in the Sky: A History of Airlines of Western Australia*, Airlines of Western Australia, Perth, 1984, p. 102.

17 Anon, 'Senior hostess weds former P.O.W', *Daily News*, 11 September 1946, p. 9. In 1961 the minimum height requirement for MMA was 5 feet to 5 feet 7 inches, 21 to 27 years, and weight no more than 124 pounds.

18 Anon, 'Air hostess to Darwin', *Western Mail*, 28 March 1946, p. 26.

19 E. Foster quoted in G. Thomas, 'Window on the world', *Weekend West,* 4 April 2009, pp. 8–14, 10.

20 Brogden quoted in Dunn, *Speck in the Sky: A History of Airlines of Western Australia*, p. 103.

21 Patricia (Fidler) Jordan flew with MMA from 1948 to 1951. Anon, 'Miss W.A. chosen', *Barrier Miner*, 18 January 1949, p. 3.

22 Anon, 'Judging concluded', *Geraldton Guardian*, 27 January 1949, p. 5.

23 British Commonwealth Pacific Airways (BCPA) was started in 1946.

24 Anon, 'Miss WA offered posts in E.S.', *Mirror*, 5 February 1949, p. 1.

25 P. Jordan, interview with the author, 15 April 2015.

26 ibid.

27 MMA was a dry airline until 1968, but air hostesses were burdened with passengers boarding inebriated, or carrying hip flasks. When alcohol came on board in the 'wild west' drinking became quite an issue, especially with the men coming off the oil rigs, which were dry. Huge amounts of alcohol were consumed while waiting at the airports, and eventually the company (under pressure from the union) decided that any person who behaved badly towards crew could face a ban travelling on the the aircraft.

28 P. Jordan, interview with the author, 15 April 2015.

29 ibid.

30 Anon, 'Ill-Fated DC-3 turned over backwards', *West Australian*, 13 December 1949, p. 8.

31 P. Jordan, interview with the author, 15 April 2015.

32 T. (Edwards) Broad and E. (Higgs) Payne, interview with the author, 15 April 2013. Payne flew from 1951 for two years and left as she had a boyfriend, later to become her husband, and it was proving too hard to see him as she was always rostered to fly on weekends. Broad flew from 1951 for almost three years when she left to marry in early 1954.

33 T. Broad, phone interview with the author, 23 April 2015.

34 T. Broad and E. Payne, interview with the author, 15 April 2013.

35 Joni Upjohn, East-West air hostess from 1950 to 1958 quoted in A. J. Smith, *East-West Eagles: The Story of East-West Airlines*, Robert Brown and Associates, Carina, Qld., 1989, p. 54.

36 ibid, p. 53.

37 R. C. Adkins, *I Flew For MMA: An Airline Pilot's Life*, Success Print, Perth, [1996] 1998, p. 15.

38 N. Graf, *Air Stewardess*, Gramercy, New York, 1938, p. 62.

39 Nuclear testing at the Montebello Islands occurred in October 1952 and in May and June 1956.

40 R. Drewe, *Montebello: A Memoir*, Penguin, Melbourne, 2012, p. 61.

41 P. Millett, interview with the author, 16 April 2013.

42 B. Butler, interview with the author, 15 April 2015.

43 Tableland Station is now managed by Australian Wildlife Conservancy.

44 During this time Ned and Dorothy 'Dot' Delower were the Tableland station managers.

45 E. Foster, interview with the author, 15 April 2015.

46 W. Georgetti-Remkes, interview with the author, 5 September 2015.

47 ibid.

48 MMA, General Instructions 'Natives', *MMA Air Hostess Manual*, September 1964.

49 'MMA Meal booklet' 1963-1966, 5 October 1964, p. 10. Courtesy of Valerie (Mason) Hall.

50 MMA, General Instructions 'Natives', *MMA Air Hostess Manual*, September 1964.

51 E. 'Dick' Evans, telephone interview with the author, 26 April 2013. MMA pilot 1957 to 1969.

52 Esplanade Hotel Advertisement, *Northern Territory Times*, 12 July 1951, p. 6.

53 D. Newell, interview with the author, 16 April 2013. MMA air hostess 1953 to 1955.

54 P. Millett, interview with the author, 16 April 2013. MMA air hostess 1965 to 1967.

55 MMA would use the foyer of the Hotel Darwin to administer the Perth services and charter flights.

56 B. Butler, interview with the author, 15 April 2015.

57 Anon, *Sunshine Festival Brochure*, Geraldton, 1961.

58 B. Butler, interview with the author, 15 April 2015.

59 E. Foster, *A Bird's Eye View: Memories and Memorabilia of MMA, 1960–1962*,

unpublished manuscript, 2007, p. 7.

60 E. Foster, interview with the author, 15 April 2015; 'How to become an air hostess with MMA, brochure, c. 1960.

61 M. Grant, interview with the author, 14 April 2015. MMA air hostess 1956 to 1957. The hammock was tied above the freight and was used to sleep in.

62 MMA 'Terms of Employment – June 1962', *MMA Air Hostess Manual*.

63 E. Foster, 'Letter to 'Folks', Christmas 1961.

64 E. Foster, interview with the author, 15 April 2015.

65 These turbo-prop planes were introduced in December 1959.

66 The weather radar meant the pilot could observe the weather conditions along a flight path up to 80 miles (128 kilometres) ahead.

67 E. Foster, interview with the author, 15 April 2015.

68 R. Johnson, interview with the author, 22 April 2013. MMA employee from 1971 until the collapse of Ansett, 2001.

69 R. Sterling, *Stewardess*, Piatkus, Loughton, UK, [1982] 1983, p. 4.

70 MMA Air Hostess Application form, c. 1961.

71 P. Ward, interview with the author, 12 May 2015.

72 E. Price, *Air Hostess in Love*, John Gresham, London, 1962, p. 57.

73 P. Asphar, interview with the author, 16 April 2013.

74 ibid.

75 P. Millett, interview with the author, 17 April 2013.

76 In 1981 MacRobertson Miller Airline Services was renamed Airlines of Western Australia.

77 P. Millett, interview with the author, 17 April 2013.

78 ibid.

79 P. Ward, interview with the author, 12 May 2015. MMA air hostess 1962 to 1967, 1968 to 1982. In 1967 Ward left MMA to do a degree but came back for the senior position. She signed a contract saying MMA would pay her university fees and she could remain flying if she married. Ward completed her BA degree while at MMA and was promoted to Manager, Passenger Services.

80 Anon, 'Glamour of the uniform', *Argus,* 16 December 1949, p. 2.

81 I. Sabey, *Challenge in the Skies: The Founding of TAA,* Hyland House, Melbourne, 1979, pp. 100–1.

82 The slogan was introduced in 1948.

83 J. Gunn, *Contested Skies: Trans Australia Airlines 1946–1992*, University of Queensland Press, Brisbane, 1999, p. 33.

84 Anon, 'Air hostess: a superintendent appointed', *West Australian*, 24 July 1946, p. 10.

85 Anon, '800 girls seek jobs as air hostesses', *Argus,* 22 August 1946, p. 3.

86 Anon, 'Aspiring hostesses', *West Australian*, 22 August 1946, p. 8.

87 Trans Australia Airlines Advertisement, *Examiner*, 17 August 1946, p. 4 and *Argus*, 17 August 1946, p. 38.

88 P. Merlehan, *Wings Away: Flying Tales to Tell*, Wings Away, Queensland, 1992, p. 9.

89 Anon, 'Took to life in air', *Courier-Mail*, 25 January 1947, p. 6.

90 P. Wright, 'Airman's widow flies the skies as air hostess', *Mail*, 22 February 1947, p. 9.

91 Anon, 'Gwladys Fogden', *Sydney Morning Herald*, 17 April 1947, p. 16.

92 Anon, 'First air hostess checking north', *Townsville Bulletin*, 28 August 1947, p. 2. Gladys (Allan) Gellie was recruited in 1946.

93 Anon, 'First air hostess England bound, *Mail*, 26 June 1948, p. 17.

94 Anon, 'Two views on modern miss', *Courier-Mail*, 29 October 1947, p. 6.

95 L. Wake, 'That air age', c. 1996, pp. 16–17, clipping.

96 Bussell worked for TAA for eighteen months before she left to join British Commonwealth Pacific Airlines (BCPA).

97 L. Wake, 'That air age', c. 1996, pp. 16–17, clipping.

98 TAA training film, Fortune Productions, c. 1948.

99 ibid.

100 ibid; Anon, 'Hostesses have ideas for improved air service', *Sun*, 17 June 1947, clipping.

101 Sabey, *Challenge in the Skies: The Founding of T.A.A*, p.104.

102 ibid.

103 D. Lauchland, interview with the author, 6 August 2013.

104 Anon, 'Advertisement', *Sydney Morning Herald*, 7 September 1949, p. 17.

105 Anon, 'Board, residence' advertisement', *Courier-Mail*, 9 May 1946, p. 10.

106 C. Locket, interview with the author, 21 June 2012.

107 D. Lauchland, interview with the author, 6 August 2013.

108 ibid.

109 P. Brinsley, telephone interview with the author, 10 April 2015.

110 TEAL was jointly owned by Australia, New Zealand and Britain.

111 Merlehan, *Wings Away: Flying Tales to Tell*, p. 32.

112 M. Avallone, *Flight Hostess Rogers*, Tower Publications, New York, 1962, p. 7.

113 Anon, 'TAA Convair bring migrants,' *Argus*, 1 October 1948, p. 3.

114 Anon, 'Advanced training for air hostess applicants', *Sydney Morning Herald*, 15 January 1948, p. 6.

115 Anon, 'Would you like to be an air hostess?', *Sun Herald*, 17 April 1949, p. 3.

116 In March 1946 a civil aviation conference was held in Wellington, New Zealand, with participants from the United Kingdom, Australia, New Zealand and Canada. The aim was to open up routes across the Pacific

Ocean. As a result of the meeting a new airline was formed, British Commonwealth Pacific Airlines (BCPA). Initially, the whole airline operations were undertaken by ANA, who supplied the planes and the crew.

117 Anon, '260 want to be hostesses', *Daily News*, 16 January 1948, p. 4.

118 There were nine crew on the DC-6, the captain, copilot, first officer, navigator, radio operator, flight engineer, purser, two hostesses (one a trained nurse).

119 *BCPA at Your Service booklet*, c. 1948.

120 A. Pfeifer, telephone conversation with the author, 28 October 2010.

121 P. Gillespie, telephone conversation with the author, 22 June 2016.

122 S. Brogden, 'The Southern Cross Route' *Aircraft,* March 1949 in H. M. Moore, *Silver Wings in Pacific Skies*, Boolarong Publications, Brisbane, 1993, p. 105.

123 Anon, 'It's hard work for the air hostess', *News*, 6 March 1953, p. 11.

124 Passengers would stay at Niumalu (Sheltering Palms) Hotel. R. Charlett, 'Cocktails with Lunch 3½ Miles, Up', *Argus,* April 2 1949, p. 3.

125 P. Gillespie, interview with the author, 3 September 2015.

126 Hostess General Rules from Manual of Instructions by E.V. Wall 1/12/1950, in Moore, *Silver Wings in Pacific Skies*, p. 109.

127 Moore, *Silver Wings in Pacific Skies*, p. 138.

128 Coleman lent the hat to Dorothy Fraser Bell to wear to her interview with BCPA. With the result: 'I wore your hat, I got the job'.

129 P. Coleman, interview with the author, 2012.

130 Hostess General Rules from Manual of Instructions by E.V. Wall 1/12/1950, in Moore, *Silver Wings in Pacific Skies*, p. 109.

131 M. Shaw, interview with the author, 4 March 2015.

132 P. Coleman, interview with the author, 3 June 2012.

133 BCPA was absorbed by Qantas, 1 April 1954.

134 P. Coleman, interview with the author, 3 June 2012.

135 Not only did Coleman and her husband Barry fly but her daughter, Debbie, and her sons, Matthew and Mark, also had long careers working as cabin crew for Qantas; Matthew is still flying.

136 P. Yeldham, interview with the author, 4 March 2013. Originally planned as thirteen fifteen-minute programs, Yeldham wrote fifty-two episodes without ever having flown in a plane. He received advice from the actor Charles 'Bud' Tingwell, who had been a pilot, and his wife, Audrey Wilson, who had been an air hostess. Also Yeldham's wife had good ideas about plots for the programs.

137 Anon, 'Passengers and pilots are out', *Courier-Mail*, 24 July 1952, p. 8.

138 P. Brinsley, telephone interview with the author, 10 April 2015.

139 Anon, 'They want to see the world before they marry,' *The Londoner*, 19 April 1950.

140 Anon, 'Qland [sic] girl for dangerous job in Malaya', *Courier-Mail*, 4 November 1952, p. 8.

141 EK [sic], 'Nursing sister on the wing again', *Barrier Miner*, 6 June 1952, p. 9.

142 P. Hawken, *Air Hostess Ann*, The Bodley Head, London, [1952] 1953, pp. 46–7.

143 N. Cummings, telephone interview with the author, 22 May 2012.

144 Anon, 'Variety for an air hostess', *West Australian,* 30 August 1949, pp. 15–16.

145 S. Catling, 'This flying business is not all flying', *Courier-Mail*, 13 August 1949, p. 2.

Chapter Four

THE WORLD COMES TO AUSTRALIA

4.1. 'A Wonderful Opportunity to See the World': the Qantas Flight Hostess

They got used to us, I think. In the beginning, the stewards
probably didn't know what to make of us.

Irma (Wharton) McLaren, ANA air hostess 1947,

and Qantas flight hostess, 1947 to 1952

In 1947, Qantas Empire Airways, which had been set up in 1920, became wholly government owned and the airline purchased a fleet of the new pressurised Lockheed Constellation L749. Badged with the 'winged kangaroo' symbol, the plane had ten crew (seven technical crew, two flight stewards and one flight hostess) with only thirty-eight passengers.[1] Irma McLaren, a veteran of the second intake of Qantas flight hostesses, thought, 'It was a lovely aeroplane with plenty of room'. And it was all first-class travel.[2] *Qantas Empire Airways* magazine was effusive in its description of the new plane: 'More than beauty is in the sleek, graceful lines of the Constellation. The redundant, the unsatisfactory, the mediocre have been discarded, and in it beauty and efficiency are complementary'.[3]

The 'Connies', as they were affectionately known, would provide the utmost in comfort, and Qantas had the only model where the seats could be laid flat and convert to twelve bunks; an option sold in-flight for £100 extra. The mechanism to convert the seats was tricky and often depended on the flight engineer checking the manual. As most of the Qantas Constellation flights left at night it was necessary to warn the passengers either seated or lying in their beds that the flames coming from the engines were merely exhaust, and there was nothing to fear. Trudy (Edwards) Broad, who worked for MacRobertson Miller Airlines, was on a stopover in Darwin and was offered the opportunity to go on board the new Constellation:

> I remember going up these steps and there were only about six steps to go up into the DC-3 and this one you went up like a two-storey building. Then I looked at the seats and they were so, sort of, small and all together, more like modern day aircraft whereas ours, we had big seats.[4]

Not only did the Constellation appear incredibly modern but flight hostesses were going to form part of the crew; a first for Qantas. Qantas had employed stewards since 1938, when they had moved operations from Brisbane to Rose Bay to begin the flying boat service to London. Now, almost ten years later, in December 1947, Qantas selected nine young women, from more than 1,000 applicants, to train to fly on the longest scheduled air route in the world, the Constellation 'Kangaroo Route' from Sydney to London.[5] It was decided to call the new crew members 'flight hostesses', as a way of distinguishing them from the domestic air hostesses.[6]

The nine women selected were Patricia Burke, Joy Bruce, Joy Daniell, Margaret Lamb, Rosetta Allison, Margaret Calf and

The First Qantas flight hostesses, January 1948

Qantas had employed flight stewards since 1938 but in December 1947 nine flight hostesses were employed to fly on the new Lockheed Constellation L749. Australia's international airline used the flight hostess to promote not only the airline but also Australian tourism to the world. Courtesy of The Australian Women's Weekly/ *Bauer Media Pty Limited.*

Adrienne Gundlinger, Irma Wharton and Marjorie 'Marj' de Tracy. They had all worked for other domestic airlines, including de Tracy, who had worked at ANA as a senior hostess. De Tracy

was appointed as the senior hostess at Qantas and, on the 8th
May 1948, was the first flight hostess to fly on the Constellation
service.[7] The new recruits all had a range of prior work experience
in nursing, physiotherapy, teaching, interior design, secretarial
work and war service with the WAAF (Women's Australian Air
Force). The criteria for the position were: age between 23 and
30 years; height to 5 feet 7 inches; weight to about 9 stone 7
pounds; education to intermediate standard; experience in handling people; ability to type and knowledge of a foreign language
was an advantage. The duties were still standard: general attention
to passenger requirements, traffic clerical work on board, and
assistance in serving meals.[8]

Patricia (Burke) St Leon had seen the Qantas flight hostess job
advertised in the paper, and she went for the interview wearing
her best clothes: 'A dress that was very smart, that I'd bought in
Melbourne but it did have a slight cleavage'.[9] The interview was
conducted by George Harmer, general manager of Qantas, Bruce
Hinchcliffe from the staff department, Bill Nielsen, the traffic
manager, and Lady Elizabeth Fysh. It was not surprising to find
Elizabeth Fysh on the interview panel. Not only was she the wife
of the co-founder of Qantas but she had been involved with the
airline right from the early days, including testing the sogginess of
the landing strip after a spell of rain with her high-heeled shoes.
Echoing the experience of Matron Holyman, she was also referred
to as Qantas's 'first caterer', as she used to make sandwiches for
passengers and crew.[10] These early Qantas flight hostesses used to
say they were 'handpicked by Lady Fysh'.

In retrospect, St Leon thinks the interview questions were
curious, compared with the type of questions they might ask
today.[11] 'What does your father do, Miss Burke?' and she replied
he was a sugarcane farmer in Innisfail, north Queensland, 'Oh,

and where were you educated?' and she replied 'mostly in a convent' as she had been a boarder at St Patrick's Convent in Townsville.[12] She wasn't asked about her experience working with TAA; they were more interested in her nursing experience. Her nursing qualifications would see her in good stead, as sometimes on layovers she would 'moonlight' at St Vincent's Hospital in Sydney for extra cash.

The successful applicants had two weeks' training at the Qantas Traffic School in Bay Street, Double Bay.[13] By the 1950s the course was five weeks long, with a probationary flying period of three months.[14] The training course was described as 'tough' with the idea that the flight hostesses would have more knowledge than they would need in practice and with the view that on board this would translate to giving the passengers a feeling of confidence.[15] The 'Kangaroo Route' would operate three times a fortnight, taking three or four days' flying time to get to London, but with all the stopovers the flight hostesses would be away for three weeks at a time. Because of the length of time away it was necessary to think carefully about the 30 pound (13.6 kilogram) luggage allowance. One of the flight hostesses suggested they may set up 'clothes dumps' with friends on the way, but in the meantime an all-purpose off-duty frock that could be dressed either up or down with accessories would be just the ticket. De Tracy thought that 'a swimsuit would be worth its weight'.[16]

The passengers had a much more considerable luggage allowance of 66 pounds (30 kilograms) and they were advised that because of the even temperature in the Constellation few changes of clothes would be necessary. What passengers should wear on these long trips across the world became the subject of many magazine and newspaper articles. A correspondent from the *Sydney Morning Herald* on the first Constellation 'Charles Kingsford

Smith' service to London on the 1st December 1947 suggested that 'extreme style should be avoided' and her choice of outfit for the flight was:

> ...a black wool bouclé suit, long-sleeved white blouse, and a small black hat aboard. Immediately the aircraft took off for England I changed into cherry red corduroy slacks, suede sandals of the same tone, a daffodil yellow silk jersey blouse, and tied my head in a patterned silk scarf which had a wide border of cherry red.[17]

The correspondent remarked that, while some men wore sports clothes, somewhat remarkably there 'were several who wore their navy blue suits complete with waistcoats, collars, and ties, for the whole journey, and landed in London just as if they had come only on a suburban train journey into the city'.[18]

I think the glamour wears off after a while.
Irma (Wharton) McLaren, ANA air hostess 1947,
and Qantas flight hostess 1947 to 1952

Irma McLaren grew up in Lismore and on leaving school at 17 travelled to Sydney to become a nurse, then worked with the Red Cross during the war. In 1947 she became an air hostess for ANA but after a couple of months she left to join Qantas. Matron Holyman was 'very cross' about the waste of training when she left. McLaren had not formally applied for Qantas; instead, she and Joy Bruce, another ANA hostess, were in Sydney for the day, and somewhat spontaneously decided to go to the Qantas office in Shell House, Carrington Street, hoping to see her brother Alan, who was a pilot with Qantas. As they were catching the lift the operator mentioned they were interviewing that day, and so, in their ANA uniforms, they met Mr Hinchcliffe, the employment officer. They 'hit it off' and both Bruce and McLaren were asked to attend two more interviews. The final interview was around a table with a panel and she thought that she would miss out as, as she gave some clichéd answers: 'I love flying' and it's 'a wonderful opportunity to see the world'. But both she and her friend were accepted. She started a fortnight's training on the 5th January 1948 at the Qantas Training School, Double Bay, but had to wait until May for her first trip.[19]

Qantas Flight Crew, Cairo, 1952
Travelling the world was part of the daily life of the Qantas cabin crew. Here flight hostesses Sue Crawford and Llyris McIntosh (right) pose alongside flight steward Joe Ellis in front of the Sphinx and Pyramid of Giza. Courtesy of Jenny Mooney.

The Constellation flight would leave Sydney at 8.30pm, and arrive in Darwin at dawn, where the passengers and crew would be driven to Berrimah Hostel to have breakfast. They would leave for Singapore that day, arriving at about 2.30 in the afternoon after a long and tiring flight.[20] Singapore was a favourite stopover, and the flight hostesses would stay in Room 66 at Raffles Hotel, on the ground floor near the outdoor area. It would only be later that they had an air-conditioned room upstairs. In the early days, the hotel would allow them to leave their summer uniforms there while they travelled through to London, collecting them on the way back. Qantas also employed ground hostesses at Singapore to help with travel arrangements and on occasion take passengers on tours of the city. From Singapore they would go on to Karachi, staying at Speedbird House, which was owned by BOAC, and then on to Cairo where they would stay at the Heliopolis Palace Hotel, wining and dining in the French restaurant and relaxing with games of golf and tennis. Depending on the time of year, they might fly to Rome instead of Cairo, staying at the Residence Palace Hotel. Once they arrived in London they would catch the train to stay at Dormy House, which was an old house on golf links at Sunningdale, Berkshire. Like Speedbird House, it was owned by BOAC.

Although there must have been expectations about appearance, Irma McLaren doesn't remember being weighed or checked for grooming and she thinks this was because de Tracy, even though she was the senior hostess, 'was one of us'. This may have been the case for the first intake of flight hostesses, but as de Tracy remained as flight hostess supervisor for twenty-seven years there were other recollections about her legacy. Many flight hostesses thought she imposed an unfair requirement to report to her office at Mascot first thing the next morning after returning from a gruelling overseas flight with a written report outlining any incidents that had occurred. Like most flight hostess supervisors, de Tracy had an eagle eye, and Patricia (Stokes) Coleman remembers coming back from a trip to Hawaii and de Tracy telling her off for having a tan. Coleman replied cheekily that there weren't many palm trees on the beach at Waikiki to provide her with shade. On another occasion de Tracy said to Coleman, 'I can't fault you in your work but what's happened to your hair? I've made an appointment for you with my hairdresser'. Coleman was sent to the fashionable Vincent DeLorenzo salon in the city where he permed her hair. On her next flight the stewards were quick to notice a difference in her appearance and one of them said, 'Stokes, what happened to your hair?' As soon as she got to Honolulu she went to a hairdresser and had it all chopped off. As long as it was short she didn't think de Tracy would mind. Being a stickler for procedure, de Tracy's influence on the Qantas flight hostesses was considerable and she set a standard that was well respected across the industry. She left Qantas on the 7th March 1975.

McLaren shared a flat at Cronulla Point with a colleague, Jean Harrison, who had worked for ANA and then BCPA. Because they were both flying overseas routes McLaren didn't see her flatmate for almost nine months as their times at home failed to coincide. The third person sharing the flat was Lilian (Heal) Macalpine, who had trained with McLaren at ANA. Macalpine was from the tiny town of Quairading in Western Australia, and she was accepted into the second Qantas intake of six on the 1st March 1948. Macalpine had always wanted to fly, and had joined the WAAF during the war as a wireless operator and had taken some flights on Tiger Moths, doing 'loop–the–loops and everything'.[21] She would have liked to learn to pilot, but it was too expensive.[22] Macalpine remembers being fitted for the military-style uniform on the sixth floor of David Jones, and then having to wait until June to fly as her uniform wasn't ready. The practicality of the navy suit was never questioned, but the white uniform would get filthy, particularly the white cloth belt. On one occasion when Macalpine was asked to do a promotional shot, she had to cover the dress with a greatcoat as it was so dirty.

In the space of a year and a half, Macalpine had flown to London twenty-two times.[23] She showed me an original seating plan from one of her trips. The plan shows the seat that Prime Minister Robert Menzies occupied when he went to London for the Commonwealth Prime Ministers' Conference in 1950. Even though his seat was at the back of the plane, as Macalpine said, 'It didn't matter as they were all good in those days'. As well as having a prime minister on board her flight, Macalpine was invited to a garden party at Buckingham Palace. The invitation read: 'Thursday July 1950, 4–6 o'clock. Men morning dress or lounge suit'. She wore a broderie anglaise frock, which had been made by a friend, with long white gloves worn over the elbows, and topped the ensemble off with a hat she had bought on a trip to Paris. She was presented to the King who had 'quite a chat with her', and one can only imagine what the small town of Quairading (population approximately 1,500 people) would have made of that.[24] After the trip, Menzies wrote a letter to Hudson Fysh praising the airline and 'the two charming hostesses', presumably meaning Macalpine on the way there, and possibly a different flight hostess on the way back.[25]

4.2. Strife on Board

For Qantas, the transition from an all-male crew was not without its problems. Almost exactly a year after flight hostesses first came on board, the stewards went on a four-day strike. They were represented by the Hotel, Club and Restaurant Union and they entered a case before the New South Wales Conciliation and Arbitration Commission, which demonstrated a degree of discontent on their part about the division of labour on board the

Constellations. A headline in the *Sydney Morning Herald* on the 20th April 1949 read, 'Air Hostesses "Stole Glory", says Steward'.[26] Senior flight steward Samuel Andrews reported to the commission that since the introduction of flight hostesses 'all the glory that was ours suddenly disappeared because we were no longer in the limelight'.[27] The stewards went on strike because Qantas had refused their request to have the flight hostesses placed under their charge rather than the captain's.

Most of the Qantas stewards were older than the flight hostesses and they were typically of a different class. They had been recruited from the surf clubs around Sydney or had worked in the merchant navy as stewards. It was this generation of stewards that would set the tone for the future generations. Their educational levels tended to be lower than the flight hostesses. It was not until 1968 that stewards had to have a minimum education requirement of an Intermediate Certificate and they had to be aged between 21 and 26.[28] The introduction of flight hostesses performing different duties to the stewards created tension on board.[29] Essentially the flight hostesses were brought on board to handle the passengers while the stewards were expected to provide the bar and food service. The stewards had already provided ten years of service from the flying boats to the Constellation services, and they were confident they still had the welfare of the passengers and the company at heart. By employing young women in their twenties and insisting they leave on marrying, Qantas exacerbated this situation by having a steady turn-over of young women, none of whom had the career opportunities offered to the stewards. Indeed, the gender dynamics of the cabin crew would become the cause of major industrial disputes in the 1980s.

Mr J. R. Donovan, the Conciliation Commissioner judging the dispute, questioned Andrews about whether it was appropriate that a woman should be in charge of other women passengers and children, to which Andrews replied, 'No. We have looked after hundreds of women and children and have been particularly successful with babies'.[30] He related an account of a recent trip where two children had thrown tea all over him, but by the time they reached London they were 'eating out of his hand'.[31] Andrews may have been referring to 6-year-old Roger Eames and his brother, who were on the first Constellation flight from London to Sydney on the 5th December 1947. Eames recalled people making a fuss of him, as along with his brother there were only three children on the plane. He spent the time playing with his Dinky Toys in the aisle and was taken to the cockpit to talk to the pilots, the navigator, radio operator and flight engineer.[32] In May, Commissioner Donovan ruled that the flight hostesses should remain under the control of the flight captain, and their duties would be carried out 'independently of the control of senior flight stewards'.[33]

4.3. 'Knockabout Blokes': Flight Stewards

Some suggested that the dispute was merely about a few personal differences. Frank Tishler, who began working with Qantas in 1949 and would stay with the company until 1957, said that he had no trouble with the flight hostesses. When he started there were sixty-six stewards and twelve flight hostesses. Tishler may have been employed because of a shortage of stewards; certainly later that year they may have needed more stewards as in August they went on strike again. The stewards were striking in the hope that two of their colleagues would be reinstated after being dismissed for unsatisfactory behaviour while on a trip to London.[34] Just as the flight hostesses seemed to be a certain type, the stewards could mostly be characterised as 'knockabout blokes', usually drinkers and full of Australian-style repartee and practical jokes.[35] Most of the stewards had nicknames: Sammy 'Trousers' Hogan and Darrel 'Atom' Budd, so-named because he was small. Tishler said, 'He should have been a jockey. But no one was too big for him. He'd fight anyone'.[36]

Qantas training class in preparation for the Boeing 707, c. 1959
The introduction of the Qantas Boeing 707 jet warranted new training to prepare for the inaugural passenger flight to San Francisco in July 1959. There was still only one flight hostess rostered on each flight compared to five flight stewards. Here the crew receive some instructions from Passenger Services Instructor Phil Penn. Courtesy of Qantas Heritage Collection.

Tishler had grown up in the working-class suburb of Newtown in Sydney, and in 1949 as a 20-year-old he had returned from the army:

...my brother was a flight steward in Qantas and I'd had a nice suit made in Japan, a nice suit to wear out. He was going out to debrief so I went out there with him.

The office was just outside the main building at Rose Bay…he was debriefing with the steward control fellow who was Ken O'Flaherty, and a girl came out from the office. She said, 'Come in out of the rain'. So I walked in out of the rain. 'Are you looking for a job?' I said, 'oh yeah, all right'. Because I just wanted to stand out of the rain. She said, 'What sort of a job? The only job I knew was a flight steward because that's what my brother was. So she handed me some papers to fill in…'[37]

He spoke to the men in charge of catering and they agreed to employ him, on the spot. He didn't tell them that he hadn't yet been discharged from the army, but this worked out alright as he had to wait a short while for the next training school. His brother, who had worked with Qantas for a couple of years, was annoyed as it had taken him six months to be accepted into the airline. Initially Tishler was the only one in his class at the training school, which was run by George Watham, then four other stewards from Brisbane came down to be retrained as they had recently closed the inland run from Brisbane to Darwin.[38] The training school lasted about a month and he graduated as a cadet flight steward in February 1949. He was paid £5 a week and £1 flight pay. Tishler remembers the flight hostesses fondly, 'They were all great girls. Some of them were on themselves a little bit, you know?' But he said, 'I don't honestly think there was one hostess that I disliked'. He remembered Margaret Lamb entering the Miss Airways competition in London in July 1950, and thought she may have been chosen because she had a 'uni degree'.[39]

She must know how to deal with any emergency – and she must know how to fend off the wolves. For an air hostess is a sitting target for every wolf, philanderer, and good-time Charlie on the loose. She can't run away from them; she can't get out and walk. She finds the best weapon against wolves is the bright smile and the sparring wisecrack. She must keep her dignity and her distance.

'It is the glamour job every girl envies', *Sunday Mail*, 1953.[40]

Tishler led a bachelor life, describing himself as being 'one of the old boys'. His favourite trip was the short-lived luxury Connoisseur flights from Sydney to Nandi, then Honolulu, and on to San Francisco. There was a week-long stopover in Honolulu, and they stayed at the Edgewater Hotel, Waikiki. For Tishler, there was the proverbial girl in every port: a girl in Honolulu, a girl in London, a girl in San Francisco and a girl in Sydney. It was obviously hard to maintain such relationships with such extended periods away; after meeting Faye Skinner Roberts on a number of flights in 1957, the 24-year-old Tishler became the first Qantas steward to marry a flight hostess. Patricia Coleman was their bridesmaid; she and Skinner Roberts had flown together with BCPA and Qantas. Shortly after Tishler and Skinner Roberts married they went to live in Perth for ten years, with Frank managing the catering department at Perth airport before leaving that job to buy a hotel.

In 2015, reflecting on his time working with Qantas, Tishler is still amazed by what an incredible life it was for a working-class lad from Newtown. No other job would have offered him the opportunity to stay at first-class hotels all over the world; hotels such as the Quirinale in Rome, 'the best hotel in Rome'. For Tishler it was the 'Best job I ever had. Wish I'd never left it'.[41]

The fellows were all against it. We'd been stewards all the time.
But they had to accept that the flight hostesses – they'd come
on board.

Max White, Qantas flight steward, 1947 to 1980

Many of the stewards had long-term careers at Qantas and Max
White is a good example of this. He began with Qantas on the
26th December 1946 and only left after forty-four years on the
25th November 1980.[42] His interest in joining the airline came
from meeting one of his 'mates' wearing a Qantas uniform, and
thinking that he would enjoy a job with the airline rather than
his present position as a mechanic. He didn't really know anything about Qantas, and he had never been out of Sydney, but
he 'knocked on their door' for a month until he was accepted.
Initially he was given a position as a ground steward:

> I'd meet the planes when they came in, so take every-
> thing off and put it through to be washed and stuff
> like that, and then stack a new lot up, get it out to the
> plane, put it on board and spread it around. Make the
> beds, because they had beds in those days, put the bunks
> down and make the bunks. Of course I tried to do it so
> it was better than the last bloke to impress them.[43]

He was still a ground steward when the Constellation L749
arrived at Mascot airport. There was huge excitement, especially
when the plane 'taxied up to the terminal, went reverse thrust
and started up the engine and drove backwards. Nobody had ever
seen a plane do that. That impressed the daylights out of everybody'.[44] Another reason the plane was so impressive was because

it was brand new. Until then, much of the Qantas fleet had been second-hand. The plane seemed huge, and White described entering the Constellation through a front door and noticing there was a lounge set up. The lounge was to have a very short lifespan because 'Qantas don't like lounges; they take them out and put seats in'.[45]

White didn't mind flight hostesses coming on board, although he knew the 'fellows were all against it'. Whatever they felt, they had to live with it. It wasn't that all the stewards had a total set against the flight hostesses. They would encounter other flight hostesses at stopovers, especially when they stayed at many of the same places as the BOAC crews. The issue there was that BOAC had more 'girls' than Qantas and they were protective of them in regard to the Qantas stewards. White remembers occasions where 'the whole crew would come out, surround the girl, and take her back to a room. That didn't impress us at all. But anyway, that's what happens'.[46]

Ed Ronsisvalle started with Qantas in May 1966, and would have a thirty-six year career with Qantas, finishing as a Customer Service Manager in 2002.[47] When he started there were about 350 cabin crew and the flight stewards had a six-week training course, which would run concurrently with the flight hostess course. When he was interviewed he was asked what football team he supported. It happened to be exactly the same team that the interviewer supported: 'We got on famously after that and he closed his notes up then and he said, "We'll be contacting you", so I think that won him over'.[48] Ronsisvalle flew with stewards who were 'the butchers, the bakers, the guy from the surf club'. He didn't think Qantas really wanted experience from the people they interviewed, rather people they could train up in their own way to follow the routine and add value with good service.

4.4. 'Company Manners' and Ansett

Hostesses are trained, not born.

Nan Witcomb, Ansett-ANA air hostess 1950,

Ansett-ANA Senior Route Hostess in South Australia 1957,

and Ansett Senior Regional Hostess to 1973

You really had to keep that grin on your face, smiling at people all the time.

Pauline (Powell) Alderman, ANA air hostess, 1951 to 1955

By the 1950s, the eight major airlines in Australia were: Qantas, MacRobertson Miller Airlines, Ansett, Butler Air Transport, Australian National Airways, Tasman Empire Airways Limited, Trans Australia Airlines and British Commonwealth Pacific Airlines. A significant change to the industry occurred in 1957. ANA had been struggling financially and the sudden death of Ivan Holyman threw the airline into a spin. In a desperate measure, the ANA board suggested a plan to 'rationalise' their services with the government-owned TAA. The merger with TAA didn't eventuate; instead, in October that year it was Ansett that came to the rescue, and ANA became Ansett-ANA.[49]

It was Ansett-ANA that now proved the biggest competitor to TAA. In an attempt to stop instability within the industry, the Civil Aviation Act was amended to create the duopoly known as the Two-Airline Agreement. The agreement meant that TAA and Ansett-ANA would operate in tandem on the major trunk routes. The two-airline policy also created a bizarre form of unity where each airline flew similar aircraft, and flights were scheduled at almost exactly the same time. This arrangement was ostensibly put in place so the government airline TAA would not enjoy competitive advantage over the privately owned Ansett-ANA.[50] The changes to the domestic aviation industry created much discussion from the media and the public. One journalist commented that Australia excelled at civil aviation – along with 'tennis, radio-astronomy, singing and making steel'.[51]

Ansett-ANA Air Hostess Shirley Boles, 1956
The first page of the flight logbook created by Ansett-ANA air hostess Shirley Boles, who flew with the airline from 1956 until 1974. Courtesy of Shirley Boles.

Even though Ansett had been operating since 1936, it was only ten years later that they employed their first air hostess. Eve Sexton started with Ansett on the 30th May 1946, having worked for ANA from January 1943 to November 1943 but had left to assist the war effort and work at the Department of Aircraft Production.[52] She became Senior Hostess with Ansett and was to have a long career in the airline industry, later working for

BCPA, and then joining Qantas when they merged with BCPA in 1954. Compared to the other Australian airlines operating, Ansett remained a relatively small airline, and by 1950 Sexton only had eighteen air hostesses in her charge.

Shirley Boles was another Ansett air hostess who would have a long career in the industry. She started with Ansett in 1956, the year before the merger with ANA. Prior to joining the airline she had lived on a dairy property at Albion Park on the south coast of New South Wales, and there was an airfield adjacent to their farm. Watching the RAAF Wirraway aircraft complete training manoeuvres made her determined to 'set her sights in the clouds above'.[53] As she was working on the farm she would watch the ANA DC-3 fly over at the same time every afternoon, en route from Sydney to Melbourne. She would even keep a scrapbook of clippings about all the air crashes and, undeterred, she applied with TAA, but missed out with the note that she 'lacked the sophistication and maturity'. But a year later, she was accepted with Ansett. There was only one other trainee in her intake and they had been recruited to help out with the 1956 Melbourne Olympics. Training included learning how ticketing worked, catering procedures and a member of staff from the Emergency Department explained the emergency exits on the DC-3 and the Convair CV-340, which were the two aircraft operating out of Melbourne.[54] Boles was given a book of 'Company Manners' and was assigned to a trainer hostess and flew with her for four weeks learning the onboard duties.

Boles was amazed when Ansett purchased ANA in 1957. 'Here was a very small airline buying a very large airline, and I was overwhelmed but very excited'. In those days Reginald (Myles) Ansett was known as 'R.M.' to all in the company. Almost a year after the merger, Ansett-ANA held Australia's first air hostess' convention with sixty Ansett-ANA air hostesses congregating at the Hotel Australia in Melbourne.[55] The convention was the first of a number to be held in different states and the issues addressed were about creating a more competitive air service but it was also to give the air hostesses an opportunity to voice suggestions and mention any concerns regarding the merger. The amalgamation had created a degree of resentment, with the ANA air hostesses feeling they were second place to the Ansett hostesses, even though they far outnumbered them. Reginald Ansett had bought out ANA so the perception was that the Ansett air hostesses saw it as 'their airline'.

Ansett-ANA, along with TAA, took over the New Guinea route from Qantas. Boles would be flying on the 'massive' four piston–engined Douglas DC-6B aircraft to New Guinea.[56] The flights to Papua New Guinea were long and hard – a cabin crew of three would leave Sydney at 8.30pm, flying via Brisbane to Port Moresby and then over the extremely rugged, mountainous terrain of the Owen Stanley Range to arrive at the coastal town of Lae at 8am. Boles would arrive 'somewhat worse for wear' but she thought the whole crew was in the same situation. If anything, the south-bound flights were worse, as there would be full passenger loadings, often with lots of children on board. The food was hot casseroles, meat, peas and mashed potatoes served on melamine plates. Alcohol would be served on board, but if passengers were drinking too much, particularly on the long flights to Darwin and Papua New Guinea, Boles would get the captains' permission and close the bar. Flying on the DC-6Bs Boles 'was aware of abnormalities':

...especially during night flights when the curtains were drawn. I always knew when we lost an engine, one of four. I felt the aircraft shudder just for a few seconds, and I knew. I would always go to straight to the flight deck to enquire if all was well...The old '6' I was told could fly on three motors without difficulties, two if necessary. But we never lost more than one engine on my flights.[57]

Boles became the Assistant Senior Regional Hostess, Sydney, and stayed with Ansett for eighteen years, leaving reluctantly in 1974 because she had reached the retirement age of 40.

4.5. 'Loud Talk and Laughter Should be Avoided': Regional Airlines

In addition to the main eight airlines, there were also smaller ones, such as Bush Pilots Airways in far north Queensland; East-West Airlines in Tamworth in northern New South Wales; Connellan Airways, Alice Springs; Butler Air Transport, flying out of Tooraweenah, New South Wales; and South Coast Aviation, a small regional airline near Wollongong. All these airlines used air hostesses on their services. South Coast Aviation flew a six-seater Avro Anson and Mrs Marjorie Gadd, who previously worked as a typist for the airline, was the sole air hostess. She received no training except for completing a first-aid course. With the 'approval' of her schoolteacher husband, her typical daily route would be a 700-mile trip from Wollongong to Cowra, then Sydney, then West Wylong and home again. On Saturdays she would fly to Jervis Bay.[58]

Butler Air Transport (BAT) was another small regional airline. It had formed in 1934 flying mainly within New South Wales but also to the southern border of Queensland. In the mid-1950s the routes were extended to Melbourne with the introduction of the twenty-four-passenger Vickers Viscount.[59] Despite the fact it flew to over sixty-three country towns, the relatively small scale of the airline meant that some of the more formal operational procedures of the larger companies didn't apply. Sometimes BAT would employ pilots on a casual basis, and this may have compromised standards at times. This was the case, as air hostess June Ashton discovered, while on a DC-3 service. With no navigational aids in place, one of the passengers remarked to Ashton that he thought they were going the wrong way. So he was taken to the cockpit and, under the captain's instructions, helped direct the plane to the aerodrome.[60] As Ashton said, it was common to fly using the roads, rivers and railway lines as navigational aids.

In 1951, BAT had only fifteen air hostesses and they would be trained on routine passenger flights. Each air hostess would have a navy blue folder containing a training manual, which they would refer to for the protocol and etiquette required both on and off the aircraft. Instructions included the following:

> Loud talk and laughter should be avoided within the hearing of passengers or public [and] conversation with other employees in the presence of passengers should be kept to a minimum and should only be on matters pertaining to business and when addressing other employees. In the presence of passengers, Christian names or nicknames are to be avoided.[61]

The BAT air hostesses were expected to 'show a genuine interest in each passenger, and to speak and converse well and intelligently'.[62] One air hostess took a serious interest in a passenger when he asked her with some urgency to go to the cockpit and find the exact position of the plane. It turned out the passenger was an apiarist and had spotted a stand of flowering gums from the plane window, and he thought the site would be a perfect place for a beehive.[63]

4.6. Wrestlers, Royal Tours and Espionage

There was always a wonderfully diverse mix of people travelling on any given flight, and it was rare to have a flight without an incident. ANA hostess Bette Hill, who graduated in March 1948, listed the wrestler Ventura Tenario 'Chief Little Wolf', Helen Keller, the Liberal politician Richard Casey and the Duchess of Grafton among the passengers she had assisted in the eighteen months she had been flying.[64] The wool buyers were still being mentioned, though their tendency to 'shout drinks for all passengers' was being replaced by the other more sober, 'portly, waistcoated businessman carrying the satchel of important papers between capital cities'.[65] Politicians continued to be regular clientele, some of them more demanding than others. A discussion about air hostesses was tabled in the South Australian parliament, when it was alleged that Labor MP Clyde Cameron was making them nervous. He had complained about only being allowed one barley sugar, instead of two, and the fact that TAA had discontinued fruit juices and poultry lunches. Making his own defence, Cameron denied he was making the hostesses nervous and added that he thought they were doing a good job.[66]

On international flights, the relationship with the passengers would change because one would spend days rather than hours with passengers. Even if a passenger was being unpleasant, the flight hostesses would often remark that by the time they had three or four days together any difficulties would disappear.[67] Over the course of the flight there may have been an increased appreciation of the flight hostesses, as passengers would observe how they managed the demands of the long and tiring flights.

Betty Isaks had one passenger who warmed to her during her first solo trip with Qantas. He proposed to her. Italian boxer Bruno

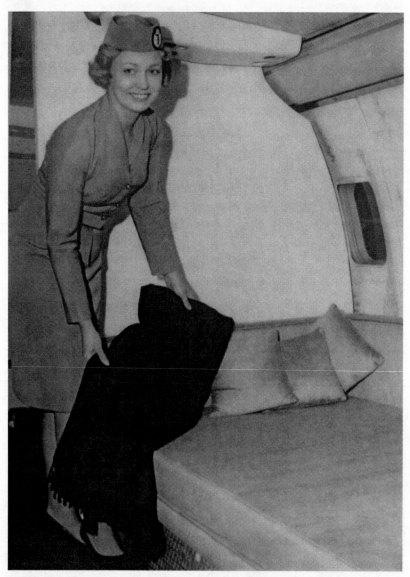

Judith (Dunstone) Potts, Princess Marina Royal Tour, 1964
It was always a privilege to be selected to be the flight hostess for a royal tour. Here Judith Dunstone prepares for Princess Marina, the Duchess of Kent, to visit Australia from the 23rd of September to the 8th of October 1964. Courtesy of Judith Potts.

Visintin later apologised, saying that it was 'one beeg mistake' but only when he realised that the story had made the papers. A fast mover in and out of the ring, he insisted that he was only trying to learn English, and wanted to know the words for 'mouth,' 'kiss' and 'heart' before he said 'I want to marry you'.[68]

Understanding cultural differences was a new aspect of international flight protocol. While ANA was flying the Air Ceylon route, it operated a charter flight taking forty Muslims from Ceylon to Jeddah, in Saudi Arabia. Lea Pike was the air hostess on board such a flight, and she was familiar with the Middle East, having worked there for four years with the WAAF. The passengers came on board with their own bedding, and kettles to cleanse their mouths. On the forward journey the men wore white and the women wore gold saris accessorised with jewels, and on the return journey the men wore green turbans and the women had a touch of green in their dress to indicate they had been to Mecca. The airline would serve special halal meals.[69]

There were other passengers who required special attention and these included unaccompanied minors. The children of expatriates living along Qantas' Kangaroo Route were often schooled in England or Australia, and in one year alone – 1952 – Qantas flew 600 school children aged between 5 and 18 to ten different countries so they could be home with their families for Christmas.[70] At the end of the school holidays in September 1955 there was almost a complete flight of school children returning to London after holidays in Sydney, Singapore and Bombay. The flight hostess Jacqueline Arunsten, in order to keep the children in order, instigated a prefect system amongst the children. It was just as well she did. There was a seven hour and twenty minute delay in Bombay, where the children were taken on a picnic, and no doubt Arunsten would have been in charge.[71]

Working for an airline was often described as feeling like being part of a big family; certainly for Mary (Letcher) Powys, who had two sisters also flying with Qantas. Neither of her sisters prepared her for the drama that happened on her first flight in 1958. As a twenty-one-year-old, on the DC-4 'Bird of Paradise' route from New Guinea to Cairns, Powys was alerted by one of the passengers that the man sitting alongside him had 'a problem'.[72] As she asked what she should do – should she put a mirror under his nose? – the passenger nonchalantly continued to eat his dinner while the crew fussed around. The passenger had in fact died, and in dealing with the situation Powys placed an oxygen mask over his face, and covered him with a blanket for the remainder of the flight. Powys saw this as a challenging start to her career as a flight hostess but she went on to fly for sixteen years, saying she 'would have cut off her arm' for the opportunity to work for the airline.

As well as keeping an eye on the passengers mid-flight, in the years before electronic scanners the air hostesses were expected to check for stowaways before each flight commenced. To this end, ANA regulations specified triple-checking of passenger numbers. In the early days of low security at airports, there was often only a low cyclone fence between the plane and the terminal, so the opportunity was there for people to sneak aboard.[73] On one occasion, Billy Hopkins, a 6-year-old boy from Fitzroy, was stopped at the gangway of an ANA plane shortly before it was due to take off for Sydney. He had been reported missing when he failed to return home from school. His mother described him as a serial absconder: 'I give him a good belting when he runs around like this, but he turns round and does the same thing the next day!'[74]

One day the air hostesses would be checking for stowaways and the next they might be preparing for royalty. The most prestigious passenger to grace an Australian plane was Queen

Elizabeth II. In 1954 she became the first reigning monarch to visit Australia. Grace 'Gay' Bury, an ex-RAAF nurse, was selected as the air hostess to accompany the Queen on her two-and-a-half-month royal tour in a specially fitted-out RAAF C-47 Dakota. She had worked as a flight officer on medical evacuation flights between Korea and Japan and in her new role she would serve the Queen's meals, arrange the flowers on the royal plane and be ready to administer first aid, if required.[75] Marj de Tracy was selected by Qantas to fly on the Queen's flights from Melbourne to Brisbane.[76] She helped train Bury, and flew with her on her preparatory Qantas flight to New Guinea.[77] Bury flew on twenty flights with the tour.

All the major airlines were given an opportunity to be part of the royal tour. Three TAA air hostesses, Beryl Oliver, Elizabeth Otter and Doris Duff, were selected to crew the Queen's flights on a Convair.[78] ANA air hostesses Joan Breadon and Margaret England had been selected for the royal trip planned for 1952, but it was cancelled upon the death of Princess Elizabeth's father. They were given a second chance and they flew with the Queen on a DC-4 Skymaster from Victoria to Tasmania. Gwyenda Gaunt, senior route hostess for ANA, was also selected for one of the Queen's flights, while Betty Pratt, Val Stack and Claire Glenn were used on a second DC-4 carrying the royal staff. It was reported that after one civic reception the Queen got on the plane and immediately took her shoes off, saying to the air hostess, 'If your feet felt like mine you'd do the same'.[79] They probably did.

All the planes on the royal tour had been specially converted to suit the royal visitors for the thirty-three flights. The Convair, which was used to fly from Hobart to Wynyard on the north-west coast of Tasmania, was divided into two compartments with the forward section arranged with twenty seats for the royal household staff and the royal visit and state officials. The royal compartment had two seats, a lounge divan, one reclining chair and a dining table with two chairs. The interior was in grey tones for the carpet and leather cabin lining, the curtains a blue-grey and the woodwork a blonde Australian timber. Two paintings were selected for the Queen's compartments: *Bush* by Arnold Shore (1947) and *Tribute by Night* by Adrian Feint (1950), a still life with a vase of flowers containing native and non-native flowers. Stationery was provided in crocodile-skin folders with a gold-and-black propelling pencil. There were two DC-4 Skymasters used to fly the royals from Launceston to Melbourne. The royal cabin on the Skymaster was towards the rear of the plane, behind the wing to ensure the best view. The cabin had a telephone so the royal couple could talk to each section of the plane, and the usual seating had been removed to include slumber lounges, a table and four chairs. At the rear of the plane was a changing room with full-length mirror. The usual ANA colour scheme of deep red, deep blue and grey dominated the furnishings.[80] Lunch was served on the flight, so there was a separate compartment with table and chairs, along with seats for the two air hostesses. The menu had a distinctly 1950s Australian flair. A fruit cocktail ambrosia was followed by a cold collation 'Bellevue' with sauce mayonnaise, and assorted salads, then for dessert 'Bombe Victoria' and sablés, and a selection of cheeses including gruyere, camembert, red coon, and coffee.[81]

The dust had only just settled from the Queen's visit when an incident on board a plane would receive worldwide attention. Air hostess Joyce Bull was at the heart of the intrigue. Bull was one of the crew on the BOAC Constellation that left Sydney for Darwin on Monday 19th April 1954. On board was Evdokia Petrova. She and her husband Vladimir Petrov had both been working at the Soviet Embassy in Canberra as a cover for their intelligence work.

In a complicated series of events Vladimir sought political asylum and defected without telling Evdokia. She, in turn, was escorted to the airport by the Second Secretary at the Russian Embassy and two armed Russian couriers. She was leaving the country believing that her husband was dead, when, in fact, he was in hiding. At the airport not only was she frightened but there was a scuffle with anti-Communist protestors and she lost a shoe. The high-heeled stylish shoe was held up by someone in the crowd as a sign of the West, and for the rest of the flight she borrowed a pair of suede sling-back shoes from Bull. During the flight Bull was asked to secretly pass on a message from Prime Minister Robert Menzies about whether she would like asylum in Australia, and also to give her assurance that her husband was still alive. Once landed in Darwin, Petrova rang her husband to confirm he was alive and, according to Bull, she was heard to say, 'No, no, no, I won't defect'. It was only when she heard their dog bark in the background that she changed her mind.[82] After this extraordinarily dramatic flight, Bull's flatmate was asked to comment about Bull's personal qualities and she described her in the following way: 'Joyce enjoys the ballet, is crazy about Van Gogh, is a Shakespeare fan, and, most of all, likes making savoury meals out of practically nothing. Joyce is a most level-headed girl. I can just imagine her doing this'.[83]

4.7. 'Glamour Air Girls Form a Union': The Airline Hostesses' Association

The fact that air hostesses were continually expected to perform under duress and with onerous working conditions, meant that when they were presented with an opportunity for industrial support they were ready and willing to embrace the offer. This came in July 1955 when the Australian Air Pilots Association (AAPA) sent a questionnaire to Australia's 500 air hostesses asking if they wanted to form a union to protect their interests. The Australian Transport Officers' Federation (ATOF) objected, saying that they looked after the air hostesses. Bruce Crofts, the manager of the Air Pilots Association, replied that the ATO only looked after government employees, covering only TAA and Qantas.[84] Despite the disagreement about who covered whom, in August 1955, the Australian Air Pilots Association announced that it would help both air hostesses and stewards form an Air Hostesses' and Stewards' Association, with branches to be formed in all states. On the 26th September 1955, TAA air hostess Elaine (Smith) Swain called a meeting and air hostesses from ANA, Ansett and TAA airlines came to elect members to form a committee for a proposed 'Airline Hostesses' and Stewards' Association'. There is no record of any of the stewards attending this meeting, nor of any Qantas flight hostesses. The stewards went on to form the Flight Stewards' Association of Australia (FSAA) in 1957, and the Qantas flight hostesses, also thinking their concerns were unique, formed the Overseas Branch of the Airline Hostesses' Association in 1963. Over the years the relationship between the domestic and the overseas branch of the association would become strained, with the domestic branch operating out of Melbourne and the overseas branch run out of Sydney. It would not be until 1992 that the stewards' union and the Airline Hostesses' Association would be amalgamated to form the Flight Attendants Association of Australia.

The first meeting of the domestic air hostesses was seen as newsworthy, as the following day an article appeared in *The Argus* with the heading, 'Committee of...AHA! Glamor [sic] Air Girls Form a Union'.[85] The article went on to describe the forty women in the newly formed Airline Hostesses' Association as 'shapely and vivacious' and lending 'glamor [sic] to the occasion'. The article also reported them as the 'most photogenic trade union'.[86] On the 2nd November 1956, the Airline Hostesses' Association (AHA) was formally registered with Elaine (Smith) Swain appointed the first president. She had a long association with the aviation industry having joined TAA in April 1949 and, after working there for eight years, had left to go to the UK where she was senior training hostess for Cunard Eagle Airways, and later chief hostess. In 1963, she returned to Australia where she became TAA's superintendent of air hostesses, setting up their training school.

The AHA was formed with a membership of 186 air hostesses, and as an affiliate of the Australian Air Pilots Association (AAPA). Although a seemingly odd alliance, later this association would often work in the air hostesses' favour in relation to industrial gains such as superannuation: 'If the pilots had it then the hosties would have it, because the hosties were basically Adam's rib in those days'.[87] Margaret Robinson, in her history of the Airline Hostesses' Association, says it was in the pilots' interests to control the AHA to prevent the air hostesses linking with ground unions, as the Transport Workers' Union (TWA) wanted. Also, as the domestic air hostesses comprised the entire crew, should they strike, they could ground the airlines; something the pilots wouldn't have wanted unless it supported their own interest. Another issue was that for a long time air hostesses were seen as a 'short-term female work-force [that] earned minimal wages from which to extract union dues'.[88] What was meant by short-term was that the marriage bar, which was in place until 1972, prevented long-term employment with the airlines as air hostesses had to resign to marry. With a perceived lack of industrial muscle, Robinson says that there was always a sense of benevolence and paternalism as a result of this association with an attitude of fixing things up for "the girls", through to the 1970s. This attitude was similar to what was happening on the planes where the pilots, as well as flying the planes, had a public-relations role with passengers, but it was often up to the air hostesses to sort out or apologise to disgruntled passengers for any dramas that occurred during or leading up to a flight (even though it was company policy to apologise for delays).

Hostesses want a Rise, c. 1966
The Airline Hostesses' Association was formed to protect the interests of the air hostesses, and the women would meet regularly to discuss the issues affecting their conditions of employment. This newspaper clipping from September 1966 shows a group of TAA air hostesses who, along with Ansett-ANA air hostesses, attended a meeting in Melbourne to discuss the possibility of strike action. Courtesy of Rochelle Sutherland.

Another issue was that some of the air hostesses resented the fact that they would have to be at the airport well in advance of a flight, because this is what the pilots had to do as they prepared for a flight. While the air hostesses had to prepare the aircraft before flights, being at the airport up to an hour before the flight was seen merely as a means whereby the airlines could save on ground transportation costs. One air hostess referred to this arrangement as the women being the 'pilot's handbags'.[89]

The advantage of forming an association meant that the AHA could negotiate their first award. The first log of claims was served on TAA, Ansett and ANA in February 1957. The issues of key concern were the standard of overnight accommodation and the unfair flight conditions of air hostesses compared to pilots. Until the award, the air hostesses had no work rules or regulation of duty hours (aside from the number of flying hours), while the pilots' hours were regulated by the government Air Navigation Orders. This meant that the airlines could ask cabin crew to stay on duty for unlimited hours, which they often did.[90] Elaine Swain remembered one duty of twenty-seven hours and other air hostesses remember 'long, cold nights' at Mangalore, an airport near Seymour in Victoria that was used when bad weather prevented landing at Essendon. The air hostesses would remain on duty helping the stranded passengers.[91] In 1953 MMA air hostess Trudy Broad had an emergency landing in a DC-3 in Geraldton. Three days later, still in the same clothes, and not expecting any passengers, she had to usher a passenger on board for the return trip to Perth, as the passenger's father was ill. She felt she had to say something when the passenger looked askance at the state of her appearance.

Elizabeth Foster represented thirty MMA air hostesses at an arbitration hearing in Melbourne arguing for higher wages and improved conditions, especially in regard to accommodation. There were conditions that were specific to Western Australia:

> When I went to that arbitration hearing in Melbourne and they started to talk about all the hotels of the eastern states and how dreadful they were. I started talking about the Wyndham pub – you had to have a pilot to take you to the toilet at night because it was 100 yards down the back of the hotel. Halls Creek, if you sat up you saw all these men sleeping in all these cubicles with low walls. Port Hedland, the men slept down one side of the verandah, the women the other and we had a room to change. It was outback flying, it was the outback.[92]

> *It was a furnished apartment, quite attractive, with a living room, two bedrooms, kitchen and bath. Dot protested at squeezing three girls into one bedroom, but Jean pointed out that all six of them would rarely be at home at once.*
>
> Helen Wells, *Silver Wings for Vicki*, 1947[93]

Suitable accommodation was an issue of major concern for the air hostesses. It was not unusual to have to share a room with another air hostess, which would be fine if travelling on the same flight but it was disruptive if one was leaving early in the morning. MMA crews had stayed at the Esplanade Hotel, Port Hedland, for many years, but by the late 1960s the crew would stay at the new Walkabout Motel near the airport. The problem was that it operated on a strict routine of 10am checkout and 2pm check-in. This would mean the crews could wait for a number of hours for a room. The motel wasn't prepared to do them any favours, even though the airline crews provided a good income for them, particularly during the wet – the off-season.[94]

One air hostess described the state of overnight accommodation, saying that the places they stayed you wouldn't put a rat into. But in northern Australia the rats were there; they chewed the hostesses' shoes.[95] In Perth in the early 1960s, the Ansett–ANA air hostesses would have three beds in one room in an old house at Wedderburn, the only advantage with the accommodation was that the housekeeper was 'rather wonderful' and you could put in requests for the type of food you liked.[96]

With early morning flights and late nights home, getting to and from the airport was a constant problem. Barbara Butler was also one of MMA's union representatives and went to Melbourne with senior hostess Julie Miller to discuss with Bruce Crofts, the Airline Hostesses' Association union representative, the issues of 'transport home, the travel allowance and hours of work'. The issue about transport home was one for all air hostesses. When the air hostesses joined MMA they were warned that it was a 'round the clock' airline but the problem was '…when you came back to Perth late at night, if the plane was delayed, or just late at night, there was no provision for you to get home. There was no taxi to get home and not everybody had a car. So we managed to get that brought in; they provided a taxi'.[97]

The Airline Hostesses' Association was to become a crucial organisation in changing the working conditions for air hostesses. The airlines had always had the advantage as they were used to a high turnover and were prepared to replace air hostesses with grievances rather than try to reach an agreement. One example of the lack of power of the air hostesses happened when the trainer hostesses in Adelaide thought the extra five shillings they earned a week was not enough, and refused to do any further training duties. The result was the training course was pulled from Adelaide, leaving the 'girls' contrite. On such issues, their loyalty towards the company and reluctance to 'rock the boat' was present even among trainees. The only real power they had was to ground the airline if they decided not to work, a direct result of a Department of Civil Aviation decision of the 18th January 1954 making the provision of cabin attendants compulsory on all regular civil aviation aircraft.[98]

The Airline Hostesses' Association was significant as it was one of the first all-female unions, and for a long time operated as a 'closed shop'. As well as achieving important industrial gains, the isolation of the profession meant the union provided an opportunity for the women to discuss common concerns, but also to meet and socialise. Given the shift hours they worked it was difficult to get the women together but there was usually good representation at the meetings. It didn't matter whether it was sleeping on the verandah of the Esplanade Hotel, shared bedrooms with no locks at Onslow, or the hair dryers not working at Raffles in Singapore, the air hostesses had challenging working conditions that were tolerated only because of their good grace and a lack of awareness for the possibility of change. But change was in the air.

Notes

1   Three pilots, two flight engineers, one navigator and one radio officer.
2   I. Wharton, interview with the author, May 2012.
3   Qantas, 'Designed for performance', *Qantas Empire Airways,* January 1949, pp. 4–5.
4   T. Broad, telephone interview with the author, 23 April 2015.
5   In 1948, Australian airlines were carrying over 1,200,000 passengers a year and Qantas alone was employing 3,332 staff. Anon, 'They all fly', *Qantas Empire Airways,* August 1948, p. 7.
6   At this stage Qantas employed fifty-four stewards with Jack Martin as head

steward. C. Burgess, 'A Story of Service', *Qantas News Special Edition*, July 1988, clipping.

7   Anon, 'World digest', *Courier-Mail*, 11 February 1948, p. 4.

8   Anon, 'First nine girls to fly Sydney-London run', *Australian Women's Weekly*, 14 February 1948, p. 17.

9   Most of the air hostesses interviewed for the book remember very clearly what they wore on the day of their interview. They were very conscious of making the 'right impression' both through what they wore and also through careful preparation in anticipation of questions they may be asked during the interviews.

10 K. Hudson & J. Pettifer, *Diamonds in the Sky: A Social History of Air Travel*, Bodley Head and British Broadcasting Corporation, London, 1979, p. 30.

11 P. (Burke) St Leon, interview with the author, 17 June 2009.

12 ibid.

13 By 1954 the course was five-weeks long, with a probationary flying period of three months in Qantas Empire Airways Limited, 'Flight Hostess Course Timetable', 1954.

14 ibid.

15 Anon, 'First nine girls to fly Sydney-London run', p. 17.

16 ibid.

17 Anon, 'Clothes for long journeys on the air', *Qantas Empire Airways*, January 1948, p. 10.

18 ibid.

19 Wharton stayed with Qantas for four years, reaching the position of hostess trainer before leaving to work with the Health Department, travelling to schools administering the Mantox test for tuberculosis.

20 I. Wharton, interview with the author, May 2012.

21 L. Macalpine, interview with the author, 2008.

22 ibid.

23 Anon, 'WA girl has flown to England 15 times', *Daily News*, 20 February 1950, p. 5; Anon, '22 Trips to London', *Daily News*, 4 November 1950, p. 13.

24 Anon, '22 trips to London', p. 13.

25 Anon, 'Tribute from prime minister', *Qantas Staff Magazine*, December–February 1950–1951, p. 14

26 Anon, 'Air hostesses "Stole Glory", says steward', *Sydney Morning Herald*, 20 April 1949, p. 4.

27 ibid.

28 Anon, 'Stewards', *Sky-Line*, vol. 2, no. 2, 1968, p. 7.

29 It was not until 1983 that the roles of the flight hostess and steward were integrated. See C. Williams, *Blue, Pink and White Collar Workers in Australia:*

Technicians, Bank Employees and Flight Attendants, Allen and Unwin, Sydney, 1988.

30   Anon, 'Air hostesses "Stole Glory"', p. 4.

31   ibid.

32   Anon, 'The long hop', *Sydney Morning Herald*, 29 November 1997, pp. 1, 5.

33   Anon, 'Qantas flight stewards', *Qantas Empire Airways* magazine, May 1949, p. 5

34   Anon, 'Air Hostesses replace stewards on strike', *Canberra Times,* 22 August 1949, p. 2.

35   W. Georgetti-Remkes, interview with the author, 5 September 2015.

36   F. Tishler, interview with the author, 19 March 2015.

37   F. Tishler, interview with the author, 19 March 2015.

38   The influence of George Watham extended to some referring to the recruits as 'Watham's Wonder School Waiters'.

39   Lamb had graduated from Sydney University and trained as a teacher. Anon, 'Australian in 'Miss Airways' quest', *West Australian,* 11 July 1950, p. 4.

40   Anon, 'It is the glamour job every girl envies', *Sunday Mail*, 5 April 1953, p. 11.

41   F. Tishler, interview with the author, 19 March 2015.

42   M. White, interview with the author, 21 October 2011.

43   ibid.

44   ibid.

45   Referring to the lounge in the Boeing 747.

46   M. White, interview with the author, 21 October 2011.

47   This was the same year that Qantas pilots went on a twenty-eight day strike, regarding a range of issues including rostering, hours of duty and seniority. See N. Blain, *Industrial Relations in the Air: Australian Airline Pilots*, University of Queensland Press, St Lucia, Queensland, 1984, p. 49.

48   E. Ronsisvalle, interview with the author, 6 September 2010.

49   Anon, 'Ansett – big new force in Australian aviation', *Financial Review*, 29 August 1957, p. 2. The airline also had a 40 per cent interest in Butler Air Transport.

50   J. E. Richardson & H. W. Poulton, 'Australia's Two-Airline Policy – law and the layman', *Federal Law Review*, June 1968, pp. 64–85.

51   C. Turnbull, 'We have reason to brag', *Sun*, 27 August 1957, clipping.

52   M. McRobbie, *Walking the Skies: The First Fifty Years of Air Hostessing in Australia 1936 to 1986*, Self-published, Melbourne, [1986] 1992, p. 29.

53   S. Boles, interview with the author, 13 November 2015.

54   The Convair been chartered from Hawaiian Airlines for the games. Ansett purchased more Convairs and they were used for the 'chicken and

champagne' flights between Sydney and Melbourne.

55 Anon, 'Ground-Level Talks', *Panorama*, September 1958, p. 7.

56 Trans Australia-Airlines and Ansett-ANA took over the route from Qantas in 1960.

57 S. Boles, interview with the author, 13 November 2015.

58 Anon, 'Former typist flies 700 miles daily on job', *Sunday Herald*, 24 September 1950, p. 11.

59 S. A. Casson, *The Yellow Canary: From Butler Air Transport to Ansett Express*, Self-published, Springfield Lakes, Queensland, 2014, p. 55.

60 ibid.

61 *Butler Air Transport Ltd. Hostess Manual*, 1956.

62 ibid.

63 Anon, 'Hostess makes flying good', *Argus*, 12 December 1955, p. 10.

64 Anon, 'Variety for an air hostess', *West Australian*, 30 August 1949, p. 16.

65 Anon, 'She prefers businessmen', *Daily News*, 17 December 1949, p. 28.

66 Anon, 'M.P. lost his lolly', *Barrier Miner*, 1 September 1952, p. 8.

67 Anon, 'WA girl has flown to England 15 times', p. 5.

68 Anon, 'Wished to learn', *West Australian* 23 June 1954, p. 2; Anon, 'Air hostess said no', *Advertiser*, 22 June 1954, p. 1.

69 Anon, 'Air hostess to go on "Pilgrimage to Mecca"', *Sunday Herald*, 16 September 1951, p. 18.

70 S. Patrick, 'The Children's Airlift…', *Australian Women's Weekly*, 24 December 1952, pp. 4–5.

71 Qantas, 'Hostess acted as a mother to kids on Operation Smallfry', *Qantas News,* October, 1955, p. 5.

72 Mary (Letcher) Powys, telephone conversation with the author, 10 October 2016. Powys flew with Qantas from 1958 to 1974.

73 Anon, 'Nobody can sneak a plane ride', *Argus*, 27 February 1950, p. 5.

74 Anon, 'Stowaway, 6, caught on plane', *Argus*, 25 February 1950, p. 1

75 Anon, 'She'll be air hostess to the Queen', *Courier-Mail*, 15 October 1953, p. 1.

76 Anon, 'People and parties', *Age*, January 29 1954, p. 5.

77 Anon, 'She will be hostess to the Queen', *Courier-Mail*, 30 December 1953, p. 2.

78 Beryl Oliver may have been a favourite with TAA, as a couple of years later she was selected for a flight to Alice Springs to attend the premier of the film *A Town Like Alice*. Screened at an outdoor theatre on the banks of the Todd River, Oliver accompanied the lead actor Peter Finch to the screening and they watched the film in a relaxed fashion: lying on deck chairs and smoking. H. Frizell, 'Bush Premier', *Australian Women's Weekly*, 8

August 1956, p. 33.

79   Anon, 'The Queen's aching feet', *Courier-Mail*, 28 January 1954, p. 2.

80   Anon, 'Royal compartment in TAA Convair', *Examiner*, 19 February 1954, p. 35.

81   ANA, 'Royal flight Launceston to Melbourne menu', 24 February 1954.

82   J. Koutsoukis, 'The spy scandal that heated up the Cold War', *Age*, 3 April 2004, accessed 20 October 2015 <http://www.theage.com.au/articles/2004/04/02/1080544695722.html>.

83   Anon, 'Hostess's part in drama', *Advertiser*, 22 April 1954, p. 1.

84   Anon, 'Rival union claims for air hostesses', *Sydney Morning Herald*, 21 July 1955, p. 3.

85   Anon, 'Glamour air girls form a union', *Argus*, 27 September 1955, pp. 1, 6.

86   A call from Lady Poynter in London to form a 'Hostess' union was suggested in 1924 with the aim to instil 'good manners' in young women. 'It is of no use one or two hostesses taking a firm line in regard to manners. What is wanted is co-operation'. In Anon, 'Hostesses's union', *Northern Star* (Lismore), 5 November 1924, p. 9.

87   M. Martin, interview with the author and Adam Gall, 25 March 2015.

88   M. Robinson, 'Qantas Cabin Crew and Their Union', PhD Thesis, Flinders University, 1996, p. 274.

89   P. Millett, interview with the author, 16 April 2013.

90   The new duty award meant that air hostesses were limited to a maximum of forty-eight duty hours a week, and eighty hours in any two weeks. The award failed to include a daily maximum or provision for rest periods, it was not until the 1960s that a daily limit of eleven hours was imposed.

91   Flight Attendants Association of Australia, 'Taking Care of Business – Union Style', draft document, 6 October 1986.

92   E. Foster, interview with the author, 15 April 2015.

93   H. Wells, *Silver Wings for Vicki*, Grosset & Dunlap, New York, 1947, p. 94.

94   R. C. Adkins, *I Flew For MMA: An Airline Pilot's Life*, Success Print, Perth, [1996], 1998, p. 210.

95   M. Robinson, 'A History of the Airline Hostesses' Association 1955–1981', Honours Thesis, Flinders University, 1990, p. 14.

96   P. Tickner, interview with the author, 6 August 2013.

97   B. Butler, interview with the author, 15 April 2015.

98   M. Robinson, 'A History of the Airline Hostesses' Association 1955–1981', pp. 18, 24.

SECTION THREE:
LANDING

Qantas World Route Map, 1957

This detail of an illustrative map highlights the exotic routes across the Indian Ocean that Qantas the 'Round-the–World' airline was flying in the late 1950s. Courtesy of Qantas Heritage Collection

Chapter Five

'SLINKY SEX SYMBOLS' AND THE JET AGE

Stewardesses like jet liners must be slinky sex symbols, pilots can be homely and bald.

Pan American Stewardess Training Film, 1969

5.1. The Speed of Change

In 1959 the Jet Age arrived in Australia.[1] The Boeing 707 jet almost halved the time of air travel, pushing global travel and transport into a new era. Even though earlier in the year Qantas had begun its first round-the-world service with the Lockheed Super Constellation L-1049, it was nothing compared to what the 707 jet could offer. Air travel was still considered a luxury; the Sydney to London airfare was the equivalent of about thirty-weeks' average weekly earnings. The 707's dramatic change in speed created the conditions for a new breed of cosmopolitan traveller to emerge, flying for business and pleasure. It was no coincidence that at this time Conrad Hilton built sixteen luxury hotels across the world to cater for these international folk with a new name – jetsetters.[2]

Qantas became the first non-American airline to operate the Boeing 707, with the inaugural passenger service leaving on the 29th July 1959. The flight took almost fifteen hours' flying time from Sydney to San Francisco, which is not that different to the flying time today.[3] The Australian Minister for Civil Aviation,

The Jet Age arrives: the Qantas Boeing 707, c. 1959
The new Qantas Boeing 707 cabin was decorated with an Australian theme of native wild flowers and an Indigenous-inspired design. Courtesy of Qantas Heritage Collection.

Senator Shane Paltridge, was present for the inaugural flight and alluded to the fact that Qantas had once again selected an American plane over a British one when he said, 'You may be flying in an American aircraft but you will literally be flying on the sheep's back'.[4] Australia had long broken with the tradition of buying British aircraft, but there was still some pressure to buy the de Havilland Comet, made in the UK. Well-known writer and plane spotter Clive James knew about the de Havilland Comet; in fact, he knew about most planes that flew to Australia. A few years earlier he had hung out in the sand dunes near his home to watch for the arrival of the inaugural flight to Sydney of the Pan American Stratocruiser. Years later, here he was again waiting for the arrival of the 707:

> Older now, the proud smoker of several cigarettes a day… the Boeing 707 landed, ushering in the intercontinental jet era that should have begun with the de Havilland Comet but tragically did not.[5]

Qantas made the right decision not to order the Comet as it was involved in a number of fatal crashes, severely tarnishing its reputation and ultimately its future. British writer, and long-term Australian resident, Nevil Shute had worked at de Havilland as an engineer and wrote the novel *No Highway* (1948), which, in remarkably prescient fashion, predicted the technical difficulties that would plague the Comet.[6] The air hostess in the novel, Marjorie Corder, is a true professional and while she couldn't change the fate of the plane she could prepare for the worst-case scenario:

> If things started to go wrong she had certain duties to perform; she sat quietly, conning her drill over…Only by the sheerest chance would she be free to fling herself down on the deck in the Men's Toilet when the crash was imminent; in any case it would be wrong for her, the stewardess, to take the only place of safety in the aircraft. She could hardly do that.[7]

And so, instead of the Comet it would be the Boeing 707 that occupied Australian skies, fanning aviation enthusiasms with its sleek lines and distinctive swept-backed wings. Its most enduring feature, something that everyone could see, was the long trail of black smoke it would leave as it took off. The plane could seat ninety passengers, divided into first class and tourist, almost twice as many passengers as the Comet. Qantas decorated its 707s in an Australian theme, using the services of the famous American design firm Walter Dorwin Teague. The plane was fitted with either turquoise or persimmon coloured wool seats, and the armrests were made of Australian hide. The cabin wall was decorated with a silk-screened print of a selection of wild flowers native to the east coast of Australia, and the bulkheads were decorated with a geometric, Indigenous-inspired design in white and gold.[8]

With the introduction of the 707, Qantas issued a new uniform for the flight hostesses. The uniform became known as 'Jungle Green', a soft green that matched the colour scheme of the native flowers decorating the cabin. It was made and individually fitted by 'Mr Henry' at the Saville Row Shirt Company, 6 Bond Street, near Wynyard station in Sydney.[9] The attention to detail was featured in the slightly cropped jacket with the nipped-in waist. For winter there was a coat in a deeper matching shade with a bold red lining. Unlike the flight hostesses, whose uniforms would usually change with every new model of plane, the stewards continued to wear navy, military-style suits and for cabin service they would don a white serving jacket complete with epaulets, cummerbund and a bow tie.[10]

5.2. 'Come Fly with Me': Gays and Lesbians

'Come fly with me, let's fly, let's fly away'.

Frank Sinatra, 1958

It was well known that many of the Qantas stewards were gay.[11] There had been an earlier generation that kept it well hidden, or it just wasn't spoken about. Many of the flight hostesses weren't even too sure what a gay person was. Dorothy (Bell) Harris, who started with Qantas in 1963, confessed that, 'It took me ages to comprehend what it meant' as she knew very little about sex and certainly didn't know that men were attracted to each other.[12]

As for lesbians working as flight hostesses, that was only a matter of speculation. Some of the flight hostesses thought Marj de Tracy may have been gay, but there is no evidence to support this. It would be the place of popular fiction to let the general public realise that there were gay women on board. Paula Christian's lesbian pulp fiction *Edge of Twilight* was published in 1959, and tells the anguish of Valerie McGregor, a stewardess for Inter-American, who has to distance herself from the fact that men find her attractive, while her desires are towards co-worker Toni Molina. The back-cover blurb of the book describes it as a 'refreshingly realistic treatment for women who are "different"'. Lesbian pulps flourished in the 1950s (as opposed to gay male fiction), and the era became known as the 'Golden Age' of lesbian pulp.[13] In *Edge of Twilight,* Christian refuses to romanticise the life of the stewardess; indeed, the emotional labour of the job is described throughout the book, while the lesbian theme is set to a backdrop of homophobia: '"Those stews look like real queers! Maybe they're lovers!" He snorted. "God-damn fruits. All the same".'[14]

It was rare for lesbian air hostesses to feature in other forms of popular culture, although in the late 1970s, in the premiere episode of Australian television soap *Skyways*, a lesbian air hostess is portrayed in an unhappy relationship.[15] Despite the series running for two years, the lesbian character didn't last and was soon disposed of when she was stabbed to death in a shower scene.[16]

Sue Love-Davies, who started flying with Qantas in the 1970s, recalls that even then it was unusual to see two women out having a drink together. She was in Honolulu on a stopover, and was at a bar with a girlfriend waiting for their Mai Tai cocktails, when the bartender presented them with two drinks:

> 'That's from the two gentlemen'. I said, 'Thank you very much'. Anyway we drank them [laughs] and then the next thing another two arrive and with that come the two men. They said, 'Can we join you girls?' We said, 'Actually we haven't seen each other for a long time. Thank you very much for the drinks but no, we just really want to catch up'. They said, 'Are you two lesbians?' I mean [laughs]– it was just not done. It was very unusual to see two women out together having a drink.[17]

In the early years of flying, and the later years of closet living, it wasn't always evident whether someone was gay or not, but eventually it was accepted that there were gays on board. Ed Ronsisvalle remembers the gay stewards, 'could put themselves in the passenger's or customer's position – probably much more so than the average Australian bloke that was working as a crew member at the time'.[18] Many of the flight hostesses would comment it was a relief to have gay stewards as part of the crew. They were good company when overseas, as they could be relied on to accompany them on outings to art galleries, on shopping trips, or to the theatre.

5.3. Kimonos and Golden Orchids: Exoticising the Air Hostess

They looked fantastic but it must have restricted their movements something terrible.

Max White, Qantas flight steward, 1947 to 1980

During the late 1950s and 1960s the look of the air hostess was exoticised not only in Australia, but on most world airlines. In 1958, Qantas began employing Japanese flight hostesses to work on the 'Cherry Blossom' route to Japan. Marj de Tracy had flown

Exotic cosmopolitanism: the Qantas Japanese flight hostess, c. 1959
A promotional photograph taken on board a Lockheed Electra shows a Japanese-speaking flight hostesses in full kimono working with flight steward Phil Penn. Courtesy of Qantas Heritage Collection.

to Japan to select, from 150 applicants, Yoshiko Watanabe, Teruko Oshima and Kazuko Otsu. Publicity photos of the new recruits, all in their early twenties, showed them arriving in Sydney wearing full kimonos, similar to the ones they would wear on the flights to Tokyo.[19]

Teri Teramoto was selected to fly on the Japan route in 1964. She started training with two other young Japanese women, and the stress of the new environment meant that none of them slept properly and each morning they left on the bus for training school without breakfast, instead each of them snacking on their own packet of Arnott's Scotch Finger biscuits. Snacking on biscuits was not a good idea but it was difficult to find Japanese food in Sydney and with a change of diet they all put on weight, and were put on the scales and reprimanded in front of the other trainees. After training they were sent one-by-one with a check hostess on a test flight to Hong Kong and if they managed that then they were put on a three-month probation. It was only after completing the probation period they were taken by Qantas' Tokyo manager to a shop in Ginza, which had been making kimonos for centuries, to be fitted for a kimono. The Japanese flight hostesses would board the plane in the 'Jungle Green' uniform, and after take-off they would go to the toilet and, with less than five minutes, change into the traditional kimono. Teramoto remembers that in Hong Kong they would have to get dressed in the kimono before the passengers would board, and without any air conditioning and with the high humidity it was difficult to put on the white *Tabi* socks, which had been starched and ironed ready to be worn with the *zori* (Japanese slippers). Qantas continued to recruit Japanese-born flight hostesses into the 1980s but in the 1970s they had stopped wearing the kimono, partly due to expense but there were also safety issues involved.[20]

Qantas also started to employ Chinese flight hostesses in the 1960s but they weren't a success as they came from more upper-class backgrounds and they were not used to providing service roles. Other major international airlines introduced Asian women on their flights, and they too would wear traditional forms of dress as well as the standard uniform. Pan American World Airways had introduced Japanese American stewardesses in 1955 and at the same time Japanese stewardesses were also flying on KLM, Air France, Air India and Thai Airways.[21] In recruiting Asian air hostesses the airlines traded on the stereotype of the subservient 'Asian girl'. For example, in 1961 Cathay Pacific had two flights a week between Hong Kong and Sydney with the airline proclaiming the use of British pilots who 'fly you efficiently' while the 'demure Oriental hostesses pamper you charmingly'.[22]

Stella was one of those girls who imagined air hostessing meant a smart uniform and a short cut to a rich husband. She had been very fed up when she discovered the truth.

Evadne Price, *Air Hostess in Love*, 1962[23]

In August 1958, *Life* magazine featured a 10-page colour feature article 'Glamor Girls of the Air'. The article included a photograph of fifty-three air hostesses representing sixty of the airlines that were flying into the United States. Margaret Cohan was the representative for Qantas, and she appeared like many of the other air hostesses in a navy blue military-style suit. The photograph, taken on the cusp of the jet age, marks a moment where the old military-style uniforms, which had dominated since the 1930s, now seemed seriously outdated. Some of the airlines were obviously taking regional conditions into account when designing their uniforms, as among the line-up were air hostesses in cowboy uniforms, kimonos and Arctic garb. The airlines in this way capitalised on the uniform as a way to sell regional and national differences to a new global market.

Earlier that year, Dawn James, a staff reporter for the *Australian Women's Weekly* was offered a special assignment to attend the Pan Am training school in San Francisco.[24] While she was there she tried on the Arctic emergency outfit (similar to that worn in the *Life* magazine by Alaska Airlines), which included snow shoes, a down fur-hooded parka, plus five pairs of gloves worn one on top of another. She was given a demonstration on how to use a gun in the event of encountering a polar bear.[25] There were eight women on the Pan Am training course, all transferring from other divisions in the airline, including one woman who had recently married. After being fingerprinted for security reasons, James attended the course for two weeks, although the course usually lasted for four weeks, with a further week flying as an observer. Her conclusion was that wading through a service training manual, which was about three inches thick, was no small matter. A highlight was when she got to wear the iconic Pan Am Tunis-blue uniform and learnt the etiquette of wearing the cap slightly tilted over the right eye.

It wasn't just the major airlines with themed uniforms. Butler Air Transport, which had formed in 1934 flying mainly to regional New South Wales and the southern border of Queensland, extended its routes to Melbourne with the introduction of the twenty-four passenger Vickers Viscount in the mid-1950s.[26] Initially the air hostesses had worn a navy military-style double-breasted suit with floppy beret hat, but by the 1960s they were operating as Airlines of New South Wales, and taking flights to the snowfields of Cooma. For these flights the air hostesses would wear 'ski bunny' trouser suits complete with calf-length vinyl boots.[27]

Other Australian airlines attempted to exoticise their air hostesses. On board Ansett-ANA's new Lockheed Electras, the air hostesses wore gold lamé dresses for the Golden Supper Club Service on the last flight out of Melbourne to Sydney at 10pm. The 'hostess' dress had a nipped-in waist, three-quarter-length sleeves and a broad collar.[28] They only came in three sizes; if the size didn't fit safety pins were used to hold the dress. The rationale behind the service was that it would attract businessmen who 'could relax 4 miles high' while 'attentive hostesses' served 'succulent spatchcock' or a 'lobster medallion' salad with 'tempting side dishes'. Free champagne, spirits and chilled ales were offered to the passengers who wore bibs printed with a logo featuring a golden roast chicken and a red lobster. The service was actually a way to fill up a 'positioning flight', where an otherwise empty plane had to be returned for the busy morning flight out of Sydney the next day. On the 'Golden Orchid' service to Papua New Guinea, the air hostesses would change into silky culottes to serve dinner.[29] From the late 1960s through to the early 1970s Qantas also had special Holomu'u dresses or long culottes (short-lived) for the Honolulu–San Francisco flights, and on the 'Qantastic Funjet' flights to Fiji, Noumea and Bali. The 'busy' floral pattern on the ankle-length hostess gowns drew the joking label of 'chunder dress'. There was no such name for the Hawaiian print floral shirts that the stewards wore.

Qantas wasn't the only airline placing their flight hostesses in decorative dresses. In 1967, BOAC introduced a paper mini dress covered with a print of a sun and large flowers to be worn on the Caribbean and Bermuda flights. Cut, literally, to whichever length wanted, the dress was worn with a flower in the hair (usually a fresh orchid), and white gloves and bright green slip-on shoes. The dresses weren't practical as they would tear easily and become transparent and disintegrate when wet.[30] They were meant to be fireproof, which was just as well as some of the more 'charming' passengers would try and stub their cigarettes into the fabric. They were never designed to last as, after the passengers disembarked, the air hostesses would put on the standard uniform and throw away the short-lived paper dress.[31]

5.4. The Discipline of Appearance

Despite the popularity of the profession, in 1959 Qantas only had eighty-five flight hostesses, but they were receiving 800 applications a year. There was still only one flight hostess on board, creating an 'aura' of exclusivity around her. With the introduction of the round-the-world service and the new Boeing 707 services, advertisements were placed in the major daily newspapers for new flight hostess positions.

> **Flight Hostess Vacancies**
> Qantas is seeking suitably qualified single young women
> for positions as flight hostesses. Here is an opportunity
> to secure a much sought-after position. The duties are
> interesting, sometimes exacting, but always rewarding.
> It is a career which offers a more than generous salary,
> the interest of overseas travel and an attractive newly
> designed uniform.[32]

In Melbourne the interviews would be held at Qantas House, 341 Collins Street, over a period of three days. Applicants were expected to have a 'pleasant personality and attractive appearance' and undergo three interviews before being selected into the training school.[33] The first interview would be with the employment officer, who would ask questions about general interests, schooling, work, topical questions and the standard 'Why do you want to be an air hostess?' The second interview would be slightly more informal with the employment officer and a senior hostess, and the third interview would include a panel including the passenger services manager, flight hostess superintendent, passenger services training superintendent and the flight hostess instructor. Once accepted, there was a medical before starting the three months' training.

In 1961, Margaret Gibson, who was hostess superintendent for TAA, went on a three-week tour to the United States to study air hostessing techniques. One of the airlines she visited was United Airlines and they were receiving a staggering 50,000 applications a year for the job of stewardess, with a success rate of one to every 150.[34] By comparison Gibson had 250 air hostesses under her control and would train about 100 a year[35] (an indication of the high attrition rate that continued in the job). She had a wealth of experience as she had started working as an air hostess with ANA in 1947, and in the 1950s she had worked as assistant for ANA's passenger services manager Stephen Kentley. Pat (McMahon) Merlehan, who had started with TAA in March 1957, remembers Gibson being appointed hostess superintendent later that year, remaining in that position until the end of 1962, when she returned to Claremont, Queensland, to take over the family newspaper. Merlehan remembers her as a 'bright lady on top of things', with 'a mind like a filing cabinet' and a tendency to 'pop up in all sorts of places'.[36] As a result of the US tour, Gibson noted and was critical of the new trend in having uniforms for 'on the plane' and 'off the plane'. She thought that changing out of a suit into a smock and from three-inch-heel shoes into 'flatties' once on the plane gave a sloppy impression.[37] Also, the new trend for three-quarter-length sleeves on the uniforms wouldn't work for TAA as they showed their rank on their sleeve. American airline training schools were conducting IQ and personality tests, but Gibson thought that commonsense was an important aspect of the profession, and there was no test for that trait. American Airlines had a 'luxurious and modern' training school in Fort Worth, with the trainees living there for six-and-a-half weeks while undertaking the training course. She thought the training was more extensive than the Australian courses, and her lasting impression was that the school gave the 'girls' a look of being cast in the same mould, something she wished to avoid with her trainees, citing the individual charm of the Australian girls as an asset. [38]

One of the greatest things in life is the smile, because it makes the face light up. It changes the tone of the voice. It makes people feel welcomed.

June Dally-Watkins

The issue of individuality alongside corporate standardisation was a constant with all air hostesses in all airlines. June Dally-Watkins, a well-known Australian model, had opened a school for deportment in Sydney in 1950 and Qantas employed her to teach deportment to its trainees. Dally-Watkins said that she had 'no idea how to tell them how to look after people' but she would teach the young trainees 'how to carry their body, and how to be charming, how to smile, how to have a good personality and eye contact'.[39] The flight hostesses would go to her studio in the city where they would also learn 'good manners', the correct way to put on an overcoat and some of them would have their hair done by two male hairdressers as part of general grooming.[40] Dally-Watkins remembers that her job was made easier as much of her work had already been done for her as Qantas 'only chose the best'.[41]

Pat Woodley, who had been Miss New South Wales in 1951, also ran a modelling and deportment school in Phillip Street,

Keeping up the national image, Qantas flight hostess with koala, c. 1959
A Qantas flight hostess with a ready smile wears the new 'Jungle Green' uniform in an image designed to capture the attention of an overseas market. Courtesy of Qantas Heritage Collection.

Sydney, which would-be air hostesses attended. Woodley advertised her school on the side of buses with the claim, 'I'll make any girl pretty'. She was familiar with the role undertaken by air hostesses, as in 1954 she, along with three other 'mannequins', went on a ten-day tour of the major cities in Australia, flying with ANA in the DC-6 Skychief showing 'holiday fashions' to passengers during the flights. Denise Rennison, who also won a Miss New South Wales competition in 1964 and later worked for Qantas, had attended a Pat Woodley course.[42] In Adelaide prospective hostesses attended the Dawne Walker Academy. Walker had an arrangement with ANA where they agreed to interview anyone who had graduated from her course. She was serious about creating an authentic environment, even arranging for her husband to build a mock-up DC-3 buffet.[43] In the late 1970s, her academy was now in Sydney, with courses now offered to flight stewards as well as air hostesses.[44]

Pat (Willbrandt) Gregory-Quilter, who started with Qantas in 1957, remembers the importance of deportment and grooming from the initial stages of applying for Qantas. With her second interview she had to walk up and down the interview room before the panel of four, remove and put on her gloves and make a PA announcement.[45] Once accepted for training, she joined an intake of five, and after training she was rostered on the flights to Papua New Guinea, only graduating to the Kangaroo Route when she was deemed 'good enough'. When she started, the flight hostesses were still wearing the white summer dress and she would hang her six spare uniforms on the back of the toilet door in the plane to avoid it getting crushed. More than once an inebriated passenger urinated over the uniform. Fortunately they could have their uniforms laundered along the way at the different stopovers. While on the Kangaroo Route, depending on the season, they would change from their winter uniform to their summer uniform at Singapore, or vice versa.

Gregory-Quilter worked with Qantas until 1961, then left to marry, and when the marriage failed came back in 1969 as trainer for fourteen years.[46] She was interested in achieving a more individualised look and so the Qantas training school created its own hair and make-up salon. As Gregory-Quilter said, '...we wanted to bring the best out in every girl. Not clone them but to have them individually at their best'. At this time Elizabeth Arden was the make-up used by most of the airlines and Gregory-Quilter was allergic to it, so she contacted Lancôme and Revlon to use as possible alternatives. The colour of lipstick, nail polish and eye make-up was always subdued and in keeping with a tone that suited the uniform. Despite Gregory-Quilter's intent to achieve some sort of individuality, the strict standards meant that the flight hostesses did tend to look very similar. The other reason for a standard look among the flight hostesses was that wigs were commonplace at the time. They too had to be approved; they had to look natural.[47] Wigs became popular because flight hostesses could keep their hair long and it was far easier to put on a wig at 4am, ready for an early morning flight, than it was to wash one's hair.

Maureene Martin joined Qantas in 1964 as a 22-year-old and she recalls one of her colleagues calling Gregory-Quilter 'Mrs Grooming Looming', as she would appear from her office and ask them to put some more lipstick on, or something along those lines. There was also an elocution specialist Mrs Brunton-Gibb who would teach them how to speak properly and make PA announcements. Training also included 'things like how to carry a book on your head, how to speak nicely, how to put on lashings of make-up and how to...clone yourself to look like a Qantas girl'.[48] She also remembers it was compulsory to join the union;

Qantas arranged medical benefits, and there was a very generous superannuation fund where for every dollar put in, Qantas would put in two-and-a-half.

5.5. Desert Island Nights!

I remember as a little girl riding on a tram with my mother somewhere in the city of Melbourne and a woman got on with a uniform and she was quite gorgeous. I remember looking at her and she had the little peaked cap that they used to wear and she was beautifully groomed. I just said, oh mummy, that's a beautiful lady, she's a soldier. Mum said no, no, she's an air hostess. She works for an airline. Then she told me all about it.

Kathy (Riley) Minassian, TAA air hostess, 1968 to 1970

The Air Hostess must retain her composure under all circumstances and must not portray excitement, hesitancy, confusion or fear. Quiet, smiling composure, with thoughtful efficiency, will promote relaxed comfort of passengers, and will instil confidence when anything unusual occurs.

MMA Air Hostess Manual, June 1962

Rochelle (Miles) Sutherland graduated with thirteen others from TAA training school in August 1960.[49] She kept a book of clippings from the time she started with the airline. When she joined, TAA had recently taken over the New Guinea route from Qantas. One of the clippings in her book suggests that TAA may have had trouble recruiting crew to fly on the New Guinea 'Sunbird' route, saying, 'Thin girls, fat girls, short girls, plain girls – all girls as long as they are over 21, hold a first-aid certificate and have personality' could apply for an air hostess position. Sutherland sees this media portrayal of the air hostesses as inaccurate and demeaning, especially as TAA was inundated with applications each week from young women wanting to join the airline, and they had such clear standards about size, weight and appearance. A transfer to New Guinea was actually a sought after position, with air hostesses seconded for deployments of three to six months. With so many modern planes in the skies the 'Sunbird' service, using converted DC-3s with jet-assisted take-off units, may not have offered the comfort or the glamour expected by a new generation of young women. It was also necessary to consider the financial benefits of flying. Sutherland earned more as a secretary than she did when she joined TAA. Margaret Gibson was the air hostess superintendent at TAA when Sutherland joined and she provided a letter to new recruits that included a section called 'Stock-in-Trade'. It said, '...you were selected because you had, or will have throughout training the following:

GOOD APPEARANCE and GROOMING
PERSONALITY with CHARM
INTELLIGENCE applied with COMMON SENSE
STRONG DESIRE to be of SERVICE
POISE to be able to meet all people'.[50]

We were told to smile at all times no matter what is happening and no matter how rude people are to you, smile at all times.
Kathy Minassian, TAA air hostess, 1968 to 1970

Kathy (Kathleen Riley) Minassian was interviewed for both Ansett and TAA, but it was TAA that accepted her first. It seems the fashionable outfit she had worn for the interview paid off: kid gloves, high heels and a kangaroo-skin mini coat. But the move from her hometown in Melbourne to a flat with two other host-esses in Cremorne Point, Sydney, made her realise that she may have been moving a step too fast for a 23-year-old:

> I couldn't boil water. There was no such thing as take-away shops in those days, no McDonald's or anything like that. I think I went to a butcher and I asked for one chop. He stared at me and so I said, 'I'll have two chops'. I brought them home – I suppose I got other things that day – and I just didn't know what to do with them. I thought, oh, I think mum puts them under the griller. I was totally unprepared for life.[51]

She couldn't ring her mother and ask her what to do as it was too expensive to have a phone in the flat. If the airline needed to contact her she would receive a telegram.

> *There's nothing glamorous about holding open a safety door in an evacuation. No, nothing glamorous at all.*
> Helen Nunn, Qantas flight hostess, 1967 to 1970

One training routine highlighted emergency procedures. Minassian's class visited an Olympic pool to learn how to inflate a raft and jump into the pool fully clothed: 'But the hardest part of all, that was climbing into it. They're so huge and we were struggling and trying to help each other. Then it was every man for himself and I think I went in head first and finally got in. But then of course, the point was now how would you go if the ocean was rough and, firstly, if you could even find it. So that was a good lesson'.[52] Minassian flew until 1970 when she left to take a secretarial position at the ABC. She had enjoyed her time flying, marred only by the last month when she had 'three abortive take-offs…a couple of very dicey landings and about two bomb scares'. She was glad that she didn't have to carry out any emergency procedures with any of these incidents.

The *Qantas Flight Hostess Manual* was almost 260 pages, and Bev Maunsell, who had previously worked at Ansett-ANA for two years, remembers sitting in the Qantas training school thinking that they took things very seriously. Along with her twenty-one classmates she had to: 'Write all these things out and do drawings of the plates with the parsley on it and everything'.[53] As well as the important placement of parsley, the flight hostesses would be instructed about what to do during stopovers or between flights. There was a special routine described in the *Qantas Flight Hostess Manual* as the 'Desert Island Night'. Flight hostesses were advised to set aside one night each week to delve into their personal appearance.[54] The order of activities suggested were:

1. Relaxing bath.
2. Finger and toenails.
3. Hair – combed and brush scrubbed clean.
4. Skin care.
5. Superfluous hair removed.
6. Odd jobs – mending etc.
7. At least eight hours restful sleep with plenty of fresh air.

The next morning it was expected they would 'not only feel healthier and cleaner, but look a different person. There is a virtuous feeling knowing you and your possessions are spic and span and you will make certain your working day matches the mood of orderliness'.[55]

Qantas may have had a rigorous training schedule but it also had standards to keep once a flight hostess graduated. The domestic airlines had a port supervisor in the major capital cities who would check to see that the air hostesses were well presented and the report sheet filled. But Qantas was an international airline, and once out of Sydney there was 'Buckley's chance of them catching you', if you did anything wrong.[56]

Smoking can be part of your conversation. If you don't know what to say, you can always pull out a cigarette...I started smoking when I was on the airlines.

Air hostess, c. 1964 in Studs Terkel, *Working*, 1972[57]

Marilyn (Philpott) Lawson was an impressionable 24-year-old when she joined Qantas in August 1963.[58] She thought that smoking was a part of the 'look' of the independent jet-setting flight hostess. In preparation for her first training flight to Nadi, Fiji, she bought a packet of Craven 'A' cigarettes. She spent much of the flight soothing a nervous passenger, not having the nerve to tell him that she'd never been on a Boeing 707 either. They arrived in Nadi at midnight, and she was surprised to see Fijians sleeping all over the terminals, but went alone to the Mocambo Hotel as the trainee flight hostess was the only crew member to disembark at Nadi. The rest of the crew flew on to Honolulu.[59] She went straight to her room and tried her hand at smoking. After the initial drawback she started to cough and thought to herself, 'I'm the only one here, who am I trying to impress?' and threw the packet away, never to smoke again. In any case, it was late and she had to get up at 3am to get ready for the flight back to Sydney.

Before joining Qantas, Lawson had worked as a secretary for a shipping company and she went for the initial interview during her lunchtime. John Ward, who later became chief executive officer of Qantas, interviewed her, and informed her that she would have a second and final interview at Mascot the following week in front of five people, including Marj de Tracy. He gave her the following advice:

1. Don't put your handbag on the table, put it on the floor.
2. You will be introduced to them and use their names.
3. Learn a thing or two about Qantas for the interview.

Dorothy (Bell) Harris was in the same intake as Lawson and four others. She was from the small Victorian country town of Colac. She applied to Qantas as she was keen to travel and felt fortunate that, unlike her dairy farmer boyfriend who was destined to take over the family dairy farm, she had the opportunity to do more with her life. She had only had one interview and it was in the Melbourne office. She was asked to leave the room while Marj de Tracy and personnel officer Harvey Ward discussed the interview. While waiting, the office staff, who had listened to the interview through the partition, told her she was doing well as she had been given the PA announcement to read. She was quite proud that she knew how to pronounce Tehran and knew where it was. Later, she found out when another applicant was asked if she knew where Tehran was, she replied, 'Never heard of it!' Harvey Ward replied, 'But you are a teacher'. Marj de Tracy obviously wanted to have her in the intake, so defended her: 'She's only a primary school teacher'. There were also general knowledge questions about prime ministers of various countries and Martin

Luther King's identity. Harris was given a scenario about racism, which she responded to by saying, 'I have Asian friends and have just been to Malaysia and Singapore for four months and stayed with Chinese families and Malay Muslims. I am used to mixing with other races'. She also elaborated that she had many penfriends from all over the world.[60]

Before Harris officially graduated and was given her wings, she was sent on a training flight from Sydney to Fiji. She was standing on the back steps of the Boeing 707 watching the passengers come on board thinking this was the most exciting day of her life: 'As you know I was a Colac girl and 1963 was the year that Geelong beat Hawthorn in the AFL Grand Final. It's my first overseas flight and across the tarmac coming towards me is the Geelong football team off on an overseas trip. Some of the boys were from Colac and they threw me a look, what are you doing here?' That was the start of Harris smiling her way 'backwards and forwards' across the world for the next four years. As for having a team of footballers on board, Harris says they behaved like perfect gentleman; it would seem that the 'ugly Australian' only appeared in the 1980s.

Harris's life as a flight hostess was not without some drama. In November 1966, Qantas pilots went on a twenty-eight day strike over a list of twenty industrial and operational differences they had with the company. Harris was stood down by Qantas, so she and another flight hostess went off and did a typing test in preparation for finding another job. One of her colleagues who was on only her second flight became 'stuck' in San Francisco. Qantas arranged for the tech crew to be brought home on other airlines but the flight crew remained. The flight hostess stayed at the Hotel Drake-Wiltshire in Union Square for three-and-a-half weeks. It was winter and she didn't have any of the right clothes, and she couldn't access her per diem money. Back home, her furious father was trying to get her a ticket home. Harris, in the meantime, had a part-time secretarial job lined up, but before she could start she was reinstated, as the court had ruled that Qantas had illegally stood down its employees.

Most of the flight hostesses were happy to adhere to the checks and the strict standards knowing that if they didn't they could be grounded and therefore lose their pay. If there was a hair out of place or the hairstyle didn't suit, where once Marj de Tracy would send the flight hostesses to her own hairdressers, now there was a hairdresser at Mascot. There was no need to instruct the hairdresser as he knew exactly how to cut hair to the 'Qantas style'.[61] Janette (Freeman) Davie AM began with Qantas in 1967 and had to stay in training school for a bit longer as she had pimples and had to wait for her skin to 'settle' before she could fly.[62] When she was finally allowed to fly she would have her skin checked on each return flight, and eventually she was sent to a skin specialist and put on the pill, which normally meant weight gain. The issue of the hostesses' weight was still a concern as they were rostered off if they put on too much.[63] This would have dire financial consequences, as Davie explains:

> We'd all moved from interstate. We all had to pay a bond to live in an apartment and we had no money left over once you paid the bond and your rent every week and fed yourself. So if someone said come back when you've lost the weight, it might take you three or four weeks to lose that half a stone and there was no salary during that period.[64]

It is easy to trace discrimination back to the airlines and their individual policies but there was also a sense that the air hostesses themselves endorsed the 'look' required to be employed with many of them thinking that you shouldn't fly when 'you're too fat or too old'.[65]Age was the other issue impacting on new recruits at this time. For most airlines the criteria to join were almost the same. While the height over the years had increased, the weight had remained much the same, and it was still necessary to have completed a first-aid course, and glasses or contact lenses couldn't be worn.[66] The only variation seemed to be the matter of age. In the late 1950s, Airlines of South Australia (ASA) became known as 'The Teenage Airline', as most of the hostesses were only 19 years old.[67] Julie Winter was one of the 19-year-olds employed by the airline and she loved the job, 'I wouldn't change it for anything…I couldn't bear to go back to a routine job, catch the same bus to town every day, work "nine to five" hours, and then catch the same bus home. It would be monotonous'.[68]

> *I think the turnover was also due to such a dramatic change in lifestyle. Most were away from home for the first time dealing with a demanding job, a culture of strict rules and cooking and cleaning at home…and learning to live with other people (flatmates). It was a bit much for some and some simply didn't like it.*
>
> Michele Reid, Ansett air hostess, 1964 to 1967

Michele Reid started with Ansett in 1964 as a 19-year-old and, as she was under 21, it had been necessary to get her parents' permission.[69] Her trainer gave her lots of valuable advice, including some things that may not have been in the training manual. They included making sure that she had a fresh outfit for overnight trips, and when out to always buy a round of drinks, something that a 19-year-old who had never lived away from home would not necessarily know to do. Training also included deportment:

> …we used to have to practice walking up and down a set of stairs, the sort they used to push to the aircraft for embarkation. We'd walk up and down those stairs with our handbag, overnight bag and umbrella and our coat over our arm, wearing a hat, of course. This exercise was to be done without looking at the stairs.[70]

The employment background of the air hostesses remained fairly consistent into the early 1960s, with a survey from TAA showing the majority were from clerical, nursing and teaching positions.[71] There were the odd exceptions, such as Brigitta Bruijnesteijn, who entered the profession in 1962 as a rollerskater. Admittedly, she had trained as nurse, but before joining MMA she had been a rollerskating hostess at His Majesty's Hotel, Perth. She and her fellow skaters would rollerskate the 50 yards from the bar to the dining room in turtleneck tops and short pleated skirts.[72]

Wendy (Moir) Georgetti-Remkes was 19 years old when she applied to join Ansett-ANA in 1963, but after the medical she was told she would have to have her appendix out, even though she had no prior symptoms. She had her appendix out without question, and after she recovered she was accepted into the airline in 1964.[73] She remembers that the Ansett-ANA hostesses were seen as 'glamour pusses', something she thought that Sir Reginald Ansett encouraged. She also felt that most of the air hostesses seemed much more sophisticated than her. Early in her flying career, on a stopover, she was with the female crew at the Southern Cross Hotel in Melbourne:

'Come on Wendy, we're going down to the bar'. I was terrified. I'd never been in that atmosphere. These girls just oozed confidence. The men flocked in because hosties were a drawcard in those days. I curled up with embarrassment. I just went back to my room and I said, 'I can't cope with this'. I felt very intimidated.[74]

She only flew with Ansett-ANA for a short while as she was homesick, and returned to her hometown of Perth and joined MMA. After a couple of years with MMA she left and became the first air hostess for Connellan Airways, a small airline set up by Edward 'EJ' Connellan flying out of Alice Springs. There were long twelve- to thirteen-hour days, and when she wasn't flying, she would help her boss, who she still calls 'Mr Connellan', with secretarial work. With the introduction of the reconditioned Heron aircraft, she trained as a radio operator, and would also do the load sheets sitting alongside the pilot. It was hot work as the planes weren't air-conditioned: 'you would not perspire, you would be dripping with sweat'. Before Connellan worked out a way to reengineer the Herons they had a habit of catching fire, particularly when starting. Georgetti-Remkes remembers, 'So one of my duties as the second crew was to stand in front of the engine with this whopping great fire extinguisher at the ready to put any fire out'.[75]

Despite the challenges, the work was satisfying. With a small airline it was clear that one's efforts were valued and one was seen as an important part of a team. Eventually, Georgetti-Remkes wanted to see more of the world and, with the encouragement of 'Mr Connellan', she joined Qantas in 1971, and stayed there for thirty-two years, resigning in 2003.

5.6. The Work of Glamour

While few would dispute the 'sheer hard work' of the job there
was also the hard work of being highly groomed and attractive; what might be called the work of glamour. This hard work
of looking good would spin off into other public spheres with
air hostesses entering charity and beauty competitions. Denise
Rennison, who, as mentioned earlier, had won the Miss New
South Wales competition, was nominated by Qantas to enter the
Miss International Air Hostess Quest held at Surfers Paradise in
November 1966. The competition had been set up in 1963 by
Alex McRobbie, the editor of the local newspaper. He said that
it was not a beauty contest and that the entrants were judged
solely on their ability as air hostesses. It would be an occasion
when airline hostesses from all the world's carriers could meet and
study how different companies handled in-flight service.[76] The
annual competition created worldwide publicity and for the 1964
event fifteen air hostesses travelled in a motorcade of open-top
sports cars to Brisbane City Hall. A couple of years later, Libby
(Wild) Panter represented Ansett Airlines in the competition, and
remembers the contestants getting together and comparing notes
about their job, including the topic de jour: the introduction of
trolleys in the cabins. If the competition was meant to be about
the profession it didn't stop photo opportunities such as Alice Lu
from Cathay Pacific posing on an ocean rock shelf in a bikini; an
image that found its way into the *Navy News* magazine.[77]

No doubt as a recognition of the standards that Qantas
achieved with their flight hostesses, Pat Gregory-Quilter was
used as a judge for beach girl competitions and the Miss Australia
contest. The winner of the Miss Australia competition would
be offered a trip with Qantas as part of her prize. June Wright
won Miss Australia 1971 and travelled for six months, flying with

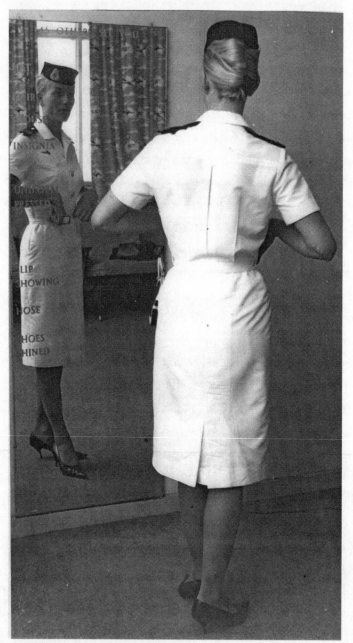

TAA air hostess check mirror, 1963
TAA air hostess Barbara Anderson checks her appearance before starting duty. The check list on the mirror reads: hat, hair, blouse, insignia, uniform pressed, slip showing, hose and shoes shined. Courtesy of the TAA Museum.

Qantas. On those trips she 'spent a lot of time chatting with the hostesses about their jobs, their social lives and the places they visit'.[78] This was enough encouragement for her to apply for the job, and in July 1972 she became a Qantas flight hostess.

With most airlines offering similar services on often identical planes, the air hostesses became the point of difference. Through careful selection and thorough training, the well-groomed, socially competent and attractive air hostess proved the perfect marketing tool to represent the public face of the airlines. In the past, airlines had often used models in their campaigns, but in the 1960s there was a trend for representing a sort of authenticity. Airlines wanted a 'girl with a smile', but it had to be genuine. It was for this reason that in September 1967, Susan (Jones) Foster became the face of Ansett-ANA. She appeared in an advertising campaign, which was pitched firmly against their competition – TAA. The slogan for the advertisement was 'How can both Airlines be the Same? We've got Susan Jones'. Foster was 22 years old and she had been flying with Ansett-ANA for three years. She thinks she was selected because she was an 'ordinary person' and even her name 'Susan Jones' fitted the brief of an everyday Australian girl.[79] Even though she was comfortable on board chatting to the passengers, Foster was very shy, and after spending a day being photographed in a studio in an old church in Melbourne, nothing could have prepared her for seeing her face on a double-page spread. Without any preparation she was sent on a promotional tour of Australia doing radio and television interviews. The campaign was highly publicised in all forms of media, with Festival records producing a 'Susan Jones' EP record to be handed out on flights. The song, about a young woman who had 'escaped' a small town to join the airline, was sung by the young, then unknown Johnny Farnham:

Autumn leaves, I wonder if you could give me some advice
I'm trying to find someone awfully nice
Susan Jones
The happiest girl used to live in our town
She got away and it's getting me down.
Susan Jones.[80]

That November, the airline knew, perhaps, that Foster was about to leave, as they ran a new advertisement, 'Whoever you are, please stop sending our Miss Jones roses', citing that they were losing 'too many good hostesses to matrimony as it is'.[81] By the end of the year Foster had become engaged to Bob Foster who had produced the 'Susan Jones' television commercial for the J. Walter Thompson agency. When the time came for Foster to leave Ansett-ANA they were able to capitalise on this by placing a full-page advertisement in every major paper with a photograph of a demure Foster in a wedding dress and veil, with the simple caption, 'I do'.

Another air hostess, Jan Elliot, replaced 'Susan Jones' as the face of Ansett-ANA. The girl-next-door look of Foster was replaced with something a bit racier: this time the new face of Ansett was represented by Elliot standing on the wing of a Boeing 727-77 in a mini-skirted uniform.[82] The idea that young, attractive and single women should represent an airline continued into the 1970s. Over at Qantas, the Customer Service Manager, John Fysh, thought that it was important to have attractive flight hostesses and suggested that the Qantas staff magazine run a series of photographs of the 'fly-birds'. The idea was not a success as, after one flight hostess appeared in her bikini alongside the caption, 'a delightful decoration for any swimming pool', it seems there were no further images in the series.[83]

5.7. The Swiss Girls and Vietnam

'You've got just what it takes,' Meg went on. 'You are over twenty-one and under twenty-seven. You speak a foreign language and have a wonderful personality. Your figure's nice, and heaven knows you're pretty'.

Jane Gerard, *Jet Stewardess*, 1962[84]

A group of Qantas flight hostesses, who became known as 'The Swiss Girls', had been recruited by Marj de Tracy on a trip to Europe in 1962.[85] There was an influx of migrants coming to Australia on Qantas charter flights and it was decided to recruit women with French and German language skills. Ruth (Wiedenmeier) Bailey, one of 'The Swiss Girls', thought that the French, German and Spanish language skills they had were an odd fit, as many of the migrants were Maltese, Italian and Greek.[86] Bailey's boss at the Swiss Credit Bank in Zurich had encouraged her to apply. She had three interviews, and at the last one de Tracy said, 'We would like you to join Qantas, but we wouldn't like you to be homesick, because it's a long way to Australia; also in Australia, there isn't much happening on the weekend – there's nothing open – there're no pubs open and no cinemas'.[87] Despite having reservations about coming to Australia, Bailey thought a job as a flight hostess would be preferable to working in the bank. Also, flying with Qantas meant that she could fly internationally, while most European air hostess jobs were on domestic airlines.

There were eighteen flight hostesses accepted out of the 200 women who applied, and one of them remembers during the interview having to stand on a table so they could check her physical stature. They were sent to Sydney, in two groups a couple of months apart. They all stayed in Manly with one group in an apartment on the ferry side and the other group on the ocean side.[88] Each day they would catch the ferry to Circular Quay, and then a bus to the training school. For some of them it felt like being on a holiday, especially as after the eight-week training school they expected to return to Europe to be based in London. Halfway through the course reality hit home when Qantas changed its mind and told them they would all be based in Sydney, also offering them a first-class trip home after nine months and, if that didn't suit them, they had the option to leave the airline. Bailey chose to stay and it was only some years later she was offered a base in London and stayed there for the next two years before returning to live in Australia.

Australia entered the Vietnam War while Bailey was flying with Qantas. During this war commercial airlines were chartered to fly troops to and from Australia. Qantas ran charter flights known as the 'Skippy Squadron', taking almost half of all Australian service personnel to Vietnam between 1965 and 1972. Flights would go from the RAAF base in Richmond, via Townsville and then on to Manila and Tan Son Nhut Air Base, Saigon. The planes would stop for only a short time to offload personnel before returning to Australia. Qantas did not roster flight hostesses on these flights, with the exception of Bailey who volunteered for one flight.[89] She was the only female on a flight to Saigon with the uniformed men, all excited and drinking a bit too much. At one stage the chief steward suggested that she stay in the crew rest area as things were 'getting a bit out of hand'.

The soldiers returning home on leave would be picked up by Qantas flights in Manila, and there would be flight hostesses on these flights. Dorothy Harris was on one of these flights and remembers, 'they drank the aircraft dry before we got to the Australian coast. So the skipper pulled into Darwin to get more beer for them'. Qantas would issue briefing notes to the returning soldiers outlining luggage allowance and a list of prohibited items, such as drugs, pornographic literature and weapons.[90] Not all the return flights home were so exuberant; many of the veterans on completing their service would fly home in total silence, physically and emotionally exhausted. Often their mates were in coffins in the cargo hold. The appearance of these thin, emotionally drained men was an image that many of the crew and the ground hostesses back in Sydney remember to this day. TAA as the domestic carrier would transport the soldier's bodies back to home states. Air hostess Kathy Minassian said they wouldn't be informed if there was a body on board, but they would know soon enough when they saw the grieving family at the airport.[91]

5.8. Indigenous Air Hostesses

After the 1967 referendum, where over 90 per cent of people voted to have Indigenous Australians included in the census, there were attempts to make Australia a more inclusive society, and to actively promote opportunities for Indigenous Australians. In June 1968, as part of a 'Your Career' section in *Dawn: A Magazine for the Aboriginal People of New South Wales*, the Department of Labour and Industry had forwarded information about the duties and qualifications necessary to be an air hostess.[92] Under 'Personal Qualifications' it mentioned that the 'work is often tiring, and the hostess must be of first-class health. She must speak fluently and clearly and have good eyesight, a pleasing appearance and personality and an ability to get along well with people'. The question of health was becoming an issue. An article from London mentioned that many air hostesses were giving up their jobs because their health was suffering from the demands of the job and medical conditions associated with flying.[93]

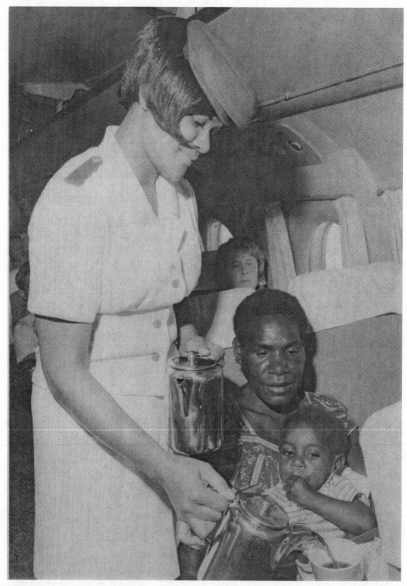

New Guinea Air Hostess, c 1969
In July 1960 TAA began flying to New Guinea, taking over the route from Qantas. In this photo New Guinea—based air hostess Helen Fletcher attends to a mother and child. Courtesy of TAA Museum.

This did not deter Sue Bryant, who became the first Indigenous Australian air hostess when she started working for Ansett Airlines of New South Wales in 1970. Bryant had grown up in the inner west of Sydney, under the flight path, and she would often gaze out of the classroom window, thinking she would like to be an air hostess. There is often an event that happens to change the direction in a young person's life. For Bryant it was when she attended the first national Aboriginal debutante ball in August 1968. She was really excited in anticipation: 'Our little five-bedroom house, was rocking'. The event was an initiative of the Foundation for Aboriginal Affairs and Bryant thinks it was the manager, Charles Perkins, who arranged for Prime Minister John Gorton to attend. In preparation for the ball she had to undergo dance classes with Ester Carol at the Foundation's office in George Street. Bryant went to the ball wearing a dress her cousin had made; a simple A-line floor-length gown with a bow in the front. The ball gave her 'so much confidence', including the confidence to become an air hostess.

After three interviews, Bryant began work on the 19th March 1970. She can't remember the panel asking her anything specific about being Indigenous, but when asked why she wanted to be an air hostess she said because she had 'always wanted to travel and as an Indigenous person she wanted to see a lot of the country'.[94] Her first uniform was a white mini dress worn with a thin tan belt and a matching pillbox hat. By the time she left in 1973, in keeping with the fashion of the day, the uniform was orange hotpants worn with a wraparound maxi skirt and brown boots. Working for Ansett Airlines of New South Wales meant Bryant flew to many of the outback towns: Dubbo, Bourke, Brewarrina and on to Charleville in Queensland. With large Indigenous populations in the towns it may have been advantageous to have Bryant on these routes but she didn't think so, as there weren't that many Indigenous passengers at that time. Other routes were to the Snowy Mountains, Griffith and Narrandera with connections to Leighton. Her favourite route was to Coffs Harbour, and on to Casino, as she would fly over her home town of Nambucca Heads. The airline also undertook charter flights with different groups such as lawn bowlers or jockeys, and bookies going to outback races at Coonabarabran. She very quickly became a senior hostess, only because the next intake of girls was immediately more junior. In 1971, she appeared in Roderick Hulsbergen's book *The Aborigine Today* wearing her uniform, and possibly a 'hostie' wig, representing a modern young woman engaged in life at work.[95]

Other Indigenous air hostesses were selected to train with Ansett and TAA. The year before Bryant began her job as an air hostess, Maria Nilson graduated with seventeen other Ansett air hostesses. Nilson was from Kwato Island off the eastern tip of New Guinea and she could speak Pidgin and two dialects, Motu and Suau. She returned to New Guinea and was appointed as the first air hostess on the Airlines of Papua and New Guinea.[96] TAA also employed local Indigenous air hostesses to be stationed in New Guinea and in the early 1970s were training Indigenous women to work as air hostesses for Air Niugini. It was not until the end of the decade, and then under the National Employment Strategy for Aboriginals and the Department of Aboriginal Affairs, that TAA employed Mary Cross from Shark Bay, Western Australia (who was living in Sydney), Jennifer Patterson from Townsville and Evelyn Schraber from Alice Springs. At the time the women were recruited TAA chairman Sir Kenneth Vial said that he hoped the three girls would be the 'forerunners of more Aboriginal hostesses with the company'.[97]

The 1960s, going into the 1970s, were a very progressive period for Australia. The postwar baby boomers were coming of age, and Australia was still an industrial country with an expanding economy. Unions were strong, and in 1972 Australia elected the most progressive government in its history under Gough Whitlam. Support for Aboriginal Australians was on the rise, along with the inclusive policy of multiculturalism that was supposed to bury the mentality of Australia's past as a xenophobic outpost of the British Empire. The airline hostesses were part of the 'boomer' demographic, and some were no doubt influenced by the atmosphere of sexual liberation and second-wave feminism. But for the most part they were professionally focused, and that suppressed any sense that sexy ad campaigns that were becoming a part of airline promotions were exploitative. That was just part of the times, and part of the fun, as they got on with the job. And it was still exciting to be taking an active role in defining this job, this profession that was still very much a work in progress, no matter how gruelling it was on the long shift home. What was sustaining for most of these young women was the *esprit de corps* that had previously started to gel with unionisation. That was a foundation, and a source of hope, to get them through the turbulent 1960s and early 1970s and into a new era of negotiation.

Notes

1   The inaugural flight of the Boeing 707 'City of Canberra' jet flight from Sydney to San Francisco.

2   A. Wharton, *Building the Cold War: Hilton International Hotels and Modern Architecture*, University of Chicago Press, Chicago, 2001, p. 1. Australia's first Hilton Hotel was in Sydney in 1974.

3   The flight time between New York and London was reduced by almost half (six-and-a-half hours, with a reduction of five hours and forty-five minutes).

4   Qantas, 'World's first round world jet service...' *Qantas Empire Airways*, vol. 25, no. 9, September 1959, pp. 1–3, 20–1.

5   C. James, 'No fear of flying', *Observer*, 10 January 1982, pp. 29, 31.

6   In 1951 the book was made into the film *No Highway in the Sky* starring James Stewart and Marlene Dietrich.

7   N. Shute, *No Highway*, Vintage, London, [1948] 2009, p. 99.

8   In 1961, Boeing created a special model 707-138B Vjet with a shortened fuselage suitable for landing on the short runway at Nadi, Fiji.

9   Saville Row Shirt Company made other uniforms for Qantas during the 1950s and 1960s.

10   For a detailed account of the Qantas uniforms see P. Black, *The Flight Attendant's Shoe*, NewSouth, Sydney, 2011.

11   For a comprehensive account of gay and male flight attendants in the US see Phil Tiemeyer, *Plane Queer: Labor, Sexuality and AIDS in the History of the Male Flight Attendants*, University of California Press, Berkley, 2013.

12   D. Harris, interview with the author, 22 November 2015.

13   Y. Keller, '"Was it right to love her brother's wife so passionately?": Lesbian pulp novels and US lesbian identity, 1950–1965', *American Quarterly*, vol. 57, no. 2, 2005, p. 388. By 1965, lesbian themes in fiction were mostly silenced as they were placed in the category of pornography.

14   P. Christian, *The Edge of Twilight*, Crest Book, New York, 1959, p. 34.

15   Anon, 'Skyways-airport', *Sydney Morning Herald*, 9 July 1979, p. 6.

16   *Skyways* was a Crawford Production, with 188 episodes aired between 1979 and 1981.

17   S. Love-Davies, interview with the author, 7 February 2015.

18   E. Ronsisvalle, interview with the author, September 2010.

19   Anon, 'Japanese in Sydney to train as air hostesses', *Sydney Morning Herald*, 11 August 1958, p. 3.

20   Anon, 'Tokyo here they come again!', *Qantas Staff News*, vol. 29, no. 17, 1981, p. 1. M. P. Laffey Inman, interview with the author, 24 March 2013 said that Northwest Airlines Japanese-speaking stewardesses stopped wearing kimonos on the Tokyo flights as there were concerns about them exiting the aircraft and assisting the passengers in an emergency.

21   C. Yano, *Airborne Dreams: 'Nisei' Stewardesses and Pan American World Airways*, Duke University Press, Durham and London, 2011, p. 4

22   Cathay Pacific Advertisement, *Panorama*, April 1962, p. 3.

23   Evadne Price, 1968. *Air Hostess in Love*. London: John Gresham, p.58.

24   D. James, 'Reporter trains as an air hostess', *Australian Women's Weekly*, 11 June 1958, pp. 8–9.

25   ibid.

26   S. A. Casson, *The Yellow Canary: From Butler Air Transport to Ansett Express*, Self-published, Springfield Lakes, Queensland, 2014, p. 55.

27   ibid, p. 214.

28   Ansett-ANA Advertisement, 'Ansett-ANA Golden Supper Club', *The Age*, 28 May 1959, p. 2. The Ansett-ANA Lockheed L-188 Electra began

service on the 18th March 1959.

29   N. Witcomb, *Up Here and Down There*, Self-published, Adelaide, 1986, p. 115.

30   L. Escolme-Schmidt, *Glamour in the Skies: The Golden Age of the Air Stewardess*, The History Press, Stroud, Gloucestershire, 2009, p. 111.

31   BOAC Paper Dresses (1967), accessed 12 January 2016 <https://www.youtube.com/watch?v=h2XkQfmjRVE>.

32   Qantas, 'Flight hostess vacancies' advertisement, *Age*, 6 November 1959, p. 11.

33   A. Dwyer, 'She's got her wings – and £14 a week', 'Teenagers Weekly' in *Australian Women's Weekly*, 8 July 1959, p. 6.

34   G. Panter Nielsen, *From Sky Girl to Flight Attendant: Women and the Making of a Union*, Cornell University, Cornell, 1982, p. 82.

35   Anon, '"Common-sense" Test for Air Hostesses', *Age*, 4 July 1961, p. 11.

36   P. Merlehan, interview with the author, 27 July 2015.

37   Anon, 'Common-sense test for air hostesses', *Age*, 4 July 1961, p. 11.

38   ibid.

39   J. Dally-Watkins, interview with the author, 9 September 2015.

40   P. Gregory-Quilter, interview with the author, 22 June 2004.

41   J. Dally-Watkins, interview with the author, 9 September 2015.

42   P. Woodley, interview with the author, 12 March 2015.

43   Witcomb, *Up Here and Down There*, p. 312.

44   Dawne Walker Academy advertisement, *Sydney Morning Herald*, 5 September 1979, p. 13.

45   P. Gregory-Quilter, interview with the author, 22 June 2004.

46   P. Gregory-Quilter left training in 1983 to become a personnel controller at Qantek (the Qantas computer section) where she worked until 1991.

47   P. Gregory-Quilter, interview with the author, 22 June 2004.

48   Ethel Brunton-Gibb was a well-known radio star having played the role of Mrs Lawson in the long-running radio play *Blue Hills*. She was employed by Qantas to teach elocution.

49   R. Sutherland, interview with the author, 3 September 2015.

50   M. Gibson, 'TAA Memo to Air Hostesses', 1960.

51   K. Minassian, interview with the author, 28 March 2013.

52   ibid.

53   B. Maunsell, interview with the author, 26 April 2012

54   M. Lawson, *Qantas Flight Hostess Manual*, 1963, p. 86.

55   ibid.

56   B. Maunsell, interview with the author, 26 April 2012.

57   S. Terkel, *Working*, Avon Books, New York, [1972] 1975, pp. 78–9.

58   Lawson flew until December 1966 when she married Terry Lawson a

Qantas flight steward.

59 The Mocambo had been built in the 1950s by a consortium of Pan American pilots, who saw the potential of having a hotel there that offered accommodation at international standards. R. G. Crocombe, *The Pacific Islands and the USA*, Institute of Pacific Studies, University of South Pacific, Rarotonga and Suva and Pacific Islands Development Program East West Center, Honolulu, 1995, p. 79. They also built The Fijian on Yanuca Island.

60 D. Harris, interview with the author, 22 November 2015.

61 R. Bailey, interview with the author, 16 November 2012.

62 J. Davie, interview with the author, September 2008. Davie flew from 1967 to 1970, then became Hostess Trainer 1970 to 1974, Hostess Controller 1974 to 1978, Qantas recruitment to 1980, then other roles, leaving in 1991.

63 In 1968 an airline sacked an air hostess for being overweight in 'Round Robin', 'Pity the hostess with the mostest!', *Australian Women's Weekly*, 13 March 1968, p. 52.

64 J. Davie, interview with the author, September 2008.

65 K. M. Barry, *Femininity in Flight: A History of Flight Attendants*, Duke University Press, Durham and London, 2007, p.137.

66 It was not until 1981 that glasses and contact lenses could be worn by air hostesses.

67 J. Evans & N. K. Daw, *An Iconic Airline: The Story of Airlines of South Australia*, Self-published, Adelaide, 2012, p. 147.

68 J. Young, 'Airline with teenage hostesses', *Australian Women's Weekly*, 29 June 1960, p. 36.

69 M. Reid, interview with the author, 22 October 2015. Ansett air hostess 1964 to 1967. At one point Qantas employed a 19-year-old but she wasn't a success so they reverted to 21 years and over.

70 M. Reid, interview with the author, 22 October 2015.

71 Statement by air hostess superintendent, TAA, November 1962 in M. Robinson, 'A History of the Airline Hostesses' Association 1955–1981', Honours Thesis, Flinders University of South Australia, p. 13.

72 E. Wynne, 'Rollerskating waitresses from Perth's His Majesty's Theatre in the 1960s: never spilled a drop', 702 ABC Perth, 10 November 2015, accessed 20 December 2015 <http://www.abc.net.au/news/2015-11-10/perth-1960s-rollerskating-waitresses-never-spilled-a-drop/6927392>.

73 W. Georgetti-Remkes, interview with the author, 5 September 2015.

74 ibid.

75 ibid.

76 Anon, 'Quest for hostess with most joins the Australian Aviation Hall of Fame', 24 September 2012, accessed 20 December

2015 <http://www.news.com.au/national/queensland/quest-for-hostess-with-most-joins-australian-aviation-hall-of-fame/story-fndo4ckr-1226479786338>.

77   Anon, 'Our choice of the week', *Navy News*, 17 September 1965, p. 7.

78   Anon, 'Beauty on the wing', *Qantas News*, vol. 20, no. 12, 14 July 1972, p. 1.

79   S. Foster, interview with the author, 16 February 2016.

80   The first time Johnny Farnham appeared on national television was on 'Kommotion' Channel 10 and he sang the Susan Jones song. <https://www.youtube.com/watch?v=UUuWXgXUF94>.

81   Ansett-ANA, 'Whoever you are please stop sending our Miss Jones roses', *The Age*, 8 November 1967, p. 3.

82   Photograph by David Mist.

83   Anon, 'Birds that fly', *PS,* vol. 2, no. 6, December 1971/January 1972, p. 8.

84   J. Gerard, *Jet Stewardess*, Lancer Books, New York, 1962, p. 13.

85   The first European intake had been recruited from Zurich and Geneva and they became known collectively as 'The Swiss Girls', even though later recruits were from Germany and France.

86   I. Legge, one of 'The Swiss Girls' recalls that there were some charter flights with Germans, and French was important on the Noumea flights. I. Legge, email correspondence with the author, 12 October 2016.

87   R. Bailey, interview with the author, 6 September 2013. Bailey flew for seven years from 1962 to 1969.

88   I. Legge, telephone conversation with the author, 3 September 2013. Legge flew from 1962 to 1965.

89   R. Bailey, interview with the author, 6 September 2013.

90   Australian Force Vietnam, Briefing Notes – Qantas Charter Saigon/Sydney, c. 1965-1972 from 'Qantas Remembering the Great Years', Facebook.

91   K. Minassian, interview with the author, 28 February 2015. TAA air hostess 1968 to 1971.

92   Anon, 'Your career – air hostessing', *Dawn: A Magazine for the Aboriginal People of New South Wales*, vol. 17, no. 6, June 1968.

93   G. Franks, 'Air hostesses make good housewives', *Press* (Christchurch, NZ), 19 August 1967, p 2.

94   S. Bryant, interview with the author, 5 June 2012.

95   R. Hulsbergen, *The Aborigine Today*, Paul Hamlyn, Sydney, 1971.

96   Anon, 'Papua's first air hostess arrives', *Canberra Times*, 13 June 1969, p. 3.

97   Anon, 'Aboriginals take to the air', *Aboriginal Quarterly,* vol. 1, no. 3, 1979, pp. 25–7.

Chapter Six

GOODBYE HOSTESSES, HELLO FLIGHT ATTENDANTS

6.1. 'A Portrait of Feminine Fury'

> *The brunette gasped. 'Air stewardesses can't marry? What is the airline thinking of?' 'Of business', snapped a reddish-haired girl.*[1]
>
> Helen Wells, *Silver Wings for Vicki*, 1947

The film adaptation of Arthur Hailey's 1968 bestselling novel *Airport,* was nominated for ten Academy Awards, including best picture, and it created a genre of disaster movies that proved popular throughout the 1970s.[2] Dean Martin stars as the captain and Jacqueline Bisset plays the stewardess, who, in the throes of a high drama with a suicide bomber on board, announces her pregnancy to the captain. It thus had the usual successful romance-action double plot. Sue Love-Davies, who became a Qantas flight hostess in 1970, remembers the film. She was living in a share house with her boyfriend at that time and his mother didn't approve of her wanting to be a flight hostess: 'I was in training school, and his mother marched me off to see this movie, saying, "this is what happens in the airline industry" '.[3] Love-Davies felt that everyone was against her career plans, so she thought, 'No, I'm just going to do what I want to do from now on'.

The profession was changing and one of the recruits in Love-Davies' year had been a Bunny in the Playboy Club in London. With second-wave feminism in the news, Love-Davies' colleague may well have thought what was good enough for Gloria Steinem was good enough for her.[4] Love-Davies sympathised with what Pat Gregory-Quilter might have thought about having an ex–Playboy Bunny as part of the training cohort, sensing that she might have a challenge on her hands. There was definitely a new type of air hostess coming on board. For Carol Locket, the decision to join an airline was based on a plan to work for two years and then be eligible for the generous staff travel discount, which included overseas travel.[5] The short-term plan was set aside and she ended up working in the job for 43 years! She was not alone in this attitude to the job, and engaging in relatively short-term employment created an atmosphere of 'girls having fun' before they would head off overseas. Air hostessing still offered a sense of independence and a very different lifestyle to the types of employment that were on offer for young women in their twenties. It was also one of the few jobs with any prestige that you could walk into without any qualifications.[6] The relative independence of the air hostess was still a challenging concept for some with expectations that young women would continue to get married in their early twenties. It was not unusual for boyfriends to be threatened by the mobile lives of their air hostess girlfriends, but most air hostesses were happy to trade Saturday-night rounds of beer at the local football club for a stay at the first-class Parmelia Hotel in Perth.

As the world changed and young women sought different types of relationships, inequalities in the workplace continued to become more apparent. Love-Davies started to see the injustices inherent in the job; for example, the pilots and stewards could marry as they pleased. It was because of issues like this, and a conversation on board a plane with Kate Heery, the President of the Overseas Branch of the Airline Hostesses' Association, that Love-Davies became involved with the union, eventually becoming Secretary/Treasurer of the Overseas Branch of the Airline Hostesses' Association:

> You would see these girls who married stewards and then they'd have to leave flying…When the girls married the pilots I suppose it was sort of to say, 'oh well I don't have to work anymore'. But there were a lot of girls that married stewards who really wanted to keep flying. I just didn't think that was fair that the females had to leave.[7]

Another issue that concerned her was that flight hostesses didn't have the same promotional opportunities: 'I could see the stewards automatically getting promotions after so many years of service – it was not based on ability – who weren't really suitable for doing the job'. Tensions thus escalated around a gendered division of labour. When Love-Davies was promoted to Senior Flight Hostess, a position she had to apply for, she would train and check the flight hostesses in a specific way, only to have some of the stewards undermine her, saying to trainees, 'don't take any notice of her love, just stick with us'.

> *Our Qantas Sheilas are Grouse, and that's the Drum.*
> *Our Qantas hostesses are the greatest and that's the truth…*
> *She wants you to feel like a guest rather than a passenger. And*
> *so does our head steward, the boss cocky of the cabin crew. He*

Anything you can do, I can do better.

They're both right. And they both have their place
on a Qantas jet. That's why Qantas introduced stewards in the
first place. Because they do some things better than hostesses.
Then again, hostesses have a few things over stewards.
It all adds up to the best service you'll find
on an airline. That's why we're the world's favourite.

QANTAS 50

'Anything you can do, I can do better', Qantas advertisement, 1970
For Qantas's 50th anniversary, one advertisement inadvertently highlighted some of the tension on board the cabins between the flight hostesses and the flight stewards. Courtesy of Qantas Historical Collection.

> *keeps a sharp eye on the whole shivoo while the stewards serve
> you the bonzer tucker and grouse grog.*
>
> Qantas advertisement, c. 1967

The gendered division in the Qantas cabin crew was portrayed in a series of advertisements in the late 1960s and early 1970s. 'Our Magnificent Men' gushed one advertisement:

Looking after you is a man-size job. That's why we have stewards. We feel they add that little extra to make wining and dining aloft a special pleasure. Our men are proud of their reputation. We can only think of one thing that will impress you as much. Our gorgeous girls.[8]

In the same period another advertisement featured a steward and a flight hostess standing back to back in a classic war-of-the-sexes pose, with the headline, 'Anything you can do, I can do better'. Under the image the text read:

They're both right. And they both have their place on a Qantas jet. That's why Qantas introduced stewards in the first place. Because they do some things better than hostesses. Then again, hostesses have a few things over the stewards.[9]

These advertisements allude to the differences in the work practices in the cabins and, while it was in Qantas's interests to defend both the flight hostesses and the stewards, they could well have been picking up on the fact that times were changing and the differences on board were becoming obvious and had to be explained. The differences extended beyond the cabins, with Qantas still operating separate training schools for the stewards and the flight hostesses.

In 1970, Qantas celebrated its 50th anniversary and a new campaign was started with an advertisement featuring a beaming flight hostess, alongside the slogan, 'The Friendliness of the Long Distance Australian'. Now, even the smile was a matter for competitive international marketing: 'Every airline has smiling hostesses. But nobody has that special open-hearted Australian smile except Qantas'. What Qantas failed to notice was that their workforce of 230 flight hostesses had stopped smiling, and on the 1st July 1970 the women started a seven-day strike over improved salaries and conditions, to match the domestic hostesses' award of the 4th June that same year. The *Australian* ran a front-page story, 'Hostesses extend strike by 24 hours' along with a page-three profile, 'The Qantas girls: a portrait of feminine fury'. Journalist Janet Hawley described the women at the inaugural strike meeting:

> The tiers of leggy, glamorous females propped in the world's latest fashions on boxes and tabletops in a small room at the back of the Air Pilots Federation Sydney offices, came to some sort of order...the girls listened, a captive vision of feminine fury.[10]

Beverley Green, who had been flying for three years, said what many of the flight hostesses were probably thinking about their role in the airlines: 'We've been idiots – we've fooled ourselves into believing the airlines advertising that we are polite, attractive, never an opposing word. We've been polite long enough'.[11] Bev Maunsell was vice-president of the Overseas Branch of the Airline Hostesses' Association and remembers the lessons learnt from the strike in terms of handling the media: 'they lined us all up and they asked us all questions and then they cut and pasted it', with the aim of making us 'look stupid'.[12] But the women learnt fast, and the industrial muscle of the Overseas Branch was recognised when the flight hostesses achieved a victory.

The strengthening of the union (both domestic and overseas) had flow-on effects. Attitudes changed about what the air hostesses were prepared to put up with, and work-practices on board also changed. At TAA, there were concerns about the quality of the service and the attitude of the air hostesses. Elaine (Smith) Swain, the TAA air hostess superintendent, sent a memorandum to all her staff asking them to reflect on the question, 'What do you think makes passengers want to travel with TAA?'[13] Her concern was about how the air hostesses were engaging with the passengers, based on a sense that the TAA 'friendly image' was being lost. A long questionnaire was attached as her attempt to correct this situation.

The real glamour wasn't on the flight; it was once you got off it.
Mary Pat Laffey Inman, Northwest Airlines US flight attendant,
1958 to 2000

Elaine Swain's concerns about the standards of the air hostesses could well have been in response to the changes in the industry. Passenger numbers were growing and staff found it hard to keep up the 'emotional labour' aspect of cabin work.[14] Global competition among airlines was increasing and, since most airlines bought the same model aircraft, it was the air hostess that provided the point of difference. National Airlines in the US ran a sexist and controversial campaign where the stewardesses wore badges saying 'Fly Me', and 'I'm Tammy. You can fly me nonstop to Miami'. Protest groups, such as the National Organisation of Women, retaliated with posters like, 'I'm Cheryl. Fly Me. Go Fly Yourself National'.

Mary Pat Laffey Inman had started in the 'white glove era' with the Minneapolis-based Northwest Airlines in 1958, the same year that Mohawk Airlines employed the first African-American stewardess.[15] She remembers the 'Fly Me' campaign and, while she found it degrading, she laughed at it as well. In some ways her reaction was understandable; she knew how the airlines were happy to trade on the stereotype of the young stewardess as glamorous and available, but she also knew that it was a marketing strategy and not a true representation of what things were like for the majority of air hostesses in their everyday working lives. But times were changing. The generations of air hostesses who were used to laughing off the behaviour of lonesome male flight crew, or passengers knocking on their hotel door at midnight with 'my wife doesn't understand me' stories, had decided that maybe they'd had enough, especially if they had Germaine Greer's *The Female Eunuch* on the bedside table.[16] As second-wave feminism was taking hold in the cabins and on the ground, a new generation of women was alert to a possible new world, and the airline companies they worked for seemed hopelessly out of touch on gender issues.[17]

In the US Laffey Inman was at the forefront of these changes. As a Northwest stewardess, she was a union representative on the Airlines Steward and Stewardess Association and as a result of the Civil Rights Act of 1964 and its Title VII, she realised that she and other stewardesses were being discriminated against because of lack of promotional opportunities compared to the male pursers.[18] In 1970, a class action suit, *Laffey et al vs Northwest*, was pleaded as a Title VII Civil Rights case and also as an Equal Pay Act case. Despite the court finding that Northwest had violated the rights of the stewardesses, the case was dragged through the courts for fifteen years until 1985, when the judgment was upheld that Northwest pay US$62 million in damages to the stewardesses. Some of the women who opted out of the lawsuit did so because they, as women and as stewardesses, 'didn't think they had rights'. There was also a fairly conservative cohort, which was not unusual for the profession in general, who didn't think they should be taking jobs from the male pursers, with the attitude, 'I'm stealing

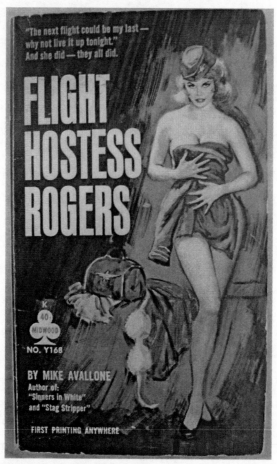

Book Cover *Flight Hostess Rogers,* **1962**
Since the 1960s airlines marketed the figure of the air hostess as a point of difference, and she was sexualised in a way that would have been impossible to imagine in relation to any other safety professional. The pulp fiction novel Flight Hostess Rogers *is an example of the stereotype surrounding the air hostess that dominated representations of air hostesses for many years. Courtesy of Tower Publications.*

the shoes from the male purser's children'. The job was still being perceived by management as a job for a family man and not for a family- or career-oriented woman. The emotional costs of these disputes took their toll, especially as the air hostesses who worked for the unions also continued to work full-time. This is commonly known in the industry as the 'triple shift': women working their jobs, organising a home life and also finding time to do the union work.

6.2. The 'Old Boilers' and Other Disputes

Carol Locket had been a secretary before she joined TAA and had taken a pay cut, so she could have what she thought would be a 'glamour job'. While it was still seen as a prestigious job, it was very poorly paid and had difficult working conditions. In 1975, International Women's Year, Locket, who was still wearing white cotton gloves to work, went on the first ever strike of domestic airline hostesses. For her to go on strike was 'so outrageous. It was so exciting'[19]. The strike famously became known as the 'Old Boilers Dispute' referring to Sir Reginald Ansett's description of the executive committee of Airline Hostesses' Association. Locket joined 1,600 women in the industrial action on the 25th March 1975 to achieve better pay, the opportunity to fly until they were three months pregnant, and to continue flying until they were 45.[20] Ansett's patronising attitude to the air hostesses included calling them 'glorified waitresses' and his rebuking them by saying, 'Frankly I've had them. We can run our airline without people to serve drinks'.[21] This comment hurt as it undercut the serious safety role the air hostesses undertook every time a plane took to the skies. The strike was strategically called at Easter, the busiest time of the year, forcing the airline to quickly resolve the issue. Agreement was reached on the day of the strike, with an apology extracted from 'Sir Reg'.

The 'Old Boilers Dispute' became a tipping point, and Shayne (Swann) Nealon who had joined TAA in 1974, and who would go on to become the Federal Secretary of the Airline Hostesses' Association, remembers the overriding sense amongst the union officials and their members of a lack of respect they had no intention of tolerating.[22] When Nealon had been recruited she was in a large cohort of about thirty-six and at that time she thinks TAA were looking for air hostesses who could be characterised as 'nice people who lived next door'.[23] The airline liked country girls, as they were often more independent, and they employed nurses for the same reason. There was also the sense that when you joined an airline you became part of an occupational community, and that the young women selected would have the ability and desire to socialise with the crew. In this way, your relationship to the airline was important. When Nealon was at training school a union representative visited on a recruiting drive and talked about the importance of rostering systems and rest breaks in terms of the Air Hostess Award, along with safety incidents and peer support through union processes.

The 'Old Boilers Dispute' mobilised a number of the air hostesses to take their careers more seriously, and Nealon decided to contribute by becoming more active in the union. But not all of the employees were staunch unionists. Nealon remembers people 'bailing me up in the lounge saying, I disagree with the fact that you're going to let people stay beyond age 35. I disagree with the fact that women should be able to stay and have maternity leave'. Despite dissent from some, the dispute and the intolerance of entrenched conditions that air hostesses had endured for so long became the start of a dynamic phase in the industrial relations of the profession. Air hostesses were pioneers not only in the sky, but also among female professionals generally.

6.3. 'Like a Town in the Sky' – The 747 Jumbo Jet

It was not only the domestic airlines that were having challenges industrially. In 1971, a storm was starting to brew in the Qantas cabins. The unrest centred around the introduction of the Boeing

747 'Jumbo Jet' in September. Rather than accept the first Boeing 747, Qantas waited for the Boeing 747B, which had been designed to suit the specific long-haul operations from Australia. The plane was huge. It could hold almost 400 passengers and was nearly three times the size of the 707. The tail was as high as a six-storey building and the cabin featured a spiral staircase leading up to the Captain Cook First Class Lounge. The lounge was a luxury that didn't last; by 1980 all lounges on the 747s were converted into business-class seating. The main impact of the Boeing 747 was that it put air travel within reach of the 'everyday' Australian. Qantas filled the seats with special holiday packages to destinations such as South-East Asia.[24]

There was a shift in recruitment with Qantas management deciding to actively recruit university-trained personnel to fill the positions on the 747s. Kate Heery was the flight hostess on board the crew that brought the first Boeing 747B from Seattle to Australia, and she represented this new type of flight hostess.[25] She had graduated with a Bachelor of Arts (Honours) from the University of Sydney. Once embarking on the career of flight hostess she became actively engaged in the Airline Hostesses' Association, and became President of the Overseas Branch of the union in 1972.[26] Lesley (Picken) Squires was another Qantas flight hostess with university qualifications, a Bachelor of Science from the Australian National University, and would become President of the Overseas Branch between 1981 and 1983. Her father had worked for Qantas for thirty-two years, and as a young child she had taken many flights overseas. She also remembers the differ-ence the 747 made to flying:

> ...as a child, travelling with my parents, I was the little junior hostie for many years. Following along, handing

249

out the menus, or the Crossing the Line Certificates, behind the hostie down the back – back in the day when you could do that. When the Jumbo arrived it wasn't possible really to have that same sort of fun relationship with the children on board because there were hundreds of them. Well not hundreds, but too many to play with. On a 707 you might have had two or three young children on the aircraft.[27]

Even with the introduction of the Boeing 747, there were still only three flight hostesses compared to twelve stewards, with four of the stewards in supervisory roles.[28] In what would become a major point of contention the flight hostesses became responsible to the Flight Service Director, a newly appointed position, and this meant the women were no longer directly responsible to the captain. Graeme Cant, who was a Qantas pilot from 1966 to 2000, said that the previous arrangement had worked well as far as the pilots were concerned with very few occasions when they became involved in anything happening in the cabin.[29] The relationships with captains tended to be a fairly benign 'gentleman-like' relationship – they may have told a flight hostess off for not wearing her hat, but usually not much more than that. The stewards were delighted to have at last achieved the control of the flight hostesses they had been seeking since the 1940s.[30] Under the new arrangements, the Flight Service Director also took over the paperwork, something which up until then had been the flight hostess's job.

Maureene Martin, a 1964 Qantas recruit, could remember the generation of flight hostesses who flew before her as being recruited, typically, on the basis of a leaving certificate, nursing qualifications or with foreign language skills, or because they had been 'lawyers' daughters or judges' daughters, or doctors' daughters'.[31] She had become a check hostess within three years, she thought because Marj de Tracy liked her, and she reciprocated, describing her as 'wonderful, very feisty, tough, [and] a bit rule-conscious'.[32] This personal aspect of the job, of whether you were liked or not by the senior management, was to play an important part in something like the roster system. Before the bid system (based on seniority) was put in place, crew were allocated a roster by senior staff and this meant that it was preferable to stay on the 'good side' of the person who did the roster. A bottle of champagne delivered to the right person was not unheard of.

Martin stayed working with Qantas for thirty-seven years, taking redundancy from the position of Director of Cabin Services in 1991. In 1974, she replaced Kate Heery as President of the Overseas Branch of Airline Hostesses' Association, and in 1976 she became Federal President of Airline Hostesses' Association. She was keenly aware of tensions around the crewing on the 747s.[33] The big difference between the 747 and the 707s was that on the 707s the stewards and the flight hostesses were used to clearly demarcated roles. On the flights, the crews would work hard together to get everything done, but the flight hostesses still felt that things were unfair. Martin outlines an example: 'the minute you got to a hotel, we got the last room in the hotel, we got the last seat on the bus...'[34] So with the 747 and the fact that the flight hostesses would be under the rule of the stewards, this was the last thing many of the flight hostesses wanted.

The domestic hostesses continued to have their own issues. In July 1976, they went on a twelve-hour strike in response to a proposal by TAA to reduce the number of hostesses by one on the Boeing 727s. Ansett became involved when it refused to confirm whether or not it was going to do the same with their air hostesses.[35] TAA's general manager, Lyndon McKenzie, said the decision to cut crew numbers was because procedures had been streamlined and the number of first-class passengers had decreased.[36] Indeed, the Australian airline industry was suffering a downturn with increased fares discouraging bookings, less businessmen flying and local holiday bookings dropping off with cheap holiday packages to South-East Asia. At the same time it was suggested that domestic airlines, which typically undertook ten hostess training schools a year, could be reduced to none after 1976.[37] With 20,000 passengers stranded by the strike, the Air Hostesses' Association reached an agreement with the airlines, with the TAA hostesses returning to work later that same day, while the Ansett air hostesses returned to work early the following morning. One air hostess described what the service would be like with the reduced numbers: 'Here's your coffee, sir, catch it if you can', and another said how the week before she had worked for twelve hours and forty minutes without a break.[38] A TAA spokesman spoke in defence of the airline, outlining the special conditions that the women had, including weekly allowances for cosmetics, hairdressing, stockings, laundering and shoes, and he went on to list free uniforms, free transport to the airport from the city, transport to and from home from 9pm and before 7am, first-class accommodation when away from home, six weeks' annual leave, and about twenty-six duty hours a week, of which only twelve are spent in the air.[39]

Grooming costs were also an industrial issue for the air hostesses. With standards to keep, Qantas flight hostesses would try to save money by having their hair cut and buying make-up overseas. As with the domestic air hostesses, they would receive a shoe and stocking allowance, and again they would often be purchased overseas to save costs. It wasn't just the women who had grooming standards: even though the men weren't weighed, they were expected to wear the uniform appropriately and be neat and tidy. While some of the stewards seem to have gotten away with the big moustaches of the 1970s, by the 1980s it was expected that beards had to be kept 'neat and trimmed' with 'good definition and naval type lines'.[40]

The issue of weight continued with air hostesses threatened with dismissal or rostered off and given ground duties until the weight came off. In the early 1970s, the TAA air hostesses were still being weighed at their first interview, and then weekly during training school, and then it was 'a three strikes and you're out'.[41] Kathy Minassian said that being overweight was the worst sin you could commit:

> Our weight was checked and God forbid that extra pound gained, we would be rapped over the knuckles and told to lose the weight immediately. Weight was strictly scaled to height, never mind one's anatomical build. We all knew 'friendly doctors' who would write prescriptions for Lasix or similar, which we would take prior to a flight when we were due to be checked. When I look back this was a very dangerous practice given a young woman's time of the month when there is a natural build-up of fluid. Still, most of us survived.[42]

Discriminatory practices around weight and appearance were minor compared to the issue that Qantas was the only international airline to employ a majority of male cabin staff. Also discriminatory was the fact that the 747 flight hostesses were doing exactly the same work as the men but in non-supervisory roles. There was another cause of unrest in relation to the 747s when it was announced that more crews would be required as the Boeing 747Bs were being reconfigured with seats replacing the upstairs lounge areas. The Airline Hostesses' Association wanted flight hostesses to fill those new positions. Arguing their case was difficult as they had to deal with the fact that the numbers were against them. Martin commented that:

> ...we were easily successful if we were dealing with issues that didn't affect flight stewards. If we were arguing with them about hairstyles, marriage, stockings, shoes, weight, we would be very successful. But the minute we started to argue with them about another girl on the aeroplane, things like that – promotion – then they would say, hmm, 1,600 of them (stewards), 400 of them (flight hostesses).[43]

Unwilling to recognise the world had changed, a Qantas spokesman, suggested the company was happy to maintain the status quo, that the present staffing arrangements dated back to when there were all-male crews on the flying boats, and that 'stewards were more likely to make careers of their jobs'.[44] The one advantage that the flight hostesses did have over the stewards was that the media preferred to have a photo of them on the front page. Martin again:

> ...a bunch of blokes strike and it's not much different to another bunch of blokes striking. But women striking was quite unusual, especially women en masse, who purposely got themselves all dollied up for the press. I mean, quite a lot of the things we managed to do we

did because we threatened to put Qantas on the front page of the *Telegraph*. I mean, that's how we got married hostesses.[45]

So the irony here was that the women could trade on their good looks as it suited them, and they also had the advantage of having sophisticated people skills, and, in particular, having practised it in the cabin they knew how to tailor their talk to deal with men, even when they were being intimidated. In this way the profession, unintentionally, had prepared them to take on disputes dealing with labour relations and men.

6.4. Lifting the Marriage Bar

As mentioned earlier, during wartime there was a small number of air hostesses who were married, but up until the 1970s the airlines operated under the policy of recruiting only single women. The exception was Bush Pilots, a small airline flying out of Cairns, which employed Pamela Watling. She was 35 years old and had three children at school. She underwent training with TAA for a 'couple of days' learning how to create an operation manual for future air hostesses. It was an exciting life as 'Bushies' would fly up to New Guinea and take charters all over Australia, including trans-porting pearl divers from Thursday Island to Broome. Unusually the air hostesses were paid by the hour, so for once, if they were delayed anywhere, they would be paid for the inconvenience.

The Qantas flight stewards had always been able to marry and most of them had the support of wives who looked after the home and children while they were away. Dianne Imison's husband, Phil, worked for Qantas for thirty-four years, mainly as an air chef working in the galley. On the London run he would be away for twelve days and then he would be at home for nine days, something the couple called 'three-quarter down time'. He was staff number 113, out of 7,000, and as a long-term employee Imison was a shareholder with Qantas, converting his bonuses to shares. As a family, they worked out the difficulties of extended periods away, with Imison able to have 'quality time' with his three children on the leave periods.[46]

Although there were other industries where women had to resign when they married, such as banks and schools, the marriage bar on women in the Commonwealth Public Service was only lifted in 1966. In the airline industry some of the resistance to married air hostesses was the fear from management that 'once women marry they go to the pack'.[47] Maureene Martin, representing the Airline Hostesses' Association, went to the manager of Qantas cabin crew, knowing that he was a staunch Methodist, and argued that they would go to the *Daily Telegraph* and say, as she put it, that 'Qantas is quite happy for us to live in sin and do nothing to us, but if I get married you'll fire me. So they changed their mind and we were allowed to be married and we didn't go to the pack [laughs]'.[48]

The marriage bar was overturned for Qantas international flight hostesses on the 4th August 1972 but not yet for domestic air hostesses. Margaret Robinson was studying to be an accountant but her university lecturer (whose wife was the chief hostess for Ansett Airlines of South Australia) said she was 'too young to be stuck in an office', and encouraged her to become an air hostess, saying there was concessional travel on both domestic and international airlines and the job was fun, interesting and lively.[49] Robinson started flying with Ansett Airlines of South Australia in 1969 and flew for fourteen years, resigning at the level of check hostess. She went on to write a PhD, 'Qantas Cabin Crew and their Union', about the history of work relations between Qantas flight stewards, flight hostesses, pilots and management. On the 29th September 1972 the marriage bar was lifted for domestic air hostesses.[50] Robinson became the first air hostess in Adelaide to marry after the marriage bar was lifted but this was in opposition to management and even some of her colleagues.[51] She argued her case to the airline, but it reached a point where the Airline Hostesses' Association advised that all domestic air hostesses were preparing to strike if Ansett Airlines of South Australia had not eventually backed down and accepted her right to continue to fly after marriage.

It would not be until the 1974 industrial award that the flight hostesses secured maternity leave, and Martin, who was chair of the Overseas Branch of the AHA, remembers the Labor government being worried about the precedent it would set in other workplaces.[52] By 1975, Qantas had fifteen married couples and a marriage roster had been introduced allowing married couples to fly together. One steward commented that under the old system three or four months could go by without seeing his wife. By the mid-1970s, TAA had 750 air hostesses, Ansett 800 and Qantas 300.[53] And by 1977 it was estimated that approximately 30 per cent of them were married.[54] The fact that air hostesses could now marry not only helped their personal circumstances, but it took away the 'single girl' status that for so long had attracted speculative comments from male passengers. Pregnancy while working was not encouraged, and clearly articulated by the fact that there weren't any uniforms for pregnant air hostesses. The union had to fight hard to get maternity leave, and in 1975 Qantas granted six weeks. One flight hostess was strongly encouraged to come back to Qantas after the birth of her baby, as the union wanted a test case. She was still breastfeeding so she had to strap her breasts and, as there was no bidding system for rosters, her first trip away was a twelve-or fourteen-day trip to London. She left Qantas after a few months.[55] By 1978, conditions had improved and Qantas flight hostesses were able to take six months off before returning to work. There was also the option to work a 'short division roster', available to married crew, meaning flight hostesses would be away no more than five days, but usually one to three.[56]

> In those days there was no entertainment on board, so you were the entertainment.
>
> Kerry-Ann Murray, Ansett air hostess, 1977.[57]

Each year thousands of young women continued to apply for this popular profession, and at Ansett hostess supervisor Janet Haley described the type of 'girl' they were looking for as one 'with an outgoing personality, interested in and able to handle people'.[58] Kerry-Ann (Mowat) Murray was just the type Haley was looking for, and she joined Ansett in 1977 after there had been a long-term lull in recruitment.[59] It was actually Kerry-Ann's mother who had the desire to be an air hostess, but she had been too short. The two of them went on a holiday to Noumea, and while on the flight Murray's mother suggested that she walk up and down the aisle to see what it was like. She gave it a try and thought 'I can do this'. After the holiday it was her mother who submitted the applications to TAA and Ansett. Murray was interviewed for TAA but she thinks she may have missed out because when they asked her to go on the scales she noticed she had a big hole in her stocking, and so did they. She found herself instead in an Ansett intake of thirty-five women. It was fun for her being an air hostess and, despite taking her job seriously, life on board the plane was not beyond the great Australian tradition of the workplace practical joke. Because of the two-airline policy, with Ansett and TAA running the same planes at almost identical times, on one occasion the air hostesses swapped uniforms and flew on the other airline. It was easy to work on another plane as they were familiar with where everything was, and of course all the air hostesses were a standard size so it was easy to swap uniforms.

In 1976, eighty-six women from fifty-five airlines met in London at the 7th International Chief Hostess Conference. Four women represented Australia: Janette Davie (Qantas), Janet Hayley (Ansett), Connie Wright (East-West Airlines) and Elaine Smith (TAA).[60] The conference addressed the issue of why women were not reaching management level, especially as 75 per cent of cabin crew were female.[61] At that time TAA and Ansett had only two female executives, although Ansett were planning to introduce a management planning program that would include women.[62] Connie Wright, who was a flight hostess superintendent, said that in her position she had '...worked for five men for six years in my operations department and not once, in all the times they went to the bar, did they think I might also like to wet my whiskers, which explains their view of management'.[63] Sir Lenox Hewitt, who became Chairman of Qantas in August 1975, recalled Qantas in those days:

It was male dominated...At the end of each monthly board meeting the board would have lunch and would invite a guest to join and also a member of staff. My first occasion I said, 'Well, who's the senior woman on the staff?' There was a sort of hushed silence. I'm not sure – Jill's [Hickson] position was a very modest one as I remember it at the time. Whether or not I invited her as the first I can't now remember.[64]

It wasn't only the air hostesses that were being discriminated against. In February 1976, Deborah Wardley applied to Ansett for a position of trainee pilot but she had to wait until the following year to be granted an interview and, despite being more experienced and qualified than other men who received positions, she was rejected. Hers became the first contested anti-discrimination case in Australia and in 1979 the Equal Opportunity Tribunal found that Ansett had discriminated against her. During the hearing Ansett raised a number of objections about why women were unsuitable for flying including that they lacked strength, the inconvenience of menstrual cycles, the possibility of pregnancy and they even discussed the jewellery Wardley wore, saying that it could restrict her leaving a plane in an emergency. Subject to orders from the Supreme Court Ansett offered Wardley a job in October 1979, but it was only when Rupert Murdoch replaced Reginald Ansett that Wardley began flying on the 4th March 1980. Wardley flew with Ansett for ten years before moving to the Netherlands to work for KLM. While this was a groundbreaking case, Christine Davy had been flying with Connellan Airways since 1963, and was the first woman in Australia to become a check captain. She went on to work as a training captain on DC-3s and as a captain on Fokker Friendships.[65]

At the end of 1977, Ansett air hostesses were averaging four years of service and TAA slightly less. Qantas figures were improving, from averaging around eighteen months only five years earlier. There were still perks to the job. Qantas crews were still staying in first-class hotels all over the world – a lifestyle famously captured in the advertisements for Peter Stuyvesant cigarettes, which for over twenty years ran with the slogan, 'The International Passport to Smoking Pleasure'. The luxury didn't just come from lounging around hotel lobbies and swimming pools as

Qantas flight hostess supervisor Ann Harper said: 'When we get to a hotel for an overnight…we stop becoming the dispenser and we become the recipient'.[66]

'Galley Curtain' Ansett advertisement, 1980
At a time when air hostesses were challenging airline companies about their conditions of employment Ansett ran this advertisement to promote the new Boeing 737 service. The award-winning advertisement proved controversial as it highlighted the type of sexism that was evident in the industry. Courtesy of Ansett Archive.

Despite making some inroads regarding working conditions on board planes, air hostesses had to battle on other fronts, for instance in the way they were represented, as women and employees, in marketing campaigns. In November 1980 Ansett made an error of judgement and was called out for exploiting its female cabin crew. The company ran a double-page advertisement in the major Australian newspapers, ostensibly to announce the new fleet of Boeing 737s. The advertisement featured an air hostess standing in an aircraft cabin, naked except for a draped galley curtain. The image was accompanied with the headline, 'If the hostess was out of uniform would you know which airline you were flying with?' Campaign Palace, the company that created the advertisement, said the rationale behind the image was that research had pinpointed that the hostesses' uniform was the key visible difference between Ansett and TAA. They also said there was no point including pilots in the advertisement as they all wore blue uniforms, and the key message would have been lost. Yvonne Troy, the Federal Secretary of the Airlines Hostesses' Association denounced the advertisement saying it 'represented an absolute contradiction of the standards of safety, efficiency and decorum which airlines demanded of their cabin staff'.[67] This advertisement created a groundswell of opinion from women (and men) against this sexist representation of the profession. Outraged air hostesses also reacted individually to the advertisement by writing letters to the newspapers, opposing the way Ansett was using their image to bolster the sexual fantasies of heterosexual men.

This period of airline history saw a rapid growth of passenger traffic, with some of the airlines challenging the traditional capacity for air hostesses to offer friendliness as a part of the service. This kind of emotional labour was increasingly recognised by their unions and associations as part of the complex set of duties they were expected to perform in increasingly demanding workplaces. But first, basic rights, like marriage equality and continuity of service, had to be achieved. In that struggle, much was achieved by these women in a relatively short period of time.

6.5. The End of an Era: Flight Attendants

The men came on board because they should…they added a dimension.

Carol Locket, flight attendant, 1973 to 2016 [68]

I think when the males came into the cabin, that was the last barrier. It was then just an open job.

Brenda Oliver Harry, flight attendant, 1967 to 2001[69]

In January 1980, the regional domestic carrier East-West Airlines appointed three men to form part of the cabin crew. TAA followed in November that same year when training course number 299 began with twenty-three women and two men, Chris Mitchell and John McCashney. Chief hostess Flora (Christian) Devery made the announcement about the two male recruits in a circular with the comment, 'Equal rights are here to stay!'[70] It was also announced that all hostess supervisor positions would be renamed with 'flight attendant' replacing 'hostess'. By 1983, cabin crew on all airlines were called flight attendants.

Men had applied to be domestic flight attendants before the 1980s, but there were always reasons why they were deemed 'unsuitable'. Most of the domestic air hostesses embraced the idea of having men on board. Michelle Higgs, who had joined MacRobertson Miller Airlines (then a subsidiary of Ansett) in 1980 when she was 19 years old, thought 'there was nothing wrong with having males on board, but it required a new way of thinking as the tradition had always been for an all-female cabin crew'.[71] The introduction of male cabin crew also instigated the annual football game between Ansett and TAA, and it would appear that at this time Ansett employed many men who were 'excellent football players' just so they could beat TAA.[72]

The relationships between the men and women on board the planes had always been complex. As mentioned earlier, some of the Qantas stewards found the flight hostesses were 'good fun birds', while others found them snobby and unprepared to roll their sleeves up to help out; some of the women found the stewards were boorish and 'okker' beyond belief, and at other times fun and likeable characters. It was not necessarily fair to blame the individual characters as it was often the corporate culture that determined the types of behaviour.

6.6. Big Trouble: Taking on the Company

As a union official, one of the pilots' representatives said to me, you need to understand, Shayne, the flight attendants need to see themselves as a profession. They need to see themselves and be more assertive in relation to that.

Shayne Nealon, TAA air hostess, then Federal

Secretary FAAA [73]

Gender matters on board continued to surface at Qantas. Industrially, the 1980s proved a challenging time for the airline with hard-fought disputes that would turn flight hostess against flight hostess, flight hostess against steward, and steward against pilot. Early in 1979, Qantas operated the last of the Boeing 707s and with it the last of the single flight hostesses as part of the crew. With the 747s not only were more women forming part of the crew; the biggest issue for the Qantas flight hostesses was they now wanted to achieve equal promotional opportunities in relation to the stewards. Many of the stewards stayed long term with the company knowing they had promotional opportunities, but there was also the belief that they hadn't been trained to move into other professions, so Qantas was their only career path.

One of the reasons that the cabin crews were so highly unionised was the fact that staff would try to sort things out with their own airline rather than leave the job or move to another airline. Moving from one airline to another meant losing seniority and 'going to the bottom of the list' in regards to rostering and other conditions. Pat Merlehan, who had a job with TAA, had a job offer with Qantas, but her response was, 'I was at the top of the heap, why go to the bottom?'[74]

There were two big industrial disputes in 1981: one involved the domestic airlines, the other Qantas. The Qantas dispute became known as the 'Boeing SP Manning Dispute'. In 1981, Qantas introduced the Boeing 747SP (SP standing for special performance), and what started out as a 'simple row' over flight stewards' pay and conditions became one of Qantas's most damaging industrial disputes.[75] The stewards went on strike because of the crew complement, galley equipment and the long-haul capacities of the new plane.[76] It was expected that the new 747SP would operate a direct flight from Sydney to Los Angeles, with less crew and therefore longer duty hours for the cabin crew (prior to this the SP Qantas crew would slip (overnight layover) in Fiji or Honolulu on route to the west coast). Qantas proposed that four crew positions would be removed on the 747SP, and the stewards thought that if anyone had to go it should be the flight hostesses. Also, the new aircraft had a business–class section, which Qantas wanted staffed by flight hostesses, while the stewards thought they should fill these positions.

Lesley Squires was the President of the Overseas Branch of the Airline Hostesses' Association at the time, and Qantas flight hostesses made the decision that it was the stewards' dispute and not theirs. Therefore the flight hostesses would keep working, though they would not perform any of the flight stewards' duties. The flight stewards, who still dominated the numbers in the crew, and liked to think they pulled some weight, saw this move as a 'total betrayal'.[77] A strike was instigated, but, in defiance of the stewards, the 747SP Sydney–Wellington service departed on the 6th February with an 'all girl' crew of twelve hostesses. Initially it was only the 747SP service that was affected and other flights continued to operate normally.

Just as it seemed the dispute would be settled, things escalated with the ACTU imposing a twelve-day black ban because Qantas had used non-union staff labour during the dispute. Qantas had secretly trained other salaried staff to work as 'volunteer' scab labour to service the aircraft during the strike action. An instructor at the training school was shocked by how many people had 'flocked to the job'. He saw this as showing contempt for the cabin crew and their training, as the scab labour delighted in the fact that they thought that in two days they could train for a job that took weeks for the cabin crew.[78]

By the 14th February there was a mass walkout of 5,000 Qantas employees, with the dispute extended beyond the issue relating to the two 747SPs. On the 19th February, despite bans by the ACTU, and in defiance of their own union, a crew of fifteen flight hostesses was formed and led by Wendy Georgetti-Remkes. Georgetti-Remkes was not supportive of the union and had only joined the Airline Hostesses' Association because it was a 'closed shop'. She was not at all sympathetic to the strike action.[79] The crew became known as 'the girls who flew for Australia', a reference to a comment made by one of the flight hostesses, 'We are going back to work, not for Qantas but for Australia'.[80] After Georgetti-Remkes flew on a second flight Qantas thought she was unsafe so they sent her back to Port Moresby where she was living, and commuting for her flights. They said, 'stay up there until we call you back. Paid for everything. They were great. I think they were removing me from the [scene] – apparently it was pretty ugly'.[81]

It was ugly. The stewards created a list of the forty-seven flight hostesses that flew, and they would question them on flights, 'coin' their cars, and make late-night phone calls.[82] Qantas would then roster the strike-breakers in pairs to protect them. Georgetti-Remkes recalls:

> They'd come up to me, the stewards, for many years. Up to ten years later, they'd say, 'Why did you fly'? Somebody said, 'Oh, she flew for Australia'. No, I didn't. I just didn't agree with it. Why hold up an airline just for the sake you didn't like something. I said, 'Idiots!' Of course, I'll fly to keep the airline in the air.

The industrial unrest created conflict between the Overseas Branch and the Federal Executive of the Airline Hostesses' Association. The executive was made up of domestic hostesses from each of the state branches, and they supported the ACTU bans. Lesley Squires and the Overseas Branch membership held the line that the issue did not concern domestic air hostesses and the overseas branch should have the autonomy in its decision-making as outlined in the constitution of the association. The dispute also divided the pilots and the stewards, as pilots continued to fly and also help perform cabin crew safety procedures. Many of the 'old time' stewards who had flown in the 1960s saw this as an act of betrayal as they had supported the pilots during their twenty-eight-day strike in 1966.

The industrial action did not finish until the 13th March, although the stewards had resumed normal duties on the 23rd February as the twelve-day 747SP ban had been lifted.[83] The decision by the stewards to return work before other members of Qantas also resulted in a great deal of animosity, as they had caused the dispute and now they had returned to work while their colleagues waited for a final outcome to the industrial action. As one Qantas employee said:

> There was a definition of courage in 1981: anyone who would put on a flight [stewards'] uniform and walk from one end of the engine overhaul shop to the other. That was defined as the most courageous thing you could possibly do.[84]

It wasn't just Qantas that was experiencing industrial unrest. Early in 1981, Shayne Nealon, who was Queensland branch secretary of the Airline Hostesses' Association, had contacted industrial sociologist Dr Claire Williams to survey the domestic union members to get a sense of their readiness to take strike action in regard to pay and promotional opportunities. The result of the survey showed that the majority of air hostesses 'felt they did not have enough control over their activities, and that their jobs had very little prestige within the company' and they were 'prepared to take strong action if negotiations regarding safety issues failed'.[85] The result would be a seven-day strike in April that year. Williams was impressed with the calibre of women she encountered: 'I'd never struck a group of workers like them before; I'd never met anything like this. They knew their award backwards...'[86] It was in the air hostesses' interests to know their current award as all their industrial rights were built into the awards, and if they were to argue for any change to their working lives then it had to be argued though the arbitration system.

On midnight Wednesday 15th April 1981 the 2,200 domestic hostesses and male flight attendants went on strike regarding 'issues of seniority, hours of duty and length of rest periods between flights, and monetary issues, including increased allowances, shift loading and across-the-board wage increases'.[87] They also wanted extra pay for supervisory duty when working on the soon to be introduced Boeing 737.[88] The strike was initially called off in response to appeals to consider the Easter holiday traffic. But on the 23rd April the domestic union went out on a seven-day strike with a 61-point log of claims. Around 30,000 passengers were grounded. The union received the help and support of John Hickey, who was the head of flight operations at TAA, who fortunately for them 'knew every cost within that business'.[89] Lyne Pike was the Federal Secretary of the Airline Hostesses' Association at the time of the dispute and said after the dispute was over: 'It makes me angry, though, that we had to ground the whole country for a week to settle these claims. It was not necessary for the airlines to push us that far. This strike has made me more militant'.[90]

The closed-shop Airline Hostesses' Association was gathering strength, and the nature of the workplace made the flight crews a strong occupational community. Crews travelling together would discuss issues in the confines of the cabin, in the foyers of hotels; the close physical nature of the job allowed fervent discussion to take place at work and on stopovers.

6.7. The Golden Girls

We were called returnees, retreads or golden girls.

Sue Love-Davies, Qantas flight attendant 1970 to 1980,

then 1995 to 2008

Another major dispute in the 1980s affected Qantas flight hostesses and their right to promotional opportunities. Up until 1983, the only promotional opportunity within the Qantas cabin was to senior flight hostess, and at that time there were only thirteen positions for the total of 450 flight hostesses.[91] Related to the issue of promotion was the fact that a group of flight hostesses who had joined Qantas in the 1970s had been given the option to sign a ten-year contract that offered the benefit of staff travel, and an escalation of superannuation, if they retired when they reached 35.[92] Many of the women had signed the contract thinking 35 was a long way off and they were unlikely to be in the job that long. Also a group of them would argue, at the time, that when they were due to retire there were no promotional opportunities open to them, and for that reason there was no point continuing in what they perceived to be a 'dead end job'. Not everyone felt the same way, as Sue Love-Davies says:

> I think there were a lot there that were just trained to think that that was our role and we shouldn't ask for anything more, that they were just happy to be flight hostesses. A lot of them just didn't seem to be able to look outside the square and see what the opportunities were and look at what other airlines were doing. So they were just happy to sit.[93]

270

The Qantas flight hostesses knew they had a right to take Qantas to the Equal Opportunity Tribunal on the basis of the *New South Wales Anti-discrimination Act 1977*, which stated that it was unlawful for employers to discriminate on the basis of a person's sex. And so it would be that during the 1980s three cases were put before the Equal Opportunity Tribunal involving some twenty Qantas flight hostesses. All of the cases resulted in favour of the flight hostesses.[94]

Lesley Squires was the President of the Overseas Branch of the Airline Hostesses' Association from 1981 to 1983. In 1982 she had lodged a complaint with the Equal Opportunity Tribunal in NSW. The lack of promotional opportunity and numerical inequality were the issues, as she said: 'It didn't matter how good we were, we were helpless'.[95] The flight hostesses were still operating under the 1974 award, which had failed to include anything about promotion. While lack of promotional opportunities for the women was a cost-cutting measure on the part of the company, there was still the view that flight hostesses should be young and beautiful. During the case, Squires recalls, 'the Qantas industrial relations representative got up in the Commission during the SP dispute and said our customers write to us and say it's a shame that the hostesses aren't quite as young and beautiful as they used to be. Could you please address this?'[96]

The case before the Equal Opportunity Tribunal went for three years, with Qantas appealing the decision. The Overseas Branch of the association, now led by Joan Worth, withdrew support for the case. In August 1985 Squires was awarded almost $40,000 in damages, which went to pay the legal fees as no costs were awarded as part of the decision.[97] In the meantime, Qantas had opened supervisory cabin positions to all crew. Pam Crocker and Joan Wurst were selected as the first female Flight

Service Directors in April 1984.[98] Approximately a hundred cabin crew had applied for the positions, with about 20 per cent of the applications from senior female flight attendants.

> *I handcuffed a 6 foot 4 Croatian. I had him on the floor, with my foot in his back. Yes, that's the kind of stuff that you don't get to experience every day.*
>
> Patricia 'Tricia' Gubbins, Qantas flight attendant,
> 1974 to 2012[99]

Patricia 'Tricia' Gubbins flew with Qantas for thirty-eight years, retiring in 2012. She was selected wearing a pink Pierre Cardin suit that she had bought specially for the interview from a high-end second-hand shop. She didn't know at the time, but the success rate of the applicants was a ratio of 1 to 350. Even if she had known, there was no point in letting this go to her head, especially with the interview outlining some of the duties:

> I remember vividly one of the questions was, was I any good at cleaning toilets? I was absolutely shocked at that. But I thought yes, I'm really good at cleaning toilets, because I'd actually just helped a friend set up a motel'.[100]

After a seven-week training course, with about twenty-eight others, she boarded the 747 and immediately realised that the job was clearly demarcated:

> So we were literally the lowest common denominator on that flight. The men got all the great jobs. We got the jobs of cleaning the toilets, changing the babies' bassinet. We got all the menial task jobs, which was

perfectly acceptable then, and acceptable in my head also because of that generation.[101]

When Gubbins joined she had signed a contract to say that she would leave when she was 35. She flew for seven years and then was based in London until 1982. When she came back from London, she found out that women were starting to be promoted but she became pregnant. Gubbins returned to work when her daughter was a year and a half, and was told that she had to leave, based only on a decision she had made almost ten years before. Qantas wasn't interested in her changing her mind, so she decided to take Qantas to court. She knew there were other flight hostesses who had experienced the same discrimination:

> I remember, I started a group and there were only going to be five or six of us. We thought, oh well, we'll hire a room in the Wentworth Hotel and we'll all meet there to decide what we were going to do. I got some lawyers involved who, I didn't realise at the time, but they thought, 'Oh God, hosties! Let's get into it'.

As it turned out, about a hundred women were interested and they had to hire a big function room at the Wentworth. They invited three lawyers from Henry Davis York, who agreed to do the work pro bono. It wasn't just the women who had signed the contracts to retire at 35 who came to the meeting:

> Some were still there. Some were planning to stay. Some had never signed it. Some wanted compensation for the fact that they weren't allowed to be an air chef. Some

wanted promotion. Some were going for promotion. It was a plethora of women that had been wronged.

Aside from the aim of receiving compensation for the years of discrimination, the women wanted recognition for their value as flight attendants and not just as 'the girls who cleaned the toilets'. In the end it was seven of the female flight attendants who took out a class action.

Our strength was our numbers and the fact that we never ever, ever, ever gave up.
Patricia 'Tricia' Gubbins, Qantas flight attendant, 1974 to 2012

It took eight years for the decision to be handed down, and Maggie Gilet had had two children in this period. The final decision was in November 1993:

We walked in, it was over within a few minutes, the judge just passed a decision that we had won the case, and then his final words as he closed the book were, 'and these women have to be offered their jobs back immediately'. We actually sat there and we were stunned because we weren't expecting that. Someone had to actually jolt us into the realisation that we had won the case and that we had been offered our jobs back if we so wished.[102]

This decision would create resentment from other flight attendants, as the women who left when they turned 35 were seen to have had left their jobs and cashed in their superannuation, bought houses and had children while others remained working. For those who had continued working during this period it didn't seem fair when this group of women had their jobs reinstated and were granted seniority.[103]

No matter what the issue the flight attendants had with the companies they worked for, there was an unusual demand for the job that was hard to shake. There was still the notion that the airlines were like a family, even if they were badly behaved at times. As Bev Maunsell says, referring to the period up until the 1990s, 'people would have crawled through hoops of fire for Qantas'.[104] Flight attendants form occupational communities because they spend extended periods away from their families and friends and they regularly talk to each other about their everyday work practices and experiences. They also talk about intimate details of their personal lives, in the many long hours flying, as a way of keeping their loved ones alive in their thoughts. This sense of community is extended to the clubs that the air and flight hostesses have formed, Wings Away (TAA), Down to Earth (ANA and Ansett) and the Flight Hostesses' Association (Qantas). The clubs mean a lot to the women, even if they only worked for a short period, as they can reflect on the experiences of a working life like none other, and as a profession that shaped them into the women they became.

Those imagined golden days of flying are long gone and the air hostess, or 'hostie' as she is often known in the Australian vernacular, is now the gender-neutral 'flight attendant'. Once perceived as a glamorous and adventurous career, the profession has in many respects been reduced to just another customer service role. The profession today is part of the new cost-cutting trends in the aviation industry, where outsourcing and short-term contract work have changed what was once the dream job for many young women to a demanding employment, like many others, with an uncertain future. New labour conditions now dominate an industry that manages an unprecedented number of flight crew and ground staff working in the global contexts of what is now a much larger, highly competitive industry. Today, airlines employ cabin crew on contracts where they work longer rostered hours and are paid less than their colleagues who were employed only a few years before. This is part of today's industrial agreements, which incorporate more of the 'flexibility' demanded by the companies. So, this story finishes at the end of the 'golden era'; the history of the contemporary flight attendant is another story that remains to be told.

Notes

1   H. Wells, *Silver Wings for Vicki*, Grosset & Dunlap, New York, 1947, p. 53.

2   R. Hogan, *The Stewardess is Flying the Plane!: American Films of the 1970s*, Bulfinch Press, New York, p. 45.

3   S. Love-Davies, interview with the author, 7 February 2015. Qantas flight attendant 1970 to 1980, then 1995 to 2008.

4   Gloria Steinem was an undercover Playboy Bunny at the New York Playboy Club in 1963.

5   C. Locket, interview with the author, 21 June 2012.

6   S. Love-Davies, interview with the author, 7 February 2015.

7   ibid.

8   Qantas, 'Our magnificent men' advertisement, *Qantas Airways*, vol. 35, no. 11, November 1969, p. 21.

9   Qantas, 'Anything you can do' advertisement, *Qantas Airways*, vol. 36, no. 5, May 1970, back cover. The advertisement ran until July 1972.

10   J. Hawley, 'Hostesses extend strike by 24 hours', *Australian*, 2 July 1970, p. 3.

11   ibid.

12   B. Maunsell, interview with the author, 26 April 2012.

13   E. J. Smith, 'Hostess Notice', 13 November 1970.

14   Emotional labour was a term coined by A. Hochschild, *The Managed Heart: Commercialization of Human Feeling*, University of California Press, Berkley, California, 2003.

15   M. P. Laffey Inman, interview with the author, 24 March 2015. Northwest had originally hired men to work 'in the belly' (the bar area) of the Stratocruiser but when the service of that plane was discontinued they stopped employing men between 1957 and 1964.

16 G. Greer, *The Female Eunuch,* MacGibbon and Kee, London, 1970.

17 Other conditions had improved over Laffey Inman's time working for the airline. When she started working for the airline in 1958 as a 20-year-old she could work about 120 hours a month and that would be reduced to a maximum of 80 hours a month. This was similar to the conditions for Australian air hostesses.

18 In the United States it was TWA and Northwest that had this issue with male pursers; Pan Am was promoting female pursers.

19 Carol Locket, interview with the author, 21 June 2012.

20 The award was shaped by the gains made by the Qantas flight hostesses before Commissioner Deverall in 1974. See M. Robinson, 'A History of the Airline Hostesses' Association 1955–1981', Honours Thesis, Flinders University, 1990. As a result of the strike there was a new award offering a pay increase, annual leave was increased to six weeks, air hostesses could work until they were twelve weeks pregnant, and could return to work six weeks after confinement, and retirement age was increased to 45 years.

21 K. Clarke 'Hostesses stop jets', *Age*, 25 March 1975, p. 1.

22 S. Nealon, interview with the author, 19 November 2014. Shayne Nealon started as a TAA air hostess in 1974 and became Federal Secretary of the Airline Hostesses' Association in 1982.

23 ibid.

24 In September 1977, Freddie Laker in the UK opened up 'no-frills' travel between London and New York with his Laker Skytrain services.

25 Heery was also the flight hostess selected to crew on the flight that took the opposition leader Gough Whitlam to the People's Republic of China in July 1971.

26 H. Veitch, 'High-flyer who was dedicated to charity', *Canberra Times*, 30 June 2008, accessed 19 April 2015 <http://www.canberratimes.com.au/zoom/archive/rSMH080630GC6EL5JUBRJ>.

27 L. and R. Squires, interview with the author, 29 October 2014.

28 Anon, 'Good morning this is your flight services director speaking', *Airways Inflight* magazine, May/June 1978, pp. 36–8.

29 G. Cant, interview with the author, 19 March 2015.

30 L. and R. Squires, interview with the author, 29 October 2014.

31 M. Martin, interview with the author and Adam Gall, 20 March 2015.

32 ibid.

33 The NSW, WA and Queensland branches of the domestic hostesses joined the overseas branch when Martin was president because of dissatisfaction with the way the Victorian branch was operating, despite the fact they had the biggest numbers.

34   M. Martin, interview with the author and Adam Gall, 20 March 2015.

35   TAA used five hostesses on the 727/76 with 120-passenger capacity, while Ansett used four with a fifth on the evening service. The 727/276 could hold 151 passengers.

36   V. Basile, 'Airlines hit by hostess strike', *Age*, 1 July 1976, p. 1.

37   J. Percival, 'Biggest slump since the 1960s hits airlines', *Sydney Morning Herald*, 4 July 1976, p. 1.

38   Anon, 'Hostesses say cuts will affect service', *Sydney Morning Herald*, 2 July 1976, p. 3.

39   ibid.

40   Sidoli, T., 'Beards' Memorandum from Tino Sidoli, Qantas Cabin Crew Line Manager, 1 December 1980.

41   C. Locket, interview with the author, 21 June 2012. Air hostess with TAA 1973 and then Qantas, to 2016.

42   K. Minassian, email correspondence with the author, 22 January 2013.

43   M. Martin, interview with the author and Adam Gall, 20 March 2015.

44   P. Derriman, 'Qantas accused by hostesses', *Sydney Morning Herald*, 8 May 1979, p. 1.

45   M. Martin, interview with the author and Adam Gall, 20 March 2015.

46   D. Imison, interview with the author, 12 June 2012.

47   Manager of Qantas Cabin Crew, quoted in interview with M. Martin, interview with the author and Adam Gall, 20 March 2015.

48   ibid. There was a view that Catholics weren't employed at Qantas, although there was the odd exception.

49   M. Robinson, interview with the author, 3 January 2013.

50   Robinson, *A History of the Airline Hostesses' Association 1955–1981*, p. 44.

51   M. Robinson, written correspondence with the author, 13 September 2013.

52   For domestic air hostesses maternity leave was secured in 1975.

53   Anon, 'How many hosties', *Australian Women's Weekly*, 10 December 1975, p. 33.

54   J. Stackhouse, 'The newest profession', *Bulletin,* 5 November 1977, pp. 51–4.

55   S. Love-Davies, interview with the author, 7 February 2015.

56   Anon, 'Good morning this is your flight services director speaking', pp. 36–8.

57   K. Murray, interview with the author, 25 July 2013. Air hostess for Ansett 1977 to 1981, Qantas ground hostess 1998 to current.

58   Stackhouse, 'The newest profession', pp. 51–4.

59   K. Murray, interview with the author, 25 July 2013.

60   East-West Airlines was a regional airline flying mainly in the north-west of NSW.

61 L. Escolme-Schmidt, *Glamour in the Skies: The Golden Age of the Air Stewardess,* The History Press, Stroud, Gloucestershire, 2009, p.184.

62 C. Osborne, 'Australia's top women in airlines' *Australian Women's Weekly,* 22 December 1976, p. 11.

63 ibid.

64 L. Hewitt, interview with the author, 11 June 2012. Jill (Hickson) Wran was international relations manager for Qantas. C. McGregor, 'The trapped butterfly', *Sydney Morning Herald,* 23 August 1986, accessed 20 October 2015 <http://www.smh.com.au/good-weekend/gw-classics/the-trapped-butterfly-20140916-10bj9j.html>.

65 E. J. Connellan, *Failure of Triumph: The Story of Connellan Airways,* Paradigm Investments, Alice Springs, 1992, p. 316.

66 Stackhouse, 'The newest profession', pp. 51–4.

67 G. O'Brien, 'Look! that airlines done it again', *Sydney Morning Herald,* 25 November 1980, p. 3.

68 C. Locket, interview with the author, 21 June 2012.

69 B. Oliver Harry, interview with the author, 15 April 2013.

70 F. Christian, *Trans Australia Airlines Flight Attendants* circular, 5 November 1980.

71 M.Higgs, interview with the author, 10 January 2014. Flew with MMA 1980, then with Ansett until 2001.

72 M. Higgs, interview with the author, 10 January 2014. Flew with MMA, then Ansett from 1980 to 2001.

73 TAA air hostess, 1974 to 1994, Federal President of Airline Hostesses' Association 1982 to 1992, then Federal Secretary (domestic/regional) of the Flight Attendants Association of Australia.

74 P. Merlehan, interview with the author, 27 July 2015.

75 K. Martin, 'From a little dispute that grew and ran away', *Sydney Morning Herald,* 19 February 1981, p. 3.

76 M. Robinson, 'Qantas Cabin Crew and Their Union', PhD Thesis, Flinders University, 1996, p. 357

77 G. Cant, interview with the author, 19 March 2015.

78 Robinson, *Qantas Cabin Crew and Their Union,* p. 371.

79 L. and R. Squires, interview with the author, 29 October 2014. Rick Squires was a flight steward (started 1972) and President of the Flight Stewards' Association of Australia 1978 to 1980.

80 Anon, 'PM backs Qantas fight', *Sydney Morning Herald,* 20 February 1981, p. 1.

81 W. Georgetti-Remkes, interview with the author, 5 September 2015.

82 Robinson, *Qantas Cabin Crew and Their Union,* p. 374.

83   N. Blain, *Industrial Relations in the Air: Australian Airline Pilots*, University of Queensland Press, Brisbane, 1983, p. 102.

84   Qantas employee quoted in Robinson, *Qantas Cabin Crew and Their Union*, p. 378.

85   J. MacKellar, 'Airline hosties come down to earth', *Telegraph*, 4 November 1982, p. 24.

86   C. Williams, interview with the author, 8 November 2013.

87   S. Cram, 'Hostess who led strike', *National Times*, 3–6 May 1981, p. 6.

88   Anon, 'Trains out now air hostesses stop the planes', *Sydney Morning Herald*, 15 April 1981, p. 1.

89   S. Nealon, interview with the author, 19 November 2014.

90   Cram, 'Hostess who led strike', p. 6.

91   In 1983 there were 1,700 flight stewards, in M. Robinson, 'A Portrait of Feminine Fury': Solidarity, Separatism and Assertion in a Middle-Class Women's Union', unpublished paper, 1998.

92   The conditions related to the retirement was something the AHA had negotiated.

93   S. Love-Davies, interview with the author, 7 February 2015.

94   *Ms Lesley Squires vs. Qantas* (1985), *Ms Thompson and others vs. Qantas* (1989) and *Ms Gubbins and other vs. Qantas* (1991).

95   L. and R. Squires, interview with the author, 29 October 2014

96   ibid.

97   Air New Zealand air hostesses contacted Squires about her case and subsequently seventeen women started their own industrial dispute around sex discrimination in regard to male cabin crew. The story of their thirteen-year dispute formed the basis for Brita McVeigh's documentary *Coffee, Tea or Me? The Surprising Story of the Underestimated Trolley Dolly*, Gaylene Preston, Wellington, NZ, 2002.

98   Anon, 'Our first ladies' *Qantas News: The Newsletter for Qantas People*, vol. 32, no. 5, 1984, p. 2.

99   P. Gubbins, interview with the author, 19 April 2012. Qantas flight attendant 1974 to 2012.

100 ibid.

101 ibid.

102 M. Gilet, interview with the author, 30 August 2010.

103 In the late 1970s there was a new Superannuation Plan B. Flight hostesses could switch from Plan A with the retirement age of 35 to Plan B where you could work until 55, or retire after 20 years of service. The men were offered Plan B too but they were offered promotional opportunities unlike the flight hostesses.

104 B. Maunsell, interview with the author, 26 April 2012.

BIBLIOGRAPHY

Books

Adkins, R. C., *I Flew For MMA: An Airline Pilot's Life*, Success Print, Perth, [1996], 1998.

Avallone, M., *Flight Hostess Rogers*, Tower Publications, New York, 1962.

Barry, K. M., *Femininity in Flight: A History of Flight Attendants*, Duke University Press, Durham and London, 2007.

Baxter Anderson, B., *Peggy Wayne, Sky Girl*, Cupples & Leon, New York, 1941.

Black. P., *The Flight Attendant's Shoe*, NewSouth, Sydney, 2011.

Blain, N., *Industrial Relations in the Air: Australian Airline Pilots*, University of Queensland Press, St Lucia, Queensland, 1984.

Casson, S. A., *The Yellow Canary: From Butler Air Transport to Ansett Express*, Self-published, Springfield Lakes, Queensland, 2014.

Christian, P. *The Edge of Twilight*, Crest Book, New York, 1959.

Connellan, E. J., *Failure of Triumph: The Story of Connellan Airways*, Paradigm Investments, Alice Springs, 1992.

Crocombe, R. G., *The Pacific Islands and the USA*, Institute of Pacific Studies, University of South Pacific, Rarotonga and Suva and Pacific Islands Development Program East West Center, Honolulu, 1995.

Drewe, R., *Montebello: A Memoir*, Penguin, Melbourne, 2012.

Dunn, F., *Speck in the Sky: A History of Airlines of Western Australia*, Airlines of Western Australia, Perth, 1984.

Escolme-Schmidt, L., *Glamour in the Skies: The Golden Age of the Air Stewardess*, The History Press, Stroud, Gloucestershire, 2009.

Evans, J. & Daw, N. K., *An Iconic Airline: The Story of Airlines of South Australia*, Self-published, Adelaide, 2012.

Foster, E., 'A Bird's Eye View: Memories and Memorabilia of MMA, 1960–1962', unpublished manuscript, 2007.

Game, A. & Pringle, R., *Gender at Work*, Allen and Unwin, Sydney, 1983.

Gardiner, L., *A Woman's Place: A History of the Homecraft Hostel*, Hyland House,

Melbourne, 1993.

George, E., *Two at Daly Waters*, Georgian House, Melbourne, 1945.

Gerard, J., *Jet Stewardess*, Lancer Books, New York, 1962.

Graf, N., *Air Stewardess*, Gramercy, New York, 1938.

Greer, G., *The Female Eunuch,* MacGibbon and Kee, London, 1970.

Gunn, J., *Contested Skies: Trans Australia Airlines 1946–1992*, University of Queensland Press, Brisbane, 1999.

Hawken, P., *Air Hostess Ann*, The Bodley Head, London, [1952] 1953.

Hill, E., *The Great Australian Loneliness*, Robertson and Mullens Ltd, Melbourne, [1937] 1945.

Hochschild, A., *The Managed Heart: Commercialization of Human Feeling*, University of California Press, Berkley, California, 2003.

Hogan, R., *The Stewardess is Flying the Plane!: American Films of the 1970s*, Bulfinch Press, New York , 2005.

Hudson, K. & Pettifer, J., *Diamonds in the Sky: A Social History of Air Travel*, Bodley Head and British Broadcasting Corporation, London, 1979.

Hulsbergen, R., *The Aborigine Today*, Paul Hamlyn, Sydney, 1971.

Job, M., *Air Crash Vol 1. 1929–1939*, Macarthur Job and Aerospace Publications, Canberra, 1991.

McRobbie, M., *Walking the Skies: The First Fifty Years of Air Hostessing 1936 to 1986*, Self- published, Melbourne, [1986] 1992.

Merlehan, P. *Wings Away: Flying Tales to Tell*, Wings Away, Queensland, 1992.

Moore, H. M., *Silver Wings in Pacific Skies*, Boolarong Publications, Brisbane, 1993.

Panter Nielsen, G., *From Sky Girl to Flight Attendant: Women and the Making of a Union*, Cornell University, Cornell, 1982.

Price, E., *Air Hostess in Love*, John Gresham, London, 1962.

Rogers Hager, A., *Janice Airline Hostess*, Julian Messner, New York, [1948] 1949.

Sabey, I., *Challenge in the Skies: The Founding of TAA*, Hyland House, Melbourne, 1979.

Shute, N., *No Highway*, Vintage, London, [1948] 2009.

Smith, A. J., *East-West Eagles: The Story of East-West Airlines*, Robert Brown and Associates, Carina, Qld., 1989.

Sterling, R., *Stewardess*, Piatkus, Loughton, UK, [1982] 1983.

Terkel, S., *Working*, Avon Books, New York, [1972] 1975.

Tiemeyer, P., *Plane Queer: Labor, Sexuality and AIDS in the History of the Male Flight Attendants*, University of California Press, Berkley, 2013.

Wells, H., *Silver Wings for Vicki*, Grosset & Dunlap, New York, 1947.

Wharton, A., *Building the Cold War: Hilton International Hotels and Modern*

Architecture, University of Chicago Press, Chicago, 2001. p. 1.

Wheeler, J., *Jane, Stewardess of the Air Lines*, Goldsmith, Chicago, 1934.

Williams, C., *Blue, Pink and White Collar Workers in Australia: Technicians, Bank Employees and Flight Attendants*, Allen and Unwin, Sydney, 1988.

Witcomb, N., *Up Here and Down There*, Self-published, Adelaide, 1986.

Yano, C., *Airborne Dreams: 'Nisei' Stewardesses and Pan American World Airways*, Duke University Press, Durham and London, 2011.

Yule, P., *The Forgotten Giant of Australia Aviation: Australian National Airways*, Hyland House, Melbourne, 2001.

Magazine and Newspaper Articles

Anon, 'Hostesses's union', *Northern Star* (Lismore), 5 November 1924, p. 9.

Anon, 'Australia's first. Hobart girl selected', *Advocate*, 12 March 1936, p. 7.

Anon, 'First air hostesses', *Advocate*, 13 March 1936, npn.

Anon, 'Tasmanian air hostess: Miss M. F. Grueber's task', *Mercury*, 18 March 1936, p. 6.

Anon, 'Few air hostesses: Australian lines would prefer stewards', *Courier-Mail*, 7 April 1936, p. 14.

Anon, 'A short flight: Bungana surprises', *Launceston Examiner*, 30 April 1936, p. 7.

Anon, 'First air hostess', *Townsville Daily Bulletin*, 4 May 1936, p. 10.

Anon, 'Douglas makes record commercial flight', *Advocate*, 4 May 1936, p. 7.

Anon, 'New airliner's fast flight', *Argus*, 4 May 1936, p. 9.

Anon 'More air hostess: careers for girls', *Sydney Morning Herald*, 15 May 1936, p. 11.

Anon, 'Versatile air hostess', *Mercury*, 27 May 1936, p. 6.

Anon, 'Girls from the south are in the clouds', *Australian Women's Weekly*, 30 May 1936, p. 39.

Anon, 'New air hostess', *Mercury*, 4 June 1936, p. 7.

Anon, 'Meet the air hostesses', *Barrier Miner*, 8 June 1936, p. 4.

Anon, 'Air hostess', *Examiner Women's Supplement*, 5 August 1936, p. 5.

Anon, 'On duty with the air hostess', *Mercury*, 5 August 1936, p. 7.

Anon, 'Air traveller appreciates Tasmania', *Mercury*, 11 August 1936, p. 6.

Anon, 'Hostesses banned: Imperial Airways prefer stewards', *Examiner*, 17 October 1936, p. 7.

Anon, 'New air hostess: Miss Dethbridge appointed', *Mercury*, 19 November 1936, p. 7.

Anon, 'Archbishop Wand in forced landing', Rockhampton, *Morning Bulletin*, 4 December 1936, p. 9.

Anon, '"Felt a slight jar": passengers not worried', *Sydney Morning Herald*, 4

December 1936, p. 11.

Anon, 'Thrills at big air pageant', *Mail*, 19 December 1936, p. 1.

Anon, 'Air hostesses to be replaced by stewards', *Mercury*, 25 December 1936, p. 9.

Anon, 'New air hostess here on Wednesday', *Advertiser*, 16 January 1937, p. 14.

Anon, 'Man makes good as deputy air hostess', *Advocate*, 30 January 1937, p. 4.

Anon, 'Air accidents do not deter women travellers', *Australia Women's Weekly*, 27 February 1937, p. 35.

Anon, 'Air Hostess', *Western Mail*, 11 March 1937, p. 32.

Anon, 'Air services criticised: Lady Haig protests to company', *Advertiser*, 15 March 1937, p. 20.

Anon, 'Bungana speaking at 180 m.p.h.', *Daily News*, 15 March 1937, p. 2.

Anon, 'Would you like to be an air hostess?', *Daily News*, 17 March 1937, p. 4.

Anon, 'Voices from the air: Lady Haig and others', *Daily News*, 22 March 1937, p. 4.

Anon, 'The flying hostess', *Morning Bulletin*, Rockhampton, 22 April 1937, p. 13.

Anon, 'Flying Hostess at Rex Sunday', *Madera Tribune*, 24 April 1937, p. 3.

Anon, 'Exciting new career for girls', *Australian Women's Weekly*, 29 May 1937, p. 2.

Anon, 'Must retire at 35: rigid code for air hostesses for Airlines of Australia', *Courier-Mail*, 9 July 1937, p. 14.

Anon, 'Air hostesses', *Mercury*, 19 July 1937, p. 6.

Anon, 'Air hostess', *Auckland Star*, 27 July 1937, p. 9.

Anon, 'Air hostess has many duties but likes job', *Courier-Mail*, 2 August 1937, p. 17.

Anon, 'Transport: women on wheels', *Time*, 16 August 1937, p. 17.

Anon, 'Housekeeping in the clouds', *Popular Mechanics*, 38 (5), November 1937, p. 712.

Anon, 'Goodwill flight', *Sydney Morning Herald,* 15 November 1937, p. 9.

Anon, 'Aeroplane to carry 43 passengers', *Courier-Mail*, 16 November 1937, p. 12.

Anon, 'Goodwill air tour', *West Australian*, 16 Nov 1937, p. 20.

Anon, 'Flying hostess' advertisement, *Camperdown Chronicle*, 18 November 1937, p. 2.

Anon, 'Air hostess to be married', *Argus*, 19 March 1938, p. 3.

Anon, 'Air hostess travels by ship to London', *Advertiser,* 15 April 1938, p. 13.

Anon, 'Sheila Lyons wants to be an air hostess', *Daily News*, 30 April 1938, p. 1.

Anon, 'Will become linguist', *Courier-Mail*, 7 June 1938, p. 3.

Anon, 'Australian hostess for world's airlines', *Advertiser*, 9 June 1938, p. 9.

Anon, 'She earns her living in the air', *Sydney Morning Herald*, 12 July 1938, p. 12.

Anon, 'Half a million miles flown by pioneer air hostess', *Herald*, 9 September 1938, clipping.

Anon, 'Terrible aviation disaster', *Kalgoorlie Miner*, 26 October 1938, p. 4.

Anon, 'Airliner victims', *Argus*, 29 October 1938, p. 2.

Anon, 'Air hostess who missed death in the Kyeema', *Australian Women's Weekly*, 5 November 1938, p. 32.

Anon, 'Up in the air', *Evening Post*, 1 December 1938, p. 19.

Anon, 'Air hostess retires', *West Australian*, 14 December 1938, p. 4.

Anon, 'Dinner party in the air', *Daily News*, 26 December 1938, p. 7.

Anon, 'Joins airways staff', *Argus*, 8 June 1939, p. 1.

Anon, 'New air hostess', *Argus*, 9 June 1939, p. 8.

Anon, 'From Perth in one day', *Argus*, 4 July 1939, p. 7.

Anon, 'Sick woman's flight', *Argus,* 7 August 1939, p. 4.

Anon, 'Two S.A girls are air hostesses' *Mail*, 19 August 1939, p. 2.

Anon, 'Fire on Bungana at 6,000ft', *Daily News* (Perth), 8 February 1940, p. 1.

Anon, 'Amazing plane landing', *Argus,* 9 February 1940, p. 1.

Anon, 'Three brave women', *Australian Women's Weekly,* 2 March 1940, p. 20.

Anon, 'Tea at 10,000ft is "Grand Fun"', *Argus*, 9 March 1940, p. 13.

Anon, 'Air hostesses: They fly for their living', *Australian Women's Weekly*, 18 May 1940, p. 2.

Anon, 'Let's talk of interesting people', *Australian Women's Weekly*, 27 July 1940, p. 2.

Anon, 'A.I.F. sister was air hostess', *Advertiser,* 10 August 1940, p. 13.

Anon, 'Failed in their duty,' *Australian Women's Weekly*, 24 August 1940, p. 14.

Anon, 'Foiled bandits', *Sunday Times* (Perth), 8 December 1940, p. 5

Anon, 'Growing importance of women's jobs in the air', *Advertiser*, 11 March 1941, p. 6.

Anon, 'Ground hostesses at Parafield', *Mail* (Adelaide) 26 July 1941, p. 9.

Anon, 'Train air hostesses: they need to be among other things, psychologists', *Daily Journal-World*, 19 March 1942, p. 12.

Anon, 'Air hostess told General Blamey', *Sunday Times* (Perth), 16 August 1942, p. 3.

Anon, 'Pioneering at Daly Waters', *Mail*, 18 September 1943, p. 13.

Anon, 'Objected to noise at flats', *Courier-Mail*, 17 May 1944, p. 5.

Anon, 'Parker Shoe advertisement, Georges of Collins Street', *Argus,* 19 August 1944, p. 11.

Anon, 'Aspiring hostesses: lack poise and diction', c. 1945, clipping.

Anon, '10th Year of air hostess service', *Mercury*, 10 October 1945, p. 8.

Anon, 'North-West air service', *West Australian*, 28 November 1945, p. 4.

Anon, 'To be an air hostess', *Daily News*, 25 February 1946, p. 5.

Anon, 'Woman's death on ANA plane', *Sydney Morning Herald*, 11 March 1946, p. 4.

Anon, 'All aboard airline believed killed in sea night crash', *Central Queensland Herald*, 14 March 1946, p. 12.

Anon, 'Horses to planes', *West Australian*, 15 March 1946, p. 9.

Anon 'Air hostess to Darwin', *Western Mail*, 28 March 1946, p. 26.

Anon, 'Bird possible cause of air crash' *Mercury*, 1 May 1946, p. 1.

Anon, 'Heard "Terrific Bang"', *Mercury*, 1 May 1946, p. 10.

Anon, 'Bird might have collided with cockpit of Plane', *Mercury*, 2 May 1946, p. 10.

Anon, 'Board, residence' advertisement', *Courier-Mail*, 9 May 1946, p. 10.

Anon, 'Air hostess: a superintendent appointed', *West Australian*, 24 July 1946, p. 10.

Anon, 'Two hours travel by air to Kalgoorlie', *West Australian*, 2 August 1946, p. 9.

Anon, '800 girls seek jobs as air hostesses', *Argus,* 22 August 1946, p. 3.

Anon, 'Aspiring hostesses', *West Australian*, 22 August 1946, p. 8.

Anon, 'Log book for flying babies', *Sunday Times*, 8 September 1946, p. 6.

Anon, 'Senior hostess weds former P.O.W', *Daily News*, 11 September 1946, p. 9.

Anon, 'Took to life in air', *Courier-Mail,* 25 January 1947, p. 6.

Anon, 'Gwladys Fogden', *Sydney Morning Herald*, 17 April 1947, p. 16.

Anon, 'Hostesses have ideas for improved air service', *Sun*, 17 June 1947, clipping.

Anon, 'Air League show has new Auster plane', *Sydney Morning Herald*, 2 July 1947, p. 1.

Anon, 'Country's First Air Hostess', *Cairns Post*, 27 August 1947, p. 5.

Anon, 'Better services', *Daily Mercury*, 28 August 1947, p. 2.

Anon, 'First air hostess checking north', *Townsville Bulletin*, 28 August 1947, p. 2.

Anon, 'Two views on modern miss', *Courier-Mail*, 29 October 1947, p. 6.

Anon, 'Clothes for long journeys on the air', *Qantas Empire Airways,* January 1948, p. 10.

Anon, 'Advanced training for air hostess applicants', *Sydney Morning Herald*, 15 January 1948, p. 6.

Anon, '260 want to be hostesses', *Daily News*, 16 January 1948, p. 4.

Anon, 'World digest', *Courier Mail*, 11 February 1948, p. 4.

Anon, 'First nine girls to fly Sydney-London run', *Australian Women's Weekly*,

14 February 1948, p. 17.

Anon, 'First air hostess England bound', *Mail*, 26 June 1948, p. 17.

Anon, 'They all fly', *Qantas Empire Airways*, August 1948, p. 7.

Anon, 'Party held without air hostess', *Daily News*, 4 September 1948, p. 1.

Anon, 'TAA Convair bring migrants,' *Argus*, 1 October 1948, p. 3.

Anon, 'Airliner crashes on Mt Macedon', *Examiner*, 9 November 1948, p. 1.

Anon, 'Miss W.A. chosen', *Barrier Miner*, 18 January 1949, p. 3.

Anon, 'Judging concluded', *Geraldton Guardian*, 27 January 1949, p. 5.

Anon, 'Miss WA offered posts in E.S.', *Mirror*, 5 February 1949, p. 1.

Anon, 'Would you like to be an air hostess?', *Sun Herald*, 17 April 1949, p. 3.

Anon, 'Air hostess "Stole Glory", says steward', *Sydney Morning Herald*, 20 April 1949, p. 4.

Anon, 'Air heroine to be rewarded', *Advertiser*, 21 April 1949, p. 3.

Anon, 'Qantas flight stewards', *Qantas Empire Airways* magazine, May 1949, p. 5

Anon, 'Air hostesses replace stewards on strike', *Canberra Times*, 22 August 1949, p. 2.

Anon, 'Variety for an air hostess', *West Australian*, 30 August 1949, pp. 15–16.

Anon, 'Advertisement', *Sydney Morning Herald*, 7 September 1949, p. 17.

Anon, 'Positions as air hostesses in keen demand', *Cairns Post*, 9 September 1949, p. 1.

Anon, 'Ill-Fated DC-3 turned over backwards', *West Australian*, 13 December 1949, p. 8.

Anon 'Glamour of the uniform', *Argus*, 16 December 1949, p. 2.

Anon, 'She prefers businessmen', *Daily News*, 17 December 1949, p. 28.

Anon, 'WA girl has flown to England 15 times', *Daily News*, 20 February 1950, p. 5.

Anon, 'Nobody can sneak a plane ride', *Argus*, 27 February 1950, p. 5.

Anon, 'Stowaway, 6, caught on plane', *Argus*, 25 February 1950, p. 1

Anon, 'They want to see the world before they marry,' *Londoner*, 19 April 1950, npn.

Anon, 'Air crash near York', *Geraldton Guardian*, 27 June 1950, p. 3.

Anon, '28 deaths in Skymaster crash', *Mercury*, 28 June 1950, p. 1.

Anon, 'Australian in "Miss Airways" quest', *West Australian*, 11 July 1950, p. 4.

Anon, 'Former typist flies 700 miles daily on job', *Sunday Herald*, 24 September 1950, p. 11.

Anon, '22 Trips to London', *Daily News*, 4 November 1950, p. 13.

Anon, 'Tribute from prime minister', *Qantas Staff Magazine*, December–February 1950–1951, p. 14.

Anon, 'Air hostess to go on "Pilgrimage to Mecca"', *Sunday Herald*, 16

September 1951, p. 18.

Anon, 'New services to travelling public', *Sydney Morning Herald*, 19 October 1951, p. 3.

Anon, 'Passengers and pilots are out', *Courier-Mail*, 24 July 1952, p. 8.

Anon, 'M.P. lost his lolly', *Barrier Miner*, 1 September 1952, p. 8.

Anon, 'Qland [sic] girl for dangerous job in Malaya', *Courier-Mail*, 4 November 1952, p. 8.

Anon, 'It's hard work for the air hostess', *News*, 6 March 1953, p. 11.

Anon, 'Women's interests on the air', *Sydney Morning Herald*, 9 April 1953, p. 7.

Anon, 'She will be air hostess to the Queen', *Courier-Mail*, 15 October 1953, p. 2.

Anon. 'No drunks on planes', *Barrier Miner*, 28 November 1953, p. 9.

Anon, 'She will be hostess to the Queen', *Courier-Mail*, 30 December 1953, p. 2.

Anon, 'Charm of Air Hostess, *Barrier Miner*, 23 January 1954, p. 1.

Anon, 'The Queen's aching feet, *Courier-Mail*, 28 January 1954, p. 2.

Anon, 'People and parties', *Age*, January 29 1954, p. 5.

Anon, 'Royal compartment in TAA Convair', *Examiner*, 19 February 1954, p. 35.

Anon, 'She gets paid for window shopping', *Sun Herald*, 4 April 1954, p. 25.

Anon, 'Hostess's part in drama', *Advertiser*, 22 April 1954, p. 1.

Anon, 'Air hostess said no', *Advertiser*, 22 June 1954, p. 1.

Anon, 'Wished to learn', *West Australian*, 23 June 1954, p. 2.

Anon, 'Air hostess saves baby's life', *Advertiser*, 11 December 1954, p. 1

Anon, 'Hostess makes flying good', *Argus*, 12 December 1955, p. 10.

Anon, 'Rival union claims for air hostesses', *Sydney Morning Herald*, 21 July 1955, p. 3.

Anon, 'Glamour air girls form a union', *Argus*, 27 September 1955, pp. 1, 6.

Anon, 'Matron Holyman retires: she set a world standard', *Air Travel Magazine*, November 1955, p. 14.

Anon, 'Ansett – big new force in Australian aviation', *Financial Review*, 29 August 1957, p. 2.

Anon, 'Japanese in Sydney to train as air hostesses', *Sydney Morning Herald*, 11 August 1958, p. 3.

Anon, 'Ground-Level Talks', *Panorama*, September 1958, p. 7.

Anon, 'Jets will make travel easier for ladies...' *Qantas Empire Airways*, 25 (3) March 1959, p. 20.

Anon, 'Dragon in the tree-tops', *Australian Women's Weekly*, 3 February 1960, p. 3.

Anon, *Sunshine Festival Brochure*, Geraldton, 1961.

Anon, 'Common-sense test for air hostesses', *Age*, 4 July 1961, p. 11.

Anon, 'Our choice of the week', *Navy News*, 17 September 1965, p. 7.

Anon, 'Stewards', *Sky-Line* 2 (2) 1968, p. 7.

Anon, 'Your career – air hostessing,' *Dawn: A Magazine for the Aboriginal people of New South Wales*, vol. 17, no. 6, June 1968, p. 5.

Anon, 'Papua's first air hostess arrives', *Canberra Times*, 13 June 1969, p. 3.

Anon, 'Birds that fly', *PS,* vol. 2, no. 6, December 1971/January 1972, p. 8.

Anon, 'Beauty on the wing', *Qantas News*, vol. 20, no. 12, 14 July 1972, p. 1.

Anon, 'How many hosties', *Australian Women's Weekly*, 10 December 1975, p. 33.

Anon, 'Hostesses say cuts will affect service', *Sydney Morning Herald*, 2 July 1976, p. 3.

Anon, 'Skyways-airport', *Sydney Morning Herald*, 9 July 1979, p. 6.

Anon, 'Good morning this is your flight services director speaking', *Airways Inflight* magazine, May/June 1978, pp. 36–8.

Anon, 'Aboriginals take to the air', *Aboriginal Quarterly,* vol. 1, no. 3, 1979, pp. 25–7.

Anon, 'Tokyo here they come again!' *Qantas Staff News*, vol. 29, no. 17, 1981, p. 1.

Anon, 'PM backs Qantas fight', *Sydney Morning Herald*, 20 February 1981, p. 1.

Anon, 'Trains out now air hostesses stop the planes', *Sydney Morning Herald*, 15 April 1981, p. 1.

Anon, 'Our first ladies', *Qantas News: The Newsletter for Qantas People*, vol. 32, no. 5, 1984, p. 2.

Anon, 'The long hop', *Sydney Morning Herald*, 29 November 1997, pp. 1, 5.

Anon, Nundle Community Newsletter, 26 March 2012, accessed 12 June 2015 <http://www.tamworth.nsw.gov.au/ArticleDocuments/1277/Nundle_Community_Newsletter_March%20_2012.pdf.aspx>.

Anon, 'Quest for hostess with most joins the Australian Aviation Hall of Fame', 24 September 2012, accessed 20 December 2015 <http://www.news.com.au/national/queensland/quest-for-hostess-with-most-joins-australian-aviation-hall-of-fame/story-fndo4ckr-1226479786338>.

Adam, N., 'Australian air hostess guarded children', *Advertiser,* 29 January 1952, p. 1.

Ansett-ANA advertisement 'Ansett-ANA Golden Supper Club', *Age*, 28 May 1959, p. 2.

Ansett-ANA, 'Whoever you are please stop sending our Miss Jones roses', *Age*, 8 November 1967, p. 3.

Ansett-ANA, Susan Jones song, accessed 14 February 2016 <https://www.youtube.com/watch?v=UUuWXgXUF94>.

Aviation Writer, 'Douglas plane: four strait flights daily?', *Examiner*, 6 February 1936, p. 6.

Aviation Writer, 'Will additional planes be needed?', *Examiner*, 9 August 1937, p. 6.

Baker, J., '"She turned up for work with debris in her hair": the women war reporters you've never heard of', *Guardian*, Accessed 12 March 2016 <http://www.theguardian.com/commentisfree/2015/oct/22/she-turned-up-to-work-with-bits-of-debris-still-in-her-hair-the-women-war-reporters-youve-never-heard-of.>

Basile, V., 'Airlines hit by hostess strike', *Age*, 1 July 1976, p. 1.

BOAC Paper Dresses (1967), accessed 12 January 2016 <https://www.youtube.com/watch?v=h2XkQfmjRVE>.

Burgess, C., 'A Story of Service', *Qantas News Special Edition*, July 1988, p/c clipping.

Cathay Pacific Advertisement, *Panorama*, April 1962, p. 3.

Catling, S., 'This flying business is not all flying', *Courier-Mail*, 13 August 1949, p. 2.

Charlett, R., 'Cocktails with Lunch 3½ Miles, Up', *Argus*, 2 April 1949, p. 3.

Clarke, K., 'Hostesses stop jets', *Age*, 25 March 1975, p. 1.

Cram, S., 'Hostess who led strike', *National Times*, 3–6 May 1981, p. 6.

Dawne Walker Academy advertisement, *Sydney Morning Herald*, 5 September 1979, p. 13.

Derriman, P., 'Qantas accused by hostesses', *Sydney Morning Herald*, 8 May 1979, p. 1.

Dwyer, A., 'She's got her wings – and £14 a week', 'Teenagers Weekly' in *Australian Women's Weekly*, 8 July 1959, p. 6.

EK [sic], 'Nursing sister on the wing again', *Barrier Miner*, 6 June 1952, p. 9.

Esplanade Hotel Advertisement, *Northern Territory Times*, 12 July 1951, p. 6.

Ferber, M., 'Picking petals off a daisy', *Daily News*, 4 March 1940, p. 9.

Foster, E., Letter to 'Folks', Christmas 1961, personal archive.

Franks, G., 'Air hostesses make good housewives', *Press* (Christchurch, NZ), 19 August 1967, p. 2.

Frizell, H., 'Bush Premier', *Australian Women's Weekly*, 8 August 1956, p. 33.

Frizell, H., 'The Petticoat Safari', *Australian Women's Weekly*, 23 October 1957, pp. 8–10.

Fubbs, T., 'Australia's first air hostesses', *Argus*, 23 January 1937, p. 30.

Gott, S., 'Flying round with the girls!', *Mirror*, September 1960, clipping.

Halstead, 'Roundabout: people and events', *West Australian*, 29 July 1938, p. 9.

Hawley, J., 'Hostesses extend strike by 24 hours', *Australian*, 2 July 1970, p. 3.

Hepzibah, 'Pretty Perth girl gains post of air hostess', *Daily News*, 13 January 1937, p. 9.

Hepzibah, 'First air hostess on Perth run', *Daily News*, Perth, 5 February 1937, p. 7.

Hepzibah, 'Aerial romance', *Daily News*, 21 March 1938, p. 7.

Hunter, M., 'Eve and modern sister are very much alike', *Courier-Mail*, 22 December 1937, p. 22.

James, C., 'No fear of flying', *Observer*, 10 January 1982, pp. 29, 31.

James, D., 'Reporter trains as an air hostess', *Australian Women's Weekly*, 11 June 1958, pp. 8–9.

Knight, M., 'What it means to be an air hostess: medicine and manners', *Queenslander*, 23 July 1936, p. 17.

Koutsoukis, J., 'The spy scandal that heated up the Cold War', *Age*, 3 April 2004, accessed 20 October 2015 <http://www.theage.com.au/articles/2004/04/02/1080544695722.html>.

MacKellar, J., 'Airline hosties come down to earth', *Telegraph*, 4 November 1982, p. 24.

Martin, K., 'From a little dispute that grew and ran away', *Sydney Morning Herald*, 19 February 1981, p. 3.

McGregor, M., 'The trapped butterfly' *Sydney Morning Herald*, 23 August 1986, accessed 20 October 2015 <http://www.smh.com.au/good-weekend/gw-classics/the-trapped-butterfly-20140916-10bj9j.html>.

O'Brien, G., 'Look! that airlines done it again', *Sydney Morning Herald*, 25 November 1980, p. 3.

Osborne, C., 'Australia's top women in airlines', *Australian Women's Weekly*, 22 December 1976, p. 11.

Percival, J. 'Biggest slump since the 1960s hits airlines', *Sydney Morning Herald*, 4 July 1976, p. 1.

Qantas, 'Designed for performance', *Qantas Empire Airways*, January, 1949, pp. 4–5.

Qantas, 'Hostess acted as a mother to kids on Operation Smallfry', *Qantas News*, October, 1955, p. 5.

Qantas, 'World's first round world jet service…' *Qantas Empire Airways*, vol. 25, no. 9, September 1959, pp. 1-3 and pp. 20-21.

Qantas, 'Flight hostess vacancies' advertisement, *Age*, 6 November 1959, p. 11.

Qantas, 'Our magnificent men' advertisement, *Qantas Airways*, vol. 35, no. 11, November 1969, p. 21.

Qantas, 'Anything you can do' advertisement, *Qantas Airways*, vol. 36, no. 5, May 1970, back cover.

Qantas, 'The friendliness of the long distance Australian' advertisement, Qantas Airways, vol. 36, no. 9, September 1970, p. 25.

Quarrell, L., 'Air hostesses consider work fascinating', *Advertiser*, 21 December 1936, p. 12.

Quarrell, L., '100 S.A. girls seek air hostess career', *Advertiser*, 12 January 1937, p. 14.

'Round Robin', 'Pity the hostess with the mostest!', *Australian Women's Weekly*, 13 March 1968, p. 52.

St Claire, M., 'Important war post for Laurie Steele', *Australian Women's Weekly*, 10 May 1941, p. 9.

Stackhouse, J., 'The newest profession', *Bulletin*, 5 November 1977, pp. 51–4

Steele, L., 'Hostess above the clouds', *Courier-Mail*, 11 June 1938, p. 9.

Steele, L., 'Air hostess over Europe', *Australian Women's Weekly*, 29 October 1938, p. 12.

Thomas, G., 'Window on the world', *Weekend West*, 4 April 2009, pp. 8–14, 10.

Tran-Australia Airlines advertisement, *Examiner*, 17 August 1946, p. 4.

Tran-Australia Airlines advertisement *Argus*, 17 August 1946, p. 38.

Turnbull, C., 'We have reason to brag', *Sun*, 27 August 1957, clipping.

Veitch, H., 'High-flyer who was dedicated to charity', *Canberra Times*, 30 June 2008, accessed 19 April 2015 <http://www.canberratimes.com.au/zoom/archive/rSMH080630GC6EL5JUBRJ>.

Wake, L., 'That air age', c. 1996, pp. 16–17, clipping.

Wright, P. 'Airman's widow flies the skies as air hostess', *Mail*, 22 February 1947, p. 9.

Wynne, E., 'Rollerskating waitresses from Perth's His Majesty's Theatre in the 1960s: never spilled a drop', 702 ABC Perth, 10 November 2015, accessed 20 December 2015 <http://www.abc.net.au/news/2015-11-10/perth-1960s-rollerskating-waitresses-never-spilled-a-drop/6927392>.

Young, J., 'Airline with teenage hostesses', *Australian Women's Weekly*, 29 June 1960, p. 36.

Journal Articles

Keller, Y., '"Was it right to love her brother's wife so passionately?": Lesbian pulp novels and US lesbian identity, 1950–1965', *American Quarterly*, vol. 57, no. 2, 2005, pp. 385–410.

Richardson J. E. & Poulton, H. W., 'Australia's Two-Airline Policy – law and the layman', *Federal Law Review*, June 1968, pp. 64–85.

Robinson, M., 'A Portrait of Feminine Fury': Solidarity, Separatism and Assertion in a Middle-Class Women's Union', unpublished paper, 1998.

Airline, Museum and Union Documents

Airways Museum, WA Airways Hostel – Forrest, accessed 17 March 2016 <http://www.airwaysmuseum.com/FRT%20-%20WAA%20hangar%20

guest%20house%202.htm>.

ANA Airways News Announcements, December 1945.

ANA, 'Royal flight Launceston to Melbourne menu', 24 February 1954.

'BCPA at Your Service' booklet, c. 1948.

'Butler Air Transport Ltd. Hostess Manual', 1956.

Christian, F., 'Trans Australia Airlines Flight Attendants' circular, 5 November 1980.

Flight Attendants Association of Australia, 'Taking Care of Business – Union Style', draft document, 6 October 1986.

Gibson, M., 'TAA Memo to Air Hostesses', 1960.

Gibson, M., 'A tribute to Stephen Kentley', clipping.

Grueber, M., Radio Interview with Les Daley c.1936, National Library of Australia.

Holyman, L., Letter to Marguerite Grueber from Ivan Holman, 11 March 1936.

MMA, 'How to become and air hostess with MMA' brochure, c. 1960.

MMA Air Hostess Application form, c. 1961.

MMA 'Terms of Employment – June 1962', 'MMA Air Hostess Manual'.

MMA, General Instructions 'Natives', 'MMA Air Hostess Manual', September 1964.

MMA Meal booklet, 1963–66, 5 October 1964, p. 10.

Pan American Stewardess Training Film, 1969, Pan Am Archive, University of Miami.

Qantas Empire Airways Limited, 'Flight Hostess Course Timetable', 1954.

'Qantas Flight Hostess Manual', 1963.

Qantas, 'Beards' Memorandum from Tino Sidoli, Qantas Cabin Crew Line Manager, 1 December 1980.

Smith, E. J., 'Hostess Notice', 13 November 1970.

Sommerville, H., 'Trans-Australia Airlines Air Hostess Notice – DC-3 Heating Apparatus', 17 May 1948, clipping.

TAA menu, 9 September 1946.

TAA training film, Fortune Productions, c. 1948.

Western Australian Airways, 'On airways magic carpet across Australia' pamphlet, c. 1930.

Theses

Robinson, M., 'A History of the Airline Hostesses' Association 1955–1981', Honours Thesis, Flinders University, 1990.

Robinson, M., 'Qantas Cabin Crew and Their Union', PhD Thesis, Flinders University, 1996.

Films

Koster, H. (director), *No Highway in the Sky*, 20th Century Fox, 1951.

McVeigh, B. (director), *Coffee, Tea or Me: The Surprising Story of the Underestimated Trolley Dolly*, Gaylene Preston, Wellington, NZ, 2002.

Roth, M. (director), *Flying Hostess*, Universal Studio, 1936.

Seaton, G. & Hathaway, H. (directors), *Airport*, Universal, 1970.

Seler, L. (director), *Flight Angels*, Warner Brothers, 1940.

LIST OF AIRLINES

Air Ceylon, 1947, Australian National Airways (ANA) acquires a stake in the airline in 1949.

Airlines (WA) founded in 1935, merged with MacRobertson Miller Aviation to become MacRobertson Miller Airlines in 1955.

Airlines of Australia (AoA), formed in 1935 as the new name for New England Airways which had formed in 1931, and in 1942 AoA became ANA.

Airlines of New South Wales formed in 1959, and in 1969 became Ansett Airlines of New South Wales.

Airlines of South Australia, founded 1959-1986.

Air Niugini, founded in 1973-current.

Ansett Airways, founded in 1935, in 1957 became Ansett-ANA, in 1968 became Ansett Airlines of Australia, and in 1990 became Ansett Australia and ceased operation in 2001.

Australian National Airways (ANA) founded in 1936 as a restructure of Holyman's Airways, in 1957 became Ansett-ANA. In 1929 Charles Kingsford Smith and Charles Ulm founded an Australian National Airways but it ceased operations in 1931.

Australian National Airways (NSW) 1928-1931.

British Commonwealth Pacific Airways (BCPA) founded in 1946, in 1954 taken over by Qantas.

British Overseas Airways Corporation (BOAC), founded in 1939 with the merger of Imperial Airways and British Airways, began operating as BOAC in 1940, then in 1974 became British Airways.

Bush Pilots Airways (BPA), founded in 1951 and in 1981 became Air Queensland.

Butler Air Transport (BAT), founded 1934 and then in 1959 as a subsidiary of Ansett Air Transport became Airlines of New South Wales.

Connellan Airways, founded in 1939 but the name was not registered until 1943, in 1970 became Connair, and then sold to East-West Airlines in 1980.

East-West Airlines, founded 1947-1993.

Guinea Airways, founded in 1927 then in 1959 as acquired as part of Ansett Transport Industries was renamed Airlines of South Australia in 1960, the airline was taken over by Ansett in 1986.

Holyman's Airways, founded in 1932 as Flinders Island Airways then in the same year became Tasmanian Aerial Services, then in 1934 registered as Holyman's Airways. In 1936 the airline became Australian National Airways (ANA).

Imperial Airways, founded 1924 then in 1939 merged with British Airways to become British Overseas Airways Corporation (BOAC), then in 1974 became British Airways.

MacRobertson Miller Aviation, founded in 1927 in 1955 merged with Airlines (WA) to become MacRobertson Miller Airlines, in 1963 became a part of Ansett Transport Industries, in 1969 taken over by Ansett Air Transport Industries and renamed MacRobertson Miller Airline Services, in 1981 renamed Airlines of Western Australia. In 1993 the company was fully absorbed into Ansett.

Pan American World Airways (Pan Am), founded 1927-1991.

Queensland and Northern Territory Aerial Services (Qantas), founded 1920, then in 1934 Qantas Empire Airways, in 1967 Qantas Airways Limited.

South Coast Aviation Service, founded 1946, then in 1947 became East-West Airlines.

Tasman Empire Airways Limited (TEAL), founded 1940 then in 1965 became Air New Zealand.

Trans Australia Airlines (TAA) founded 1946 then in 1986 became Australian Airlines, then operating as Qantas Airways in 1993.

Western Australian Airways (WAA) founded 1921, became West Australian Airways in 1926, in 1936 was acquired by Adelaide Airways Ltd., and in the same year became part of Australian National Airways.

Unions
1955 Airline Hostesses' Association (registered 1956)
1957 Flight Stewards' Association of Australia (registered 1958)
1963 Airline Hostesses' Association (Overseas Branch)
1984 Australian Flight Attendants Association
1992 Flight Attendants Association of Australia. International Division and National Division

INDEX OF PROPER NAMES

INDEX